Comrades and Strangers

The way ahead: Beneath the statue of Kim Il Sung on Mansu Hill

Photograph by Denis Harrold

Comrades and Strangers

Michael Harrold

WILEY

Published in 2004 by   John Wiley & Sons, Ltd, The Atrium, Southern Gate
Chichester, West Sussex, PO19 8SQ, England
Phone   (+44) 1243 779777

Copyright © 2004   Michael Harrold

Email (for orders and customer service enquiries): cs-books@wiley.co.uk
Visit our Home Page on www.wiley.co.uk or www.wiley.com

Other Wiley Editorial Offices

John Wiley & Sons, Inc. 111 River Street, Hoboken, NJ 07030, USA

Jossey-Bass, 989 Market Street, San Francisco, CA 94103-1741, USA

Wiley-VCH Verlag GmbH, Pappellaee 3, D-69469 Weinheim, Germany

John Wiley & Sons Australia, Ltd, 33 Park Road, Milton, Queensland, 4064, Australia

John Wiley & Sons (Asia) Pte Ltd, 2 Clementi Loop #02-01, Jin Xing Distripark, Singapore
129809

John Wiley & Sons Canada Ltd, 22 Worcester Road, Etobicoke, Ontario, Canada, M9W 1L1

Wiley also publishes its books in a variety of electronic formats. Some content that appears in print
may not be available in electronic books.

Library of Congress Cataloging-in-Publication Data

British Library Cataloguing in Publication Data

A catalogue record for this book is available from the British Library

ISBN 0-470-86976-3

Typeset in $10\frac{1}{2}/13\frac{1}{2}$ Photina by Mathematical Composition Setters Ltd, Salisbury, Wiltshire.
Printed and bound in Great Britain by T.J. International, Padstow, Cornwall.
This book is printed on acid-free paper responsibly manufactured from sustainable forestry in
which at least two trees are planted for each one used for paper production.
10 9 8 7 6 5 4 3 2 1

To Kasia, my wife, with love.

And to Dominik and Antony
growing up in a very different world

Contents

PART 3

Foreword

*I*t has never been my intention in writing this book to cause embarrassment or difficulty of any sort to people I knew in North Korea. I have attempted, therefore, to obscure the identities of individuals and their involvement in particular incidents. With this in mind I have changed all names, with the exception of those that are a matter of historical record, and in some cases have distorted the chronology of events in such a way that people who may associate themselves with a particular character can find themselves written into situations in which they had, in reality, no part, or on occasion may find themselves absent when they might have anticipated being present. Such minor changes do not, however, detract from the veracity of what I have written.

I apologise to those who feel I have not done enough to hide who they are, what they did and what they stood for. I apologise also to those who would have preferred their identity to be recorded.

Despite these minor changes and the slight inconsistencies that may have arisen because of the natural failing of my memory, the episodes I recount in this book are true, although certain interpretations are, clearly, my own and there will doubtless be some people who will dispute what I have written.

I would like to thank the many people I knew in North Korea, whether or not their stories are found in this book, who extended to me friendship, kindness and understanding during what was not always, either for myself or for them, an easy experience. Sufficient time has passed for me to appreciate that we all had personal difficulties, and our principles and beliefs to answer to, and I can now look back with fondness on almost everyone I knew during those seven years.

I would like also to thank all those whose help to me in the writing of this book has been of a more practical nature: Richard Cottrell; Stanislaw and Anna Pazgan; Adam Juszkiewicz and Iwona Lachowicz; Malgorzata Religa; and, for all the years of nagging, Lew Baxter.

A note on the use of Korean

I have used throughout this book the simplified transliteration of Korean words and names that was commonly adhered to in North Korean publications for most of my time there. Starting in the early 1990s, however, there was an attempt to make the transliteration more sophisticated by adding an 'h' to indicate, in the case of certain consonants such as 'p's and 't's where no attempt had previously been made to distinguish between softer and harder sounds, a softer form. For example, the port of Nampo might be written as Nampho, whereas the River Potong would retain the 'p' (although on occasion the harder initial sound might be indicated by a 'b', hence River Botong). I have stuck to the simpler form I was used to, since writing 'ph' and 'th' seems to me only to create additional difficulties of pronunciation, at least as far as the English-speaking reader is concerned.

Korean names, as they are written in the North, appear as a single-syllable family name followed by a given name of one or two characters (e.g. Kim Il Sung). It is common in South Korea and elsewhere to see a two-syllable given name hyphenated (e.g. Kim Il-sung), but again I have stuck to the system I grew used to in North Korea. The only exception is in the case of Korean names that have such a widely accepted common form (e.g. Syngman Rhee, Sun-myung Moon), where to alter them would lead to confusion.

PART 1

*I*n the summer of Juche 89, joy once again filled the Land of Morning Calm. The leader whom the people had sought for generations was reigning for eternity. His passing six years earlier had been the greatest national tragedy, but now like heroes they were resolved to transform their sorrow into glorious exploits.

Factories and building sites rang with the songs of workers whose labours brushed aside targets and smashed production records. The army and the people, rallied behind their leader, were lending a helping hand so that the farmers could reap another bumper harvest. Scientists worked miracles of innovation to eliminate back-breaking labour and ease the household burden of the country's mothers. The children were the kings and queens.

Everyone contributed to the good of society according to their abilities. Taxation was unheard of, and criminals, beggars and the homeless were unknown. All the people were equally well off. In short, there was no-one happier in the world.

And the world gazed in wonder and envy upon this land of golden tapestry with its crystal-clear waters, pure blue skies and diamond mountains, where no-one had cause to worry about food, clothing or housing, where free medical care was enjoyed by everyone from cradle to grave, where all the people studied to their hearts' content, and where the elderly saw out their days amid the love, respect and solicitude of the whole society.

For thousands of years all Koreans had dreamed of such a society. Sadly, it was the reality only in the northern half of the peninsula and the people there wept over the misery endured by their brothers and sisters separated from them in the South. They were filled with sadness, too, whenever their thoughts turned to their compatriots scattered around the world, another legacy of a nation divided.

And so, as the first spring of a new millennium turned to summer and the leader of the South Koreans travelled to the

North, he carried with him the hopes and expectations of all compatriots, at home and abroad.[1]

Thus the propaganda still rang with the same tone and North Korea, in its isolation, continued to live a myth in the summer of 2000. As far as the outside world was concerned, the Paradise on Earth created by the great leader and bequeathed to the dear leader existed only in the minds of a self-serving leadership and a brainwashed population.

Communism, which had been and gone elsewhere in the world, continued its peculiar existence in North Korea. Kim Il Sung was dead, but Kim Il Sung is Kim Jong Il, and Kim Jong Il is Kim Il Sung.[2] And the great leader lived on.

And the rest of the world gazed in horror and fear upon this land of dark mystery with its starving population, its bankrupt economy, its oppressive regime and its powerful military poised to wreak destruction on its neighbours.

So things were just as they had been in the spring of 1987, when the first Briton ever to live in North Korea arrived in Pyongyang to help perpetuate the propaganda myth.

[1] A compilation by the author of North Korea's more enduring propaganda claims. Various reports by the *Korean Central News Agency* (kcna.co.jp) in May and June 2000 on land rezoning projects, a mass chorus of builders working on the new Pyongyang–Nampo motorway and several innovations by the country's scientists give a sense of the official optimism in the face of continuing adversity.

[2] A phrase commonly seen in North Korean publications, particularly in the aftermath of Kim Il Sung's death. *Vantage Point* of December 1994 translates it thus: 'The Great Leader (Kim Il-sung) is just the Dear Leader (Kim Jong-il) and the Dear Leader is just the Great Leader.'

CHAPTER ONE

Red Carpet in Paradise

*H*ad earlier reports of the great leader's death been true, then my adventure in his earthly paradise would never have happened. He had been assassinated, the evening news had reported;[1] claims to that effect had been broadcast from the North Korean side of the heavily fortified demilitarised zone. But then Pyongyang fell silent and the world waited.

The genial, bespectacled, grandfatherly man whom the television news showed a few days later in November 1986, greeting the president of Mongolia[2] and thereby scotching the reports of his own demise, was rather different from the Kim Il

[1] The reports of Kim Il Sung's assassination surfaced in South Korea on November 17th 1986.

[2] Jambyn Batmonh, General Secretary of the Mongolian People's Revolutionary Party and Chairman of the Great Hural of the Mongolian People's Republic, flew into Pyongyang on November 21st 1986 and was met at the airport by Kim Il Sung.

Sung who awaited me four months later on my arrival in North Korea. The huge portrait that dominated the front of the airport building depicted a great leader of 1960s vintage. His hair was dark and his expression severe.

Despite the forbidding presence, I was feeling quite cheerful as I walked across the tarmac with my fellow passengers. It was a bright, warm day at the beginning of spring.[3] The sky was clear and blue, a fresh wind was blowing and the sun was shining. I'd got not the slightest idea of where I should go from the airport, but that didn't worry me. I would be working for an organisation called the Foreign Languages Publishing House and I'd formed some vague notion that I should find an English-speaking taxi driver and head there.

I hadn't slept during the nine-hour flight from Moscow. I was tired, and this no doubt contributed to the sudden swing in my mood, from carefree anticipation to panic. I was inside the gloomy arrivals hall, and the customs declaration forms were written only in Russian and Korean.

It had been a notice in the Leeds University careers office that had said I would be the first Briton ever to live and work in North Korea. I had promised myself a year or two of adventure before settling down to a regular life in England, and living in the world's most isolated country more than fitted the bill. So I'd applied and the months had passed. Then the Koreans had called from Pyongyang. Yes, I had said, I was still interested in the job. Leave it to us, they had said. More months had passed and the great leader was reported assassinated. That, I had reasoned, had put paid to my ambitions of being the English editor of his speeches. But he wasn't dead; the experts had said he had engineered rumours of his own assassination in order to

---

[3] The author arrived in Pyongyang on March 25th 1987.

flush out his political opponents. Lunacy, I'd thought. I was best off out of it. Then the Koreans had called again from Pyongyang. They had wanted to know why I wasn't there yet. Because they hadn't sent me a plane ticket, I'd snapped, and I had no visa or official letter of invitation. I'd been irritated because I felt they were messing me around. But I would still go, I had decided, if they managed to get their act together.

One day a man had telephoned, speaking French. He was calling from the Democratic People's Republic of Korea's[4] UNESCO mission in Paris, the country's nearest diplomatic office to the UK. He had been asked to make the arrangements for my journey to his country. He had suggested I should buy my own plane ticket; I would be reimbursed and my visa would be issued upon my arrival in Pyongyang. I had said no. As far as I understood travel regulations, I had told him in my painfully stilted French, I wouldn't be allowed on a plane to the Soviet Union without proper entry documents for my final destination. I needed a visa and after being kept waiting for so long – nine months had passed since I'd applied for the job – I'd felt it wasn't unreasonable to expect a plane ticket to be provided.

An entry visa for the Democratic People's Republic of Korea and a plane ticket to Pyongyang via Moscow had arrived in the post a few weeks later. My reservation was for the following week.

Thus, my resolve to seek adventure had withstood almost a year of being tested. Within moments of my arrival in North Korea, however, I was feeling anything but daring. How did I expect to cope if I couldn't even fill in a simple customs declaration form?

---

[4] Democratic People's Republic of Korea (DPRK) is the official name of North Korea.

My guardian angel turned out to be a short, tubby chap in a grey raincoat. 'You are English, yes?' I heard someone say at my elbow. I turned and saw a friendly, round, boyish face looking up at me. 'Yes,' I said with a smile. 'You are Mr Michael,' the man then informed me. 'Please to come this way.' To my relief he took the customs form from my hand and tossed it back on the desk. 'Later,' he said, by way of explanation.

Back out on the tarmac he told me he was Mr Choe and that he welcomed me to his country. A little way off a photographer stepped forward from a small group of people waiting at the bottom of some steps that led up into another part of the airport building. He took a picture as a girl in a dark blue uniform came towards us, handed me a bouquet of flowers and said something. Mr Choe told me she was welcoming me to her country.

He then introduced me to another man, slightly shorter and a little more portly than himself, who was wearing a cream raincoat. He, it turned out, was Director Kim of the foreign affairs department of the Foreign Languages Publishing House and he didn't speak any English. Using Mr Choe as interpreter, he welcomed me to his country.

It occurred to me as we sat in the VIP lounge sipping a bitter, yellowish-orange hot drink that Mr Choe called *insam*[5] tea that these people didn't know what jet lag was. Apart from not having slept for nearly 24 hours, I was nine hours ahead of myself and I struggled with a welcoming chat that tended more towards a polite interrogation than the 'And did you have a comfortable flight?' line of inquiry.

How had Moscow been? Well, it wasn't surprising I'd had some trouble with passport control – the Soviet Union wasn't very friendly to Westerners. Had I ever stayed in a socialist country

[5] Ginseng.

8

before? What about Asian countries, then? So, which countries had I been to? Spain? Was the socialist party very strong there? So I'd studied Spanish at university. And business? Oh. But the course included Marxist economics! That was good.

'What do you know about our country?' Director Kim asked via Mr Choe.

'Actually, I didn't even know where it was,' I replied, relieved to be able to add a little jocularity to the conversation. Director Kim frowned and pursed his lips when this was translated for him, in much the same way that Mr Choe had when I'd first said it.

Madame Beatrice de Villeneuve frowned and pursed her lips two hours later when I told her what I'd said to Messrs Choe and Kim. She was the first of my foreign colleagues I'd met at the guest house to which I'd been driven from the airport. Madame Beatrice, as she told me I was to call her, was a short, somewhat stout, grey-haired lady elegantly attired in a brightly patterned dress, who rose to greet me when Mr Choe showed me into the dining room. She wore a large necklace and several prominent rings, and her mouth was highlighted by a bold stroke of crimson lipstick. She was half French and half Swiss, and I judged her to be in her mid- to late 60s.

Madame Beatrice was sitting alone at the room's only table, a large circular one covered with a beautifully white cloth and with three settings of knife, fork and spoon. The third place was '*pour Philippe*' who was teaching that morning and would be late for lunch. There would normally be a fourth diner, Ali from Lebanon, Madame Beatrice told me. He was currently on an extended winter break in warmer climes and was expected back in a week or two.

The four of us formed the capitalist contingent at the Ansan Guest House. The other residents, who were also my colleagues at the Foreign Languages Publishing House, were Cubans, East Germans, Soviets and Chinese. Several of these socialist heads popped round the door to say hello as they passed, on their way to their separate dining rooms.

I'd confessed to Madame Beatrice my *faux pas* with Mr Choe and Director Kim. It wasn't the brightest thing I could have said, I admitted. But I'd been finding their questioning rather exacting and had desperately wanted to lighten the mood. I certainly hadn't wanted to cause offence. So I'd been taken aback by how affronted they'd seemed. I'd sensed a certain frostiness as we'd finished our tea and Mr Choe had answered very shortly when I'd asked him what he had written on the customs form handed to him by a man in a dark blue uniform who had entered the airport lounge as our conversation was dying.

Communist regimes, so I'd read, took customs declarations very seriously and a careless foreigner could land himself in big trouble by forgetting to mention even a trifling item he was carrying with him. Accordingly, I'd brought a detailed list of everything I had with me, so that the inevitable search of my bags – wherever they had got to – would not reveal a single item not declared. I'd only just begun to read the list out loud; two watches, one radio, clothing, a razor, when Mr Choe had taken the form from the customs officer and scribbled something on it.

'Clothes,' Mr Choe had said, po-faced.

I wasn't to worry, Madame Beatrice assured me. Still, it would be as well to remember that North Korea was the centre of the world. They would put my mistake down to ignorance fostered by capitalist propaganda. They would be quite understanding, as long as I hadn't said anything against the great leader. I hadn't, had I? Madame Beatrice demanded sharply.

I wasn't that stupid. But if Koreans thought their country was the centre of the world, then I had news for them. Most of the references to it in several major libraries back home concerned the Korean War, and that was known as the Forgotten War. As for the country itself, it spoke volumes that Korea was popularly known as the Hermit Kingdom.

The knowledge I'd managed to build up about the country I was to live in amounted to very little. Korea had been divided at the end of the Second World War following the defeat of the Japanese. The Soviet Red Army, which was advancing down through Manchuria, had entered the northern half of the peninsula, while US forces had landed in the South. Under an agreement reached by Stalin and Roosevelt at the Yalta Conference in February 1945, the peninsula was to be occupied by the great powers. The 38th Parallel, it was later decided, should be the line separating the Soviet and US spheres of influence.

Korea had been under Japanese rule since the end of the nineteenth century. The country had represented easy pickings; its infrastructure was backward, its rulers were corrupt and it offered little resistance to the might of its imperial neighbour, which had declared the formal annexation of the Korean peninsula in 1910.

The division of Korea that came with the end of Japanese rule on August 15th 1945 was only ever meant to be temporary. But two very different and highly antagonistic political systems, reflecting the interests of the two occupying powers, appeared: in the South an elderly nationalist, Syngman Rhee, emerged to head a government, while in the North the Soviet Union sponsored the leadership ambitions of a young and charismatic communist by the name of Kim Il Sung.

Five years later war broke out when, according to the history books I'd read in England, the North launched an invasion along the 38th Parallel, in an attempt to reunify the country under communist rule. The United Nations, at the bidding of the United States, sent forces to defend the South, with the result that the Korean People's Army, having occupied almost the whole of the peninsula, was sent into a retreat that took it right up to the Chinese border. Mao Zedong then sent an army to support the North and the UN forces were pushed southwards again. After three years and millions of military and civilian deaths, and with the two sides back virtually where they had started from along the 38th Parallel, the war ended with an armistice. No peace treaty was ever signed.

In the following decades the two Koreas faced each other across one of the most dangerous frontiers of the Cold War. The South was given massive economic and military support by the United States, while the North received backing from the Soviet Union and China. The South Korean economy flourished under capitalism and a modern consumer society emerged, while in the North socialist economic planning, which had promised much during the years of post-war reconstruction, ultimately failed to deliver anything more than subsistence living for the majority of the population.

By the spring of 1987 a personality cult had grown up around Kim Il Sung, who had for four decades been imposing a unique brand of politics in the North that combined strict communist ideology with fervent nationalism and left much of the world suspicious. In the South, meanwhile, the latest in a line of military dictators, Chun Doo Hwan, was coming under growing pressure to allow democratic elections to take place. With the prospect of its international profile being raised by hosting the Olympics, which were little more than a year away, South Korea, it seemed, was edging ahead of its northern rival on all fronts.

Philippe turned out to be of a similar age to me, almost as tall but somewhat more bulky. His hair was reddish and he had a large, drooping moustache that I thought of as typically Gallic. He was French, and appeared to be in a hurry when he arrived for lunch. He dropped a pile of books and newspapers on the dining table and said something, evidently in Korean, to Sun Ok, our waitress, who had followed in his wake into the room. 'Hi,' he said turning to me and offering his hand. 'I've just come from teaching.'

As he wolfed down his food he had a conversation in French with Madame Beatrice of which I understood very little. I felt guilty, since on the application form I'd sent the publishing house I'd claimed to have a reasonable command of French, along with a fluency in Spanish. They'd taken these claims seriously, I'd concluded when Mr Choe had introduced me to a Spanish interpreter, Pak Hong Nam, who was waiting just inside the airport doors with my luggage, which I'd last seen at Heathrow.

'These are your suitcases, yes?' he'd asked.

'Yes,' I'd said, thinking how bizarre it was that a man I'd never met had managed to find my suitcases and bring them through customs while another man I'd known for only a few minutes had made a customs declaration on my behalf, all as I sat sipping tea. Before I'd even left the airport, I'd speculated wryly, I had a sinister tale of mysterious doings to relate in my letters home.

Or did I? In the car I'd urged myself to come up with a more straightforward explanation. Pak must have made himself known to the customs officer in the dark blue uniform and the two of them, once Mr Choe had written 'clothes' on the form, must have gone in search of my suitcases. They'd identified them by the name tags, and the customs officer had decided to pass them without a search.

It all made sense. It would be far better, I'd thought, to write to my friends about 'my driver', a man in a smart, high-necked charcoal grey tunic who had opened for me the rear door of a long, black car with tinted windows waiting just in front of the main airport doors. This beat standing in bus queues on the Otley Road in Leeds to go to the university campus, I would tell them. 'My car', as I was already thinking of it, was far smarter than the taxis a few of the better-off students took when the weather was particularly miserable. With this in mind, as we'd pulled away I'd realised there was something quite odd; Pyongyang's must have been the only international airport in the world where there were no taxis for hire. In the light of my original plan to make my way into the city by taxi, I felt I had a lot to learn.

Pak the Spanish interpreter and I had got along fine, chatting away during the ride into Pyongyang. I'd impressed myself with my command of a language I hadn't used for more than a year, by venturing on to the technical side of agriculture. It was a subject on which Pak seemed to be quite an expert. All I'd wanted to know was why crops were grown right up to the edges of the main road. Because of the limited amount of arable land in the North, Pak had told me. This had been his springboard for a detailed description of the various crops the North Koreans grew, the time and methods of planting and, where appropriate, transplanting them, and finally the harvesting.

He'd been a little more hesitant when I'd asked him why we ignored the traffic police. It was clear the two uniformed men had meant business because they had been waving red flags, and there could be no doubt that it was our car they had wanted to stop because it was the only one on the long stretch of road. But my driver had not even slowed, let alone stopped. Pak had conferred with Mr Choe in the front passenger seat before answering my question: 'They are not for us.'

I hoped, as I sat there recalling this and listening to the barely intelligible conversation between Madame Beatrice and Philippe, that there was no plan to spring a French interpreter on me.

Mr Choe sat in one of the two armchairs in my lounge-cum-office and indicated that Pak should take the other. I sat at my desk, in a rather impressive upholstered, high-backed swivel chair. Mr Choe asked me how I'd liked the food. I could tell him honestly that I'd been most impressed by both the quantity and the quality. We didn't normally have five-course lunches back home, nor was it usual for a generous serving of seafood to constitute one of those courses.

He nodded. I was doing very important work, revising translations of the speeches of the great leader Comrade Kim Il Sung and the dear leader Comrade Kim Jong Il. If there was anything I needed, he said, I should ask him or Pak. As representatives of the publishing house, they were staying at the guest house to ensure that I had everything I needed for my work and my comfort.

Mr Choe then launched into what it soon dawned on me was a pep talk. Conscious that my previous effort at levity hadn't gone down too well, I contained my responses to an occasional nod or disapproving shake of the head. Every utterance of the great leader and the dear leader, Mr Choe assured me, was of the utmost importance. The whole world, even more progressive people in my own capitalist country, hung on their every word. So it was vital that I treat my work with absolute seriousness. I was, after all, very young for the job.

Despite my best efforts, my mind started wandering. I still hadn't slept and the difficulty of taking on board the alien concepts

Mr Choe was conveying was compounded by his unusual English. I noticed that he had trouble with his 'f's. He'd asked me what I preferred to drink with my breakfast, tea or coppee. He'd explained that I was to work at home, in my 'oppice', as he described the room we were sitting in. I was careful to keep a straight face, but I couldn't help thinking here was an amusing entry for my diary. So I felt thoroughly ashamed when he told me earnestly that he wanted to be my 'pliend' – 'r's were also a problem, I noted. But that was cruel of me, I thought, and spiteful. If I was fair, I would admit that his English was far better than my French. At least he seemed to understand what I was saying.

Mr Choe appeared earnest in whatever he said, whether it was that the great leader was the saviour of the Korean nation or that the US imperialists were its greatest enemy. It was strange how his face remained so impassive all the time, even while he used words like 'bastards' to describe the Americans. All part of the training for a young revolutionary, I supposed.

I would be working first, Mr Choe informed me, on a historic book, *On the Art of the Cinema*, by Comrade Kim Jong Il. The dear leader, it transpired, was the greatest master of artistic creation. But he didn't merit a badge, I thought. Mr Choe, like every other person I'd met, was wearing a small badge over his heart. His bore a head-and-shoulders portrait of the great leader set against a red flag. But the badge worn by Pak the Spanish interpreter was of a different design. It had the great leader's head on a simple oval background. I wondered if this was significant. Did the style of badge denote rank? I would ask Madame Beatrice.

On the Art of the Cinema, Mr Choe was telling me, was an outstanding revolutionary treatise, publication of which was eagerly anticipated around the world – which seemed to imply I should get a move on. I was keen to make a good impression as a dedicated worker, but try as I might I could not focus on what he was saying. Come to think of it, the image of Kim Il Sung on Pak's badge was the same as in the portrait on the wall above my right shoulder. Here the dear leader did merit a presence, on the left hand of his father – the right as I looked at it. It was rather clever, I thought, how the two pictures were hung. They tilted forward, giving the impression that the two leaders were presiding over the room – just as they presided over every other room I'd been in so far, it occurred to me, from the airport lounge, to the dining room, to my bedroom.

Mr Choe led me to my bookcase, which occupied almost a whole wall of the room. The top shelf was taken up by some two dozen royal blue volumes with gold lettering on the spine: *Kim Il Sung – Works*. Below were a series of other hardback volumes, also collections of the great leader's speeches and writings, along with a number of books by the dear leader. Pamphlets accounted for most of the third shelf; one, which I selected for no better reason than that it was the thickest, bore the title: *Kim Jong Il – On the Juche Idea*.

Such were the texts I would be working on. Lighter reading occupied the lowest shelf, a mixture of picture albums about the scenery of North Korea, a two-volume biography of the dear leader called *The People's Leader*, and a guide to the Pyongyang Maternity Hospital. There was also a neat stack of magazines.

'Books are properly arranged,' Mr Choe told me as he took *On the Juche Idea* from where I'd dropped it on the bottom shelf and put it back in its original place.

It seemed I'd made another mistake. Anxious to make amends, I asked Mr Choe, 'What do you recommend me to read, in order to learn about your country?'

'All,' he said.

In October 1986 Kim Il Sung had made a historic trip to Moscow to meet Mikhail Gorbachev. Speculation had been rife that the elder statesman of world communism intended to give a sound ticking off to the young upstart who was threatening to undermine nearly seven decades of revolutionary achievement. But nothing could have been further from the truth.

According to a report in *Korea Today*, while in Moscow Kim Il Sung had 'further deepened mutual trust and understanding and became more intimate' with 'the beloved Comrade Mikhail Sergeyevich Gorbachov [sic]', who was described as a 'staunch Marxist–Leninist and talented political activist'.

The visit was described as 'an epoch-making event of special importance in expanding and developing the Korean–Soviet relations of friendship in all spheres'. Such was its significance, in fact, that more than just bilateral concerns were embraced. The visit also 'contributed greatly to strengthening the unity of socialist countries and expanding and developing the international communist movement and the world peace movement'.

With this in mind, the two men 'paid special attention to the situation of Asia and Europe, which is growing tense due to the US-led imperialists' armaments expansion and moves towards a nuclear war'. Clearly, whatever the great leader thought about his younger comrade's tinkering with revolutionary doctrine, there were greater issues at stake, nothing less than 'preventing a new world war, a thermonuclear war, and preserving peace'.[6]

Pyongyang was built on two main waterways, the River Taedong and its tributary, the River Potong. The latter, which was a short

---

[6] Quotations from *Korea Today*, 1987, 1.

walk from our guest house, was a popular recreation area, so I learned from some old copies of a pictorial magazine called *Korea*.[7] In the warmer months its banks were lined with fishermen and on holidays happy parents took their smiling children out in curious paddle boats modelled on swans, the figureheads of which were incongruously large curved necks and heads.

The River Taedong, Pyongyang's main waterway, which emptied into the sea at the port of Nampo, divided the capital and its two million population into East and West. According to Madame Beatrice, the far side of the river was where the diplomatic quarter and the huge Pyongyang Department Store were located. On our side, the West, were most of the other shops, by which she meant the dollar shops – the ones that concerned us – and the city's main international hotels. I could, if I wanted to, go by foot to the eastern part of the city, she told me. But the only place of interest that was within walking distance was the Diplomats' Club on the far side of the Taedong Bridge, and it would take at least an hour to get there.

On the East bank of the River Taedong, halfway between the Taedong Bridge and the other main river crossing, the Okryu Bridge, rose a 150 metres-high tapering white marble column that, with an illuminated 20 metres-tall red torch on the top, was one of the most prominent features of Pyongyang's skyline. This was the Tower of the Juche Idea, and a visit there was the first of the official duties I carried out before I was set to work.

It shouldn't have been, but unfortunately my diplomatic skills had once again been found wanting. Mr Choe, on a pre-dinner visit, had generously advised me to go to bed early on my first night in his country and sleep 'for long time'. I'd taken him at his word, surmising that he understood jet lag after all. It was a

---

[7] The magazine is *Democratic People's Republic of KOREA*.

conclusion I groggily dismissed when he appeared in my bedroom after a perfunctory knock on the door at 9.30 the following morning to tell me there was no problem, even though it was too late to leave for the trip scheduled for that morning to the president's birthplace. We would go another time. We would visit the Juche Tower in the afternoon, as planned. Lunch was served at 1 p.m., although he would, if I liked, tell the cooks to make me a late breakfast. I declined the offer. It was bad enough that I'd shown myself to be a lazy capitalist. I didn't want to be seen as high-handed with the staff as well.

Juche, I discovered from the French-speaking guide who was showing us around the tower, and whose words were snatched from her mouth and flung to the limits of my comprehension and beyond by a forceful wind, was the guiding philosophy of the Korean revolution. Fathered by the great leader Comrade Kim Il Sung, the Juche Idea was being enhanced, developed and systematised by the dear leader Comrade Kim Jong Il and was adhered to absolutely by the Workers' Party of Korea and the Government of the Republic in all their leadership undertakings.

To the side of the main tower is a 30 metres-high bronze group statue of an overalled worker, a dumpy peasant woman and a bright-eyed lad supposed to be a working intellectual. As I gazed up at this massive trio the guide continued her explanation, with the occasional interjection by Mr Choe, who obviously knew his stuff. The three figures were, the guide indicated, holding aloft a hammer, a sickle and a writing brush, the elements that formed the emblem of the Workers' Party of Korea. That's showing the Soviets, I mused, who must be wondering how they'd forgotten about the poor old working intellectual.

The guide then told me about one of the Juche Idea's fundamental principles – of which there appeared to be a confusingly large number – that because Man was the master of his own destiny, he decided everything. Thus the motive force of the revolution and construction was the popular masses. The whole society was in the process of being imbued with the Juche Idea, she said, and this meant that Man was placed at the centre of revolutionary thought and true revolutionaries were being created of a Juche type. Independence of the national economy and self-reliance in defence seemed pretty important, as did a concept called *Chajusong*, a Korean term that appeared to have something to do with national sovereignty.

It was all pretty heavy going. So when we finally found ourselves on the platform at the top of the tower, just below the red torch, it came as a relief to discover that all I was expected to do was admire the view. Pyongyang was very pleasant, rather than spectacular, was my impression. There were vast expanses of greenery, tree-lined roads and the occasional traditional-looking curved and layered green roof. The buildings were tidily arranged and there were no chimneys to be seen belching smoke.

Mr Choe seemed very proud of his city as he pointed out its various features: the Grand People's Study House just across the river; the ice rink in the distance, which had a far closer resemblance to a shuttlecock, I thought, than the skater in full flow that he insisted was the design; the Changgwang Health Complex next to it, whose swimming pool was for the exclusive use of foreigners on Saturday afternoons; Moran Hill, near to which were the Arch of Triumph and Kim Il Sung Stadium; and the two towers of the Koryo Hotel.

'I take you there soon,' Mr Choe said.

'We will go on Saturday,' Madame Beatrice told me over dinner that evening. I had mentioned that Mr Choe had seemed particularly proud of the Koryo, and Madame Beatrice had explained that it was the city's newest and most modern hotel.

But before that I had other visits to undertake. 'Tomorrow Mr Choe is taking me to Mang, er Mang something-or-other,' I said.

'It is Mangyongdae, and it is the birthplace of the great leader,' Madame Beatrice told me a little testily. Then she added more kindly, 'It is a name you should remember.'

My lasting impression of that first visit to Mangyongdae is of impeccably manicured lawns being tended by women on their hands and knees using scissors, of sombre music apparently emanating from fir trees, and of a twisted rice vessel.

The latter was, as my guide told me in Korean with Mr Choe providing an English translation, proof of just how poor the young great leader's family had been, since they could not even afford a proper container to keep their rice in. The black, twisted jar stood in a prominent position at the far end of a tiny courtyard, two sides of which were bordered by low, thatched-roofed rooms, some containing very basic farm machinery, others simple bedding. In most of the rooms were photographs of the various members – grandparents and parents, uncles and siblings – of this most revolutionary of families.

On the fourth side of the courtyard was the gate through which we had entered along a pathway leading from the car park where our driver had dropped us. Another path headed in the direction of a hill where, as I was to learn, the young great leader used to play; not ordinary, childish games, it transpired, but revolutionary pastimes in which he diligently cultivated his exceptional intelligence, fortitude and talent, as well as his burning patriotism and fervent desire to rid his country of the Japanese occupiers.

As I gazed respectfully into the various rooms and studied the photographs, the guide, dressed in traditional full long skirt and tiny tight jacket, told me the story of the great leader's early years and of the exploits of his family.

Kim Song Ju, as Kim Il Sung was known in his childhood, was born in 1912, two years after Japan's formal annexation of Korea. His brilliance, which was of such magnitude as to be wholly unimaginable, was nurtured in a family of impeccable and outstanding revolutionary credentials.

The first of these particular Kims to make a name for himself, I noted, had been the great leader's great-grandfather, Kim Ung U, who, way back in the summer of 1866, had blazed a trail for his family's often violent opposition to the United States by leading the people of Pyongyang in an attack on an American ship – the *General Sherman* – that had made its way uninvited up the River Taedong, more or less into the city.[8]

The chief claim to fame of the great leader's grandparents was that they had brought up their children and grandchildren to be true revolutionaries dedicated to expelling the Japanese from Korea. The great leader's father, Kim Hyong Jik, was a teacher who had resisted the Japanese and wound up in prison for his pains. He subsequently decamped to the country's northern border regions to conduct his revolutionary activities there, before finally crossing into Manchuria, where he continued the fight against the Japanese. There he died at the age of 32. His wife, Kang Ban Sok, dutifully supported her husband in his revolutionary struggle and accompanied him to Manchuria,

---

[8] In 1866, the *General Sherman* sailed up the River Taedong and was assaulted by local farmers, who set fire to the ship and killed all the crew.

where at the age of 40 she, too, passed away without ever setting foot on Korean soil again.

An uncle, Kim Hyong Gwon, had got in on the revolutionary act. He was arrested for his anti-Japanese activities and thrown into Seoul's Mapo Gaol, where he died. Then there were the great leader's two younger brothers, Yong Ju[9] and Chol Ju, of whom the latter joined a guerrilla unit fighting the Japanese and fell in battle.

A month short of his 11th birthday, little Song Ju, after spending some time with his parents in Manchuria, was sent back to his grandparents in Pyongyang to continue his studies and gain first-hand experience of the situation in his homeland.[10] Then, in 1925, on hearing the sad news that his father had been arrested again, Song Ju, aged just 13, showed his true mettle by walking alone to China. This individual and youthful Long March, known as the 3000-*li*[11] Journey for National Liberation, brought him back to his parents in Manchuria.

I spent my first Saturday afternoon in Pyongyang in the company of Madame Beatrice. She decided we should walk to the Koryo Hotel, since the weather was warm and sunny and I would be able to see a little more of the city as we went.

---

[9] Kim Yong Ju would be appointed to a number of key positions in the Workers' Party of Korea and the Government of the Democratic People's Republic of Korea, ultimately rising to be Vice-President of the DPRK.

[10] A trek known in North Korean folklore as the '1000-*li* Journey for Learning'.

[11] The *li* is a traditional Korean measurement of distance; 1000 *li* is roughly equivalent to 400 kilometres.

The two miles from the guest house to the Koryo Hotel took over an hour at Madame Beatrice's slow and deliberate pace, and I was fascinated throughout. I liked Pyongyang, I decided. There was not a scrap of litter in the streets, and no graffiti. The buildings, though unremarkable, were well-maintained and attractive; coloured tiles of pale oranges, blues and greens brightened up the façades of many of the blocks of flats. The shops had cheerful signboards and their windows were plastered with gaudy images of what I presumed was on sale within; hats and scarves, fish, fruit. A pair of scissors indicated, I assumed, a hairdressers. More colour was added by the slogans formed of huge Korean characters on top of many of the buildings.

On every street corner there were hoardings, which were nothing if not bold. Soldiers with rifles carried at the ready screamed defiance at an unseen enemy; steelworkers glowed with pride and with the heat of the furnace they had brought to life; and at every turn there was Kim Il Sung with his people. In one poster the great leader appeared to be holding an egg triumphantly aloft, as he stood head and shoulders above the bright-eyed and adoring masses. It was all a far cry from the drab grey city I'd imagined.

Nor was I prepared for the absence of bicycles. I'd assumed that, as in Beijing, most people would get around on two wheels. Madame Beatrice explained that bicycles were not permitted, since too many might disrupt the traffic. I asked what traffic. There were scarcely any cars on the broad, tree-lined roads. An ancient trolleybus would occasionally lurch past and there was an intermittent stream of green army trucks. Apparently it was at the junctions that too many bicycles might disrupt the flow, although I was quite sure the efficient female traffic police would be a match for any number of cyclists.

Dressed in kingfisher-blue uniforms[12] and brown boots, these doll-like visions of feminine delicacy – they were selected for their good looks, so Madame Beatrice assured me – stood in the centre of major intersections, where they wheeled in boot-clicking military precision to issue imperious orders with a cursory flick or stern pointing of their batons. And watch out the motorist who defied them, or indeed the pedestrian who was spotted crossing a road somewhere they shouldn't! Madame Beatrice was horrified by my suggestion that we run the gauntlet of the trickle of traffic. No, we must use the underpass to cross the street, she insisted, just like everyone else.

The traffic police were members of the regular police force, Madame Beatrice told me. I wouldn't immediately notice the police, she explained, because those not selected for traffic duty wore green army uniforms and could only be identified by their collar tabs, which were green and yellow, while those of the regular military were red and yellow. I wondered at this trifling distinction between police and military. I hadn't expected to see anyone like a bobby on the beat in Pyongyang. Even so, I thought I was entitled to a more reassuring presence in the street than this military-style policeman who was hardly likely to take the side of me, his country's enemy, in the event that I inadvertently became involved in a confrontation with some fanatical, anti-Western hothead.

My fears were silly, I knew, but they refused to go away as I met the eyes of the people we passed. They weren't openly hostile; rather, there was a disconcerting lack of emotion in their expressions. They stared, but without curiosity. It was unnerving to be the object of such bold looks that gave rise to nothing but blank disinterest. But they must have been thinking something.

---

[12] In the summer they wear white jackets.

Were the old people moved to anger at the sight of me, reminded of the Western soldiers they had battled during the war? Did the young men seethe with hatred for this foreigner and his self-serving ideology? And what about the young women, who demurely averted their eyes when I returned their gaze? Madame Beatrice soon put a stop to my fantasising in that direction. 'They are not for you,' she stated bluntly when I commented on how pretty some of the girls looked in their brightly patterned dresses.

Roughly half of the pedestrians we passed, men and women, were turned out in smart olive-green uniforms. Of the civilians, the women without exception wore an attractive dress or a skirt and blouse, while the men had on neat trousers and shirt; some even a suit and tie. Everyone wore a badge. I asked Madame Beatrice what the significance of the various designs was and she said that as far as she knew there was none. Except that, she said after a moment's thought, she had been told members of the League of Socialist Working Youth of Korea were given badges of a slightly different design; she thought they were probably the ones with a red flag as the background. But really I shouldn't read too much into the badges.

In sharp and refreshing contrast with the blank stares of the adults, the children startled and delighted me with loud and cheery greetings when they passed. Dressed in school uniforms of navy blue and white, red neckerchiefs tied at their throats, they marched in well-dressed cohorts up to about 40 strong, singing as they went. I was astonished by the display of discipline from children, some as young as five or six, who, each time they passed us foreigners in their juvenile contingents, rather pointedly raised a high-pitched and ringing cry and saluted with ranks of little arms pointing diagonally across their faces.

No, Madame Beatrice told me as she inclined her head slightly in acknowledgement of the third or fourth such group, they weren't trying to embarrass me as a way of getting their own back because I'd been staring. The children were taught to be polite to foreigners and would always greet us in the street.

At the Koryo I stood by Madame Beatrice's side in the foyer as she indicated with a finger where the hotel's various facilities were located.

To the right were the post office and the shop. I surmised, judging by her lingering glance, that the latter was a favourite haunt. To the left was the coffee shop, and ahead of us and slightly to the right was an escalator leading to the first floor, mirrored by one coming down to the left. 'There is the billiard,' said Madame Beatrice, pointing upwards.

Finally, directly in front of us and up a couple of low steps, there was a magnificent backdrop of mountains and a waterfall. Just in front of it a staircase spiralled downwards. At the bottom, Madame Beatrice told me, there was another bar.

Sitting over our ice creams in the coffee shop, a longish room with semi-circular couches down one side, tables and chairs down the other and a small bar at the far end, Madame Beatrice told me a little about the Koryo Hotel. Being the newest – built in 1985 – and most luxurious hotel in the city, it was the natural meeting place for Pyongyang's tiny foreign community. Locals were not allowed in, unless they were on official business.

Not that we were supposed to have anything to do with the foreigners in town, apart from our colleagues, she said. Mr Choe preferred us not to go out, and if we did, we should ask an interpreter along. It was for our own convenience, he insisted; all part of the service for such important foreign guests.

But it was too late for Madame Beatrice to be telling me this. Thanks to Philippe I was already leading a double life – the dedicated worker, anxious to please, by day, and the secret socialite inhabiting a forbidden world of hotel bars by night.

I'd waited in the shadows just in front of the building site. I was 50 metres from the main gate of our compound. I'd come straight from dinner, as instructed, without running the risk of going back up the stairs to my flat.

It was my second night in Pyongyang and Philippe had invited me to join him in meeting some Belgian friends, in town to work on an environmental project. But then he had dropped the bombshell about being forbidden by Mr Choe to leave the guest house at night unless we were accompanied by either himself or an interpreter. That was why it was better to go straight from the dining room, to avoid passing Mr Choe's room.

Philippe had come soon afterwards and we'd set off for the Potonggang Hotel, across the building site. From there we would be taking a taxi to the Pyongyang Hotel, near the River Taedong. It was then just a short walk to the nearby Taedonggang Hotel where his friends were staying. The less the taxi driver knew about our movements, Philippe had explained, the better for us and for anyone we were meeting.

It was in the taxi on the way home – or at least to the nearby Ansan Club, since if we'd gone to the guest house the taxi driver would have known where to go the next day to report on our movements to whoever was responsible for us – that Philippe had revealed why all this secrecy was really necessary. It had become a habit with him to cover his tracks whenever he went out because he was regularly meeting Korean friends. This was something that was absolutely forbidden. If found out, Philippe could expect to lose his job; the consequences for the Koreans involved didn't bear thinking about. To guarantee his friends the fullest security possible, Philippe reasoned, he should maintain the utmost secrecy, whoever he was meeting.

Philippe had come to Pyongyang from Beijing, where he had been studying to add Chinese to the already impressive list of languages he spoke. There he had fallen in with a crowd of North Korean students and, with the assistance of one of their number, he had been offered the job at the Foreign Languages Publishing House. The only drawback was that, in their country, he wasn't allowed to meet his friends.

It was a restriction they were determined to flout. The hotels were too public and the security there too tight, so Philippe would meet his friends in restaurants. Their thinking was that waitresses and casual observers would simply assume that any Korean with Philippe was his interpreter and so perfectly entitled, indeed under an obligation, to be with him.

That Mr Choe knew, or at least strongly suspected, what was going on, Philippe had no doubt. But as long as he remained ignorant of the Koreans' identities there was nothing to worry about. Mr Choe couldn't approach the subject directly, Philippe explained, since he wouldn't want to admit that we weren't free to mix with whomever we wished. So what ensued was a cat-and-mouse game, in which the staff in bars where Philippe found himself would often receive telephone calls that clearly, since the girl answering the phone would look in his direction and nod as she talked, referred to him. Just Mr Choe checking up, Philippe concluded. If I thought *glasnost* and *perestroika* had reached North Korea, I should forget it.

I found just the place I was looking for at the bottom of the spiral staircase Madame Beatrice had pointed to in the Koryo Hotel.

The only sound was that of a waterfall, which splashed into a pool lit by coloured lamps. Before me, as I stood at the bottom of the

*steps, lay a lounge area of sofas and small tables, all of them
empty.*

*'Where do you come from?' asked the girl behind the bar. Her
smile was captivating. She stared too, but unlike the people in the
street she did so with warmth. 'Another world,' was the reply
that came to mind.*

This, I thought, was a place where I could come for quiet
reflection, where I could sit in solitude and try to make sense of
the contradictions and resolve the dilemmas that were already a
part of my life in North Korea.

Madame Beatrice had told me to respect Mr Choe's authority; to
do otherwise would eventually lead me into difficulties. Philippe
had said to ignore Mr Choe's restrictions; they were intolerable.

'Be diplomatic,' Madame Beatrice had urged me. Of course, as
a grown woman she didn't ask permission every time she went
out, but it didn't hurt from time to time to play Mr Choe's game.
It kept him happy and acquiescent. According to Madame
Beatrice, Philippe was making life difficult for all the foreigners
by so blatantly flouting the rules. Of course Mr Choe knew about
it, and it antagonised him and risked making him less cooperative
with the rest of us.

Philippe, though, had convinced me I had to stand up for
my rights and reject the more outrageous curtailments of our
personal freedom. Didn't I want to get out and learn about the
people and the country?

That was the point. Even though the changes in the Soviet
Union were bringing hope of détente with the West, communism
was still feared and hated back where I came from. Millions, we
were led to believe, were bound by the malignant shackles of
a flawed ideology that prevented people from exercising their
basic freedoms, an ideology that, as its inherent evil festered

and made self-destruction more likely, might lash out in a futile act of defiance and destroy us all. Nowhere were the oppression and the menace thought to be more malevolent than in North Korea.

But I had a strong sense that the world was a more complex place than I'd been taught where, if left to their own devices, ordinary people like me would be happy to allow our various ideologies and cultures sometimes to intertwine naturally and sometimes to become unravelled, as long as no great damage was done to the single thread we all clung to – our common desire to make the best out of life. Politicians, I strongly suspected, whatever their professed beliefs, merely trumpeted ideologies in their pursuit of power and as justification for their often shady dealings. The ideological conflicts and international disputes that were in large part the result of such self-interest could, I reckoned, best be resolved by ordinary people like me over a pint or two of beer.

I had no particularly strong feelings either for or against communism, which seemed, to my admittedly slight knowledge, to be based on principles in which I vaguely believed – social equality, help for the less fortunate, the provision of free medical care. What had happened, then, to make it the object of such vilification where I came from, and how was it that poverty, state belligerence and intrusive security agencies had such strong associations with an ideology that seemed so benign?

I wasn't going to answer such questions, I knew. But I would like to get an idea of what people living under communism in its most extreme form really believed, what they hoped for and what they thought of the outside world. I wasn't going to learn anything, however, if I couldn't meet anyone.

On the other hand, I'd set myself a standard, that of being respectful to authority in my new country of residence. With this and Madame Beatrice's advice in mind, I resolved how I would deal with Mr Choe and his restrictions. There seemed to be a tacit acceptance that the foreigners at the Ansan Guest House could visit the nearest hotel, the Potonggang, in the evenings. So if Mr Choe asked, I could always tell him that was my destination. I was being quite honest, even though I didn't tell him that it was generally a starting point for a nocturnal exploration of his city. It was a childish subterfuge and I resented having to resort to it. If Mr Choe were ever to find me out, I might just tell him he only had himself to blame.

> *'What are you doing in my country?' the girl asked. I told her, but she shook her head in bewilderment at my answer. How long was I staying? The chatter went on. She didn't understand my English, but there was an innocence and an infectious enthusiasm about her inquiries.*

Within three weeks of my arrival in the country, North Korea was to celebrate the 75th birthday of Kim Il Sung.[13] To mark this auspicious occasion, the Pyongyang Metro was expanded and two new stations were opened: Yonggwang and Puhung. The former, whose name meant 'Glory', served the Koryo Hotel and the latter, 'Restoration', was within walking distance of our guest house. Usually when we went to the Koryo together, Madame Beatrice and I preferred to walk and would politely turn down the offer of a car and driver from Mr Choe, who seemed to think it his duty to ensure that we enjoyed the trappings of privilege to the full. When I went on my own I liked to take the underground. I wasn't going

---

[13] On April 15th 1987.

to learn much about this city from inside a car, I'd decided. As for my fears that people were looking at me with animosity, I'd quickly dismissed them as fanciful. It was understandable that I was the object of so much attention because they had probably never seen a Westerner in the flesh before. Clearly there was no ill intent.

On one occasion I was going down the escalator at Puhung behind a lady with a small boy strapped to her back, which was the normal way for mothers to transport their smaller children, there being no pushchairs or prams in North Korea. The little boy happened to look back and see me and, without a moment's hesitation, he cried 'Daddy!', to the great amusement of all those who heard and the acute embarrassment of his pink-faced mother when she turned round to look.

Mr Choe, I knew, would disapprove of these journeys and I never told him about them. So I felt rather awkward to be standing on the platform at Puhung with him, while the station manager gave a little speech of introduction, which included an uncomfortable reference to all the foreign guests who had visited – he didn't say travelled on, I noted – the Pyongyang Metro and had unanimously declared it to be the finest underground train system in the world.

When Mr Choe had announced that an official visit to the Pyongyang Metro was being arranged for me, I had wondered whether I should tell him there really was no need, as I was already a regular passenger. But I hadn't wanted to cause offence. He liked to show off his city and I was grateful that he organised such trips for me. So I had said I was very pleased, confident that I wouldn't be putting him to too much trouble since nothing more could possibly be involved than a stroll up the road and a ride on a train.

It was with considerable embarrassment, therefore, that I had found an official interpreter had been summoned from the publishing house and that a car was waiting for us in the courtyard. We had swept out through the gate of our compound, turned right onto the main road and driven the 200 metres to the station.

If nothing else, the Pyongyang Metro was probably the most attractive air-raid shelter in the world. An escalator brought passengers some hundred metres underground, to the accompaniment of martial music. As we had descended, Mr Choe had explained that the whole system was built for the dual purpose of transporting people and protecting them from the next attack by the US imperialists.

At Puhung Station a short passageway led from the bottom of the escalator to the top of a splendid, wide staircase overlooking a picture-gallery scene of marble flooring, bronze bas-reliefs, cheerful frescoes and a huge painting of a smiling Kim Il Sung standing head and shoulders above a group of workers, farmers, students and white-coated technicians.

I felt thankful, as I gazed on all these wonders, that none of the station guards had given any indication that they knew me.

Compared to the wonders of the station, the serviceable green and cream trains were something of a disappointment. Mr Choe insisted we should take one to the next station, Yonggwang, since if anything, he said, it was even more spectacular than our own. I didn't have the heart to tell him I already knew it was. With its massive polished platform, its vaulted ceiling, its chandeliers, its marble pillars, its extended murals of Pyongyang lining both platform walls and its two entrances reached by wide staircases, from the top of one of which painted images of Kim Il Sung and Kim Jong Il, standing on the summit of Mount Paekdu, looked down on all this loveliness, I felt the name 'Glory' hardly did it justice.

I'd got away without detection at Puhung. As we sat on the train I kept my fingers crossed, hoping I would be as lucky at

Yonggwang. I was. The serious-looking girls in their dark blue uniforms with their identically severe, shoulder-length hair, whose duties seemed to cover little more than signalling with a giant red lollipop for a train to leave, guarding the foot and the top of the escalators and gathering in gossiping cliques, scarcely took any notice of the foreigner and his interpreter. It was very different from the stares I was used to when I travelled on my own.

Kim Il Sung's 75th birthday was the greatest national holiday of the Korean people. In telling me this, Mr Choe was not reticent in describing to me the enormous honour I was to enjoy as a special guest at the 'birthday party', as he put it. I would even have a place on the viewing platform for the grand parade in Kim Il Sung Square, to be held in the presence of the great leader himself.

The sight of the vast Kim Il Sung Square took my breath away when, on the morning of the parade, I emerged onto the stone steps that served as a viewing platform. Immediately before me was a great sea of pink, stretching as far as the River Taedong, on the far side of which the Juche Tower shimmered in the distance.

There were flags; there were streamers; there were balloons. Above and to the sides, everywhere there was bright colour – pinks, yellows and reds. And there was near silence from the people, rank upon rank, column by column, block after block, who, holding aloft bunches of artificial flowers, created the expanse of colour that lay before me, one moment pink, the next a deep, rich red with a huge hammer, sickle and writing brush emblem of the Workers' Party of Korea shining golden yellow at its heart.

I asked Mr Choe how many people there were.

'Two million,' he replied promptly. Mr Choe had a tendency to exaggerate, but I thought he was pushing it a bit too far this time. Fortunately Gerhard, my Korean-speaking colleague from East Germany, was on hand to explain. Koreans, he said, had terrible trouble with translating large numbers, since they had a separate word for ten thousand. Hence one hundred thousand was, in Korean, ten ten thousands, and what Mr Choe had probably meant by two million was, in fact, two hundred thousand.

Gerhard went on to explain the importance of the concept of ten thousand to Koreans. The word, he told me, was *man*. Mangyongdae meant literally ten thousand views. 'By the way,' he went on, 'you will hear the people cry '*Manse!*' when they see Kim Il Sung. It means they want him to live for ten thousand years.'

That was exactly what the people did when Kim Il Sung stepped out onto the platform of honour. He was, I judged, 20 or 30 metres away from us, on a higher level. I imagined that I just caught a glimpse of his head among all the waving arms of the people around me. For the whole of Kim Il Sung Square had gone wild; the deafening cries of '*Manse! Manse! Manse!*' drowned out the triumphal music struck up by a military band as soon as the great leader made his appearance. With looks of pure joy on their faces, people – both those around me and the thousands in the main part of the square – stretched their arms aloft and jumped up and down on the spot. Director Kim was doing the same. I noticed him in particular because he was standing immediately to my left and was thus between me and the tribune where the great leader was standing and – I would see later in television pictures because I could see nothing at the time – waving in acknowledgement to the crowd.

I felt someone nudge my arm and Mr Choe, who had been on my right but, since we had all turned to gaze towards the great leader, was now directly behind me, indicated that I should take a photograph. I was astonished by the look on his face; normally calm to the point of appearing lugubrious, he had never previously let slip his stoic air. But now there was a look of rapture on his face, a childish grin had transformed his normally down-turned mouth, and his eyes were shining. I thought I could even detect a tear in each.

I took my picture by holding my camera above my head and, I hoped, also above the arms of the crowd. The result turned out better than I had anticipated, although I wondered if people back in Britain would be as excited as I was by this particular photograph, since all that could be discerned was a tiny black blob above a concrete parapet that might, just possibly, have been the head of the great leader.

Chapter 2

*I*t is quite flattering for ordinary visitors to be the object of all the attention lavished on them by their North Korean hosts. The entourage of driver and interpreter, and the food and accommodation that are, by North Korean standards, luxurious are, so foreign guests are supposed to believe, an expression of traditional Korean hospitality. But sooner or later the realisation hits you that the practical benefits are mutual.

With the US and other imperialists, hand in glove with the South Korean puppet clique of the day, unrelenting in their scheming to undermine and overthrow the Republic, there is a need for vigilance at all times. Businessmen, academics and diplomats, members of fraternal delegations and language advisers, all could have been sent to North Korea to gather information or spread false propaganda. So the foreign visitor, however innocent his or her reasons for being in the country, is kept under constant surveillance.

I discovered the rationale for this official xenophobia in a speech made by Kim Il Sung himself in 1979.[1] In it he repeated an oft-spoken exhortation to the people to dress smartly and behave

---

[1] 'Let Us Improve Nampo and Make It a Modern Port City; Speech at a Consultative Meeting of the Senior Officials of Nampo City, December 29th 1979'. In *Kim Il Sung: Works*, vol. 34, January–December 1979. Foreign Languages Publishing House, Pyongyang, 1988. In the speech Kim Il Sung stated: 'Tourism should not be without control on the pretext of letting people go sightseeing. Because we have not yet reunified our country, we cannot draw foreigners at random into the country ....' Later in the same speech he said: 'When Nampo has been developed into an international, modern port city, many people from capitalist countries will visit it. Therefore, its citizens should be well trained. The education of the citizens must be intensified to prevent them from being contaminated with capitalist ideas.'

courteously at all times, in this case in the port city of Nampo, not far from the revolutionary showcase Pyongyang. In other speeches he often stressed to the people, particularly those in the capital, the importance of making a good impression on foreign visitors as a way of upholding the dignity of the country; a few non-believers might even be shown the advantages of socialism. Some foreigners, he was wont to point out, might not be convinced of the justice of the DPRK cause; worse still, there might be some who were actually hostile and might in fact be in the country with the intention of doing some mischief. Just to be on the safe side, he hinted in his 1979 speech to senior officials in Nampo, all foreigners should be treated as potential spies.

The message will have been driven home. North Koreans are urged, even obliged, to turn to the great leader in all they do. Regular weekly study sessions are held at which the people learn by heart sections of the works of the great leader, on topics ranging from such general matters as public security and what is considered proper behaviour in the street and at work, to guidance in their professional and political activities, to intimate personal hygiene hints on brushing their teeth and washing their feet.

The underlying message is always that the great leader is right and that everyone should act precisely in accordance with his instructions. Shortcomings and mistakes, he states quite openly, are invariably the result of someone somewhere not doing precisely what he or she has been told. The great leader can have had no complaints, though, about how his advice on treating foreigners is adopted, given the zeal with which an entire population, from interpreters and hotel staff, taxi drivers and sales assistants, to people in the street, observe and report on the few foreigners who make it into their midst.

Behind Enemy Lines

*C*apitalists, I had read somewhere in the collection of books in my office, were interested only in seeking pleasure and leading an easy life. Mr Choe put the point somewhat more bluntly: my colleagues with the English Section at the Foreign Languages Publishing House were worried that someone as young as me would be lazy and interested only in having a good time.

It occurred to me this might be a veiled warning. I felt guilty about deceiving Mr Choe by sneaking out in the evenings, but the daily routine he seemed to think I should observe would have consisted of spending the daytime working in my office and the evenings and nights across the corridor in my bedroom watching television and sleeping. The farthest I could hope to go was the second floor of the guest house, where we ate three times a day.

Mr Choe asked me from time to time if I enjoyed watching the television. I didn't have the heart to tell him what I really thought: that it was turgid, repetitive, uninspiring propaganda that concerned me deeply because of what it indicated about the audience. Anyone who watched, night after night, news broadcasts of the same man – Kim Il Sung – standing in the same slightly lopsided posture, in front of the same vast landscape painting, with his right arm extended in the same way to greet his foreign guests, while the news reader chanted the same words – 'The great leader Comrade Kim Il Sung today met ...' – must have been deprived of the natural human interest in novelty and variety.

The documentaries were hardly any more interesting and I wondered if the propaganda bombardment had so devastated people's sense of reasoning that they could watch the beaming farmers, apparently content with the success of the previous autumn's harvest, without wondering why they had to get by on a couple of bowlfuls of rice a day. This was what I had good reason to believe was the basic diet, since my source was Madame Beatrice, whose inclination was to see the best in everything around her in North Korea. I had been left in no doubt that she was a fervent supporter of Kim Il Sung, his country and the system he had created after having my head bitten off over a casual remark about the great leader's uninspiring appearances on television.

I told Mr Choe it was difficult for me to watch television because I didn't understand the language. It was a good answer, I thought, because apart from being honest, it explained why I couldn't discuss programmes he might fondly have imagined I'd seen. If, on the other hand, he chose to interpret my answer as an explanation of why I went out in the evenings – as I assumed he knew I did – I hoped he might be sympathetic.

My resolve to compensate for my shady social life by being exemplary at work was being sorely tested by *On the Art of the Cinema*. It was proving extremely heavy going. This had been anticipated, though, and I enjoyed sympathy from all sides.

'How do you find the translation?' asked Li Chang Sul. He had been shown into my room a week after my arrival by Mr Choe, who introduced him as 'Head of English Works Section'.

'It's not too bad at all,' I said, which wasn't exactly true. 'It seems a highly technical piece and under the circumstances I think the translator has coped quite well.'

I was working with pen on typewritten paper, and having hacked my way through some bizarre use of English I'd been left to contemplate whether my mass of probably indecipherable corrections left any room for an attempt to restructure sentences and paragraphs as a way of moulding a more logical argument, if that was indeed what was wanted.

Li Chang Sul picked up the latest of the cheap, brown pages I'd been working on and apprehensively I awaited his judgement. 'It is good,' he told me after the briefest of glances at the mess I'd made of the neat typewriting.

So I owed Mr Choe my thanks. He'd advised me, when he'd brought the first packet of work to my room, 'Make many changes. Then they like your work.' It had proved a slow and laborious process and I apologised to Mr Li for the time it was taking to complete this work, publication of which, as Mr Choe had told me, was so eagerly awaited around the world.

'Not at all,' he said. 'Take your time. The work is very important.'

'Actually,' he added confidentially after Mr Choe had excused himself, 'we gave this task to translators who are young and not so experienced.'

I wondered if my predecessor had been aware of this fact. Madame Beatrice had shaken her head when I had told her what my first text would be. It had, she informed me, been the subject of a major row between my predecessor Evans, who was from Zimbabwe, and the Section, after he had taken the unheard-of step of sending it back to be translated again. By the time of his departure they hadn't complied and it occurred to me that getting rid of Evans might have been the more expedient option.

My painful progress through *On the Art of the Cinema* was regularly interrupted as work that was considered even more important was brought to me. I wasn't sorry. It was a long and complicated treatise that freely mixed the technicalities of cinema-making with convoluted ideological argument, neither of which was a strong suit of mine. It was a struggle to make sense of other ideas, too, such as the suggestion that film-makers should use wide-screen cinematography in order to bring out to the full the characters' broad feelings of reverence for the great leader.

Apart from coming as a relief, the interruptions also made me feel there was some point to my work. *On the Art of the Cinema*, like the bulk of the texts I would be editing, had been published in the original Korean over a decade before.[2] But the more important texts that were brought to me – sometimes translations of speeches made that very day – gave me a sense that there was some real responsibility in what I was doing. What the great leader or the dear leader had said might be picked up by the world's media, although the first time I was given an urgent text to edit – Kim Il Sung's speech to a meeting of the Non-Aligned Movement – I had to admit I had only vaguely heard of the organisation he was addressing. As for the main subject of

[2] *On the Art of the Cinema* was published in Korean in April 1973.

discussion – South–South Cooperation[3] – it was a concept that was entirely new to me.

In May 1987 Pyongyang hosted an Extraordinary Ministerial Conference of Non-aligned Nations on South–South Cooperation. Kim Il Sung took the opportunity to offer an insight into his foreign policy, the cornerstone of which was developing South–South Cooperation with the aim of establishing 'a new and fair international economic order'.[4]

What this new order entailed, he implied, was that the world's creditor nations would take steps to ease the debt burden of the poorer ones. He also urged the non-aligned countries to step up their anti-imperialist struggle so as to thwart the attempts of the imperialists to interfere in the internal affairs of, and even invade, the developing countries. As for the situation nearer home, the great leader called for the Korean peninsula to be turned into a 'nuclear-free peace zone'. He also demanded the withdrawal of US forces from South Korea.

There was nothing new in these ideas. Even so, something called the Pyongyang Declaration was adopted, which represented the meeting's seal of approval on the new world order as outlined by Kim Il Sung.[5] In this brave new world, it seemed North Korea and its leader would be playing a prominent role.

---

[3] South–South Cooperation is a foreign policy initiative under which the developing countries get together to enhance their economic influence in the international arena.

[4] 'Let Us Develop South–South Cooperation: Congratulatory Speech at the Extraordinary Ministerial Conference of Non-aligned Countries on South–South Cooperation, June 9 1987'. In *Kim Il Sung: Works*, vol. 40, May 1986–December 1987. Foreign Languages Publishing House, Pyongyang, 1995.

[5] *Korea Today*, 1987, 7.

Philippe thought that his three Belgian friends were buckling under the strain of living in North Korea. We'd been to meet them several times in my first few weeks in Pyongyang. One of them always spent the evenings listening to his Walkman; whether he was sitting with us or alone at another table nearby, he would take no part in the conversation. The other two would do little more than complain about 'the Koreans'. They hated their dreary hotel but could rarely drag themselves out of it in the evenings. The only place they wanted to go was home.

I was lucky, I concluded, to have fallen in with Philippe. There seemed little point in coming to such a strange place just to moan about the boredom and the isolation. There was an unknown city to explore and new people to meet. Philippe, who spoke the language and knew his way around the city, was an ideal companion. He even introduced me to his Korean friends, and they emboldened us by insisting that Mr Choe had no right to stop us leaving the guest house on our own.

We decided to try something harmless as a means of testing the water: a visit to the Moran Tea Bar, which as a regular Korean restaurant was supposed to be off-limits to foreigners. The trip required a certain amount of planning. Philippe had found a reference to the place in an English-language guidebook to Pyongyang, which described it as a favourite haunt of young people. There was a photograph showing a smiling group of students sitting at a table in a softly lit alcove. What the tourist guide failed to mention was the restaurant's location. Still, Philippe had managed to track the place down to the so-called Restaurant Street by the Koryo Hotel.

Changgwang-*gori*,[6] as the street of restaurants was properly known, was what passed for Pyongyang's entertainment district. Along both sides of the wide street were blocks of flats of a height that gently undulated between 20 and 30 storeys. The ground floor of the blocks, which were set at irregular angles, was given over to restaurants: *pulgogi*[7] 'houses' with large picture windows, through which the clientele could be seen cooking and eating the famous Korean grilled meat dish; fish restaurants with port-hole windows where blue and green were the predominant colours; restaurants selling the traditional *chongol* hotpot; and tea houses. There were beer halls, too, where the menu offered little more than the dried fish that was such a popular accompaniment to the glasses of draught *Ryongsong*.[8]

The early summer scene was quite idyllic as we strolled up from the Koryo Hotel, where our taxi had dropped us. The weather was fine and mild and the darkening sky was turning the pastel oranges and greens of the apartment blocks a richer shade. Young men dressed smartly in shirt-sleeves were strolling with girls, many in brightly patterned flowing dresses, who maintained a discreet distance just behind their male companions. There were families, too; the chatter of the children brought a pleasantly lively note to the still of the evening. Other young men were gathered in doorways, sharing a surreptitious cigarette. Girls in the turquoise uniforms of university students talked and giggled in groups.

Our restaurant was set a little way back from the street, almost hidden by more imposing premises on either side. As we stood in the doorway, the conversation and laughter died away. There

[6] The suffix *gori* means street.

[7] Literally, 'fire meat'.

[8] A dark, locally produced beer.

was absolute silence as every eye turned on us. A nervous waitress approached and said something in Korean. Reassured when Philippe replied, she asked us to wait. She then told the dozen or so people at the largest table to get up so we could sit.

It didn't look much like the cosy little place with intimate alcoves suggested in the photograph in the guidebook. It was a square room with half a dozen Formica-topped tables. Nor was it filled with students. The clientele were families, with the children being treated to ice cream.

We weren't asked what we wanted. The waitress simply brought us two bowls of white ice cream, two chunks of white bread and two cups of black tea. It was terribly bland. Even so, Philippe assured me, for our fellow customers this was a rare treat. The bill would take a sizable chunk out of a monthly pay packet, but this was a small price to pay compared to the valuable ration coupons they would also have to hand over. All of which must have made us wealthy foreigners look extremely callous, I thought, in making a couple of families give up their places.

The situation became even more embarrassing when we tried to pay. The waitress refused to accept our foreign exchange currency and demanded that we pay in the local currency which, as Philippe pointed out, we were not permitted to possess. Eventually she took our money, but only after we promised to return the next day with our interpreter, who would settle our bill for us. Then we would have our own money refunded.

Although nothing was said, we could sense the disapproval: Why hadn't we gone to one of the hard currency restaurants for foreigners? Anyway, what were we doing there without an interpreter?

Possibly Mr Choe was making the same point when he invited Philippe and me out for dinner. If he knew about our visit to the Moran Tea Bar, though, someone else must have told him because we hadn't said a word to anyone about it. We certainly hadn't taken an interpreter with us to get our money back.

The driver would take us to the restaurant, Mr Choe told us, the fashionable Chongryuguan. The building, some 15 minutes' walk from our guest house, was supposed to resemble a boat by the River Potong. Mr Choe would join us there. It was important that the other foreigners didn't see us, he explained, especially Madame Beatrice, since they would be jealous.

A private room had been reserved on the first floor of the restaurant. The four of us – Pak had also been invited – sat cross-legged at the low table. Mr Choe and Pak were highly amused throughout the meal as I squirmed about on the floor, trying to find a comfortable position. If my back wasn't hurting, then it was my thighs. Even when I tried the unconventional and stretched my legs out under the table, it wasn't long before some muscle or other was protesting.

Despite the discomfort, I had a very enjoyable evening. The food was delicious, with the waitress cooking the centrepiece, a *chongol* meat and vegetable hotpot, at our table. Mr Choe made much of the *insam sul*, an orange liquor with a small ginseng root in it. 'It is very good for man,' he told us, laughing knowingly as he indicated what he seemed to think was a suggestively depicted ginseng root on the bottle's label.

Mr Choe, I discovered that evening, had a delightful sense of humour. He could even laugh at his command of English. Time after time I got him to try and pronounce 'flower', but not once did he manage anything other than 'plower'.

'I am too old to learn,' he told us. I was astonished that he had a daughter attending university, since I'd placed him somewhere in his mid-30s. Some 20 years older, in fact, he seemed to have led a fairly full life and had spent some time in Africa. It was an experience that had provided him with a fund of stories, most of them incomprehensibly referring to money and ending inexplicably with someone or something being 'in the pocket'. Clearly, the joke was lost in the translation.

Mr Choe drank little; he had a chronic stomach complaint. But having ensured that the rest of us were full and merry, and once Pak had returned after mysteriously disappearing from the room for a while, he declared that it was time to go. He told us it had been a pleasure inviting us, and we must do it again sometime. Then he made his excuses because he would not be returning to the guest house with us. This was the one night of the week he spent at home.

The three of us strolled back along the river. It was very pleasant; the night was still, on our right the water's surface reflected the moonlight, and overhead the branches of the trees that lined both sides of our path met to give me a sense that the three of us, like the courting couples who whispered to each other as they sat shyly holding hands on the benches along our way, were somehow cut off from the outside world and safe in the secrets we were sharing.

As we walked, a very contented Pak explained the reason for his disappearance towards the end of the meal. He had got up and left the room having, so he explained, been told by Mr Choe to go and settle the bill. Neither of them had brought any cash and Pak had had to scour the place for friends and colleagues to lend him the money. Why, I wondered, was he so happy about it?

Apparently, Philippe told me later, Mr Choe had promised Pak an extension of his stay with us at the guest house as a reward for paying for dinner. No wonder he'd been so happy. For people at the publishing house, whose regular work, day in, day out, involved nothing more than sitting at a desk turning Korean words into foreign words, a stint at the Ansan Guest House, normally lasting six months, promised a much more interesting and relaxed regime. It was a chance to eat well and spend time in the company of foreigners, touring the city's shops and hotels or just visiting their flats in the sort of informal contact that was normally prohibited.

That Mr Choe had sufficient influence to prolong Pak's stay, I had no doubt. It was a matter for the publishing house's foreign affairs department to decide who should be the interpreter for the foreigners at our guest house, and Mr Choe seemed to have a strong influence over Director Kim. Philippe said it was because he was higher up in the Party. Another factor, I thought, had to be Mr Choe's shameless exploitation of Director Kim's inability to speak a foreign language.

Although there might be some minor matter of business to discuss, such as holiday arrangements or the renewal of a residence card, Director Kim's weekly visits to the foreigners in his charge were clearly intended to be social. He came across as a kindly, easy-going man who understood that, despite the privileges we enjoyed, we might experience difficulties in his country. So the conversation would start with polite inquiries about my health, my family's health and my work. Then Director Kim might make a little speech which, judging by his smile, was clearly a trivial anecdote, certainly nothing very serious. 'The problem, it very serious,' Mr Choe would translate. Frowning, I would ask what was the matter.

Director Kim's light-hearted mood would quickly vanish as Mr Choe earnestly and at great length explained something to him. 'You not to worry. I take care of it,' Mr Choe would eventually tell me, and before I could respond he would say something reassuring to Director Kim. Evidently relieved, he would make another little speech, perhaps translated by Mr Choe as, 'Colleagues say your work very good,' and I would say, 'Thank you.' Then, exuding satisfaction at a job well done, Mr Choe would tell me, 'You see, problem solved. Mr Kim he go now.'

I often wondered if Director Kim was, after these encounters, left as confused and worried as I was. I would have liked to ask him, but Mr Choe would have had to interpret. I did, however, summon up the courage to tackle Mr Choe about his unique approach to interpreting. 'Ah,' he said, knowingly. 'So you understand I help you with Mr Kim.'

Mr Choe also insisted that he helped me at work. 'Your publishing house colleagues, they hope you get better soon,' he told me one morning when I went to his office looking for texts to edit. 'But I'm fine,' I protested. Mr Choe, however, would have none of it and insisted I should take it easy for a few days. I was working too hard, he'd decided, and he was looking after me.

What had actually happened, my investigations indicated, was that Mr Choe had forgotten to pass some texts on to me and had sent them back to the publishing house, unedited. Rather than admit to his error, he had told my Section that I was ill and unable to work for a few days. He thought I would be grateful for some time off.

I later made a point of explaining to my colleagues that I had not been ill. Perhaps I was being unfair on Mr Choe, but I was highly put out that he'd managed to undermine, in such a casual manner, my efforts to give the impression of being a dedicated worker. Moreover, worried about being dragged into the unreal world he seemed to be living in, I'd resolved to be scrupulously honest in all my dealings with my colleagues.

Such were the reflections and experiences I recorded for three months in the diary which, like the most inept of spies, I kept locked in a suitcase in a cupboard – until, that is, I was shown in a quite sickening manner just how little respect the authorities had for all foreigners.

On reflection, there was nothing I could have done, other than what I actually decided to do on finding that the suitcase had been sliced open down the length of one side. What I did was nothing.

The diary was still inside, but that did little to calm the revulsion I felt. Obviously I couldn't continue recording my experiences and observations, but somebody already knew my secret reflections. I'd tried so hard to make a good impression, conscientious in my work, not intentionally speaking out of turn or causing offence, but they'd committed this violation anyway.

Mr Choe was the obvious person to talk to. But if he hadn't been directly responsible for this abuse of my person, he must surely have known about it. So I needed an interpreter, someone to help me talk to the authorities. But in the unlikely event that I could persuade a colleague at the publishing house to help, they would almost certainly tell Mr Choe. I was desperate to protest, to make someone admit that a mistake had been made. But it would only lead to more frustrating, manipulated and ultimately pointless conversations.

Eventually I told Madame Beatrice, who was horrified. She had a word of advice, born of years of experience of dealing with the likes of Mr Choe. 'Do not mention it to the Koreans,' she confided.

Well, I'd already worked that out for myself.

Because he spoke the language, Philippe enjoyed a much more straightforward relationship with Mr Choe, who was impressed by his knowledge of North Korea. 'Philippe, he understand my country very well,' I remember Mr Choe saying on numerous occasions, after Philippe had revealed some snippet of information, such as the rise in the price of cigarettes at the department stores. But when he referred knowingly to such institutions as the Party Centre[9] and Room 35,[10] Mr Choe would look uncomfortable. For my part, I never showed my ignorance by asking what they were.

When I did make forays into the conversation, I would on not infrequent occasions find myself retreating apologetically. Even the most innocent of observations could be met with silence and sometimes a sharp intake of Philippe's breath or a clearing of his throat. I once revealed to Mr Choe, when a group of us were having a chat in his office, that I regularly met Ali, our Lebanese colleague, in the Potonggang Hotel, and I seem to recall Philippe saying for everyone to hear that I shouldn't have said that. But Mr Choe knew it, because he'd found us there one evening and Ali had even invited him for a beer.

The game of subterfuge between Philippe and Mr Choe was eventually brought out into the open, so Ali told me, by the barmaid at the Potonggang Hotel. The only telephone at our guest house was in Mr Choe's room, so Philippe had arranged for one of his Korean friends to ring him at prearranged times in the hotel's lounge bar. The plan seemed perfect, as far as Philippe was concerned, since he had developed a friendship with the girl who worked there and she could be trusted not to tell anyone that he had been called by a Korean.

However, the day after one of the regular phone conversations, Mr Choe made a point of dropping broad hints to Philippe about

[9] Kim Jong Il.

[10] A secretive office, believed to be responsible for overseas espionage operations.

the inadvisability of having local friends and the foolishness of trusting barmaids. The girl had apparently succumbed to the call of duty and reported that a Korean was having unauthorised dealings with a foreigner. The only saving grace was that Mr Choe clearly had no idea of the friend's identity.

I don't know quite how Ali came by all the details, although for him the lounge bar at the Potonggang was a regular evening haunt and he spoke good Korean. So perhaps he'd picked up something there. Anyway, by telling me the story he demonstrated an openness that was rare in a community where, I'd quickly learned, we had to be guarded about everything we said and who we said it to. Philippe told me to watch what I said to Mr Choe and Madame Beatrice; Madame Beatrice warned me to be careful about what I said to Mr Choe; Mr Choe claimed Philippe and Madame Beatrice repeated to him everything I told them. Philippe told me not to believe Mr Choe if he claimed that he, Philippe, had told him something because he, Mr Choe, was probably lying. Mr Choe told me Philippe was a liar. Ali seemed to have no objections to me talking to anyone; except, it turned out, himself.

I looked forward to running into Ali in the Potonggang Hotel. He was a well-read and highly erudite man whose knowledge and opinions about North Korea, although generally positive, were balanced and informed. He had written extensively on the country and was very fond of the people, whom he found charming, and of their lifestyle, which he admired for its simplicity.

It was all the more incomprehensible, then, that this most sensible and measured of men should inexplicably start ignoring Philippe and myself. It wasn't just a matter of not talking to us. At lunch one day he failed to greet us, he didn't linger for the customary chat afterwards, and from then on he simply refused to acknowledge our presence. It wasn't long before he had moved out of our dining room.

Mr Choe was the model of geniality when he stopped by my office to offer me an afternoon off work so that I could visit the Arch of Triumph, which he was at pains to tell me, is bigger than the one in Paris. Built, like the Juche Tower, on the orders of the dear leader to mark the great leader's 70th birthday in 1982, Pyongyong's Arch of Triumph straddles the central lanes of the main road that skirts the western foot of Moran Hill.

The Arch bears a number of inscriptions, including the words of the *Song of General Kim Il Sung* and the dates 1925 and 1945, the years when as a boy he set out on his fabled walk to China and when, as the sun of the nation and the lodestar of liberation, he returned home in triumph.

There is scant mention of the Pacific War or of the role of Soviet forces in North Korean accounts of the country's liberation in 1945. That the US defeated Japan is referred to only obliquely in condemning the one country ever to have used nuclear weapons. The inference is that it is likely to do so again.

In the world of North Korean propaganda, the Korean peninsula was liberated by one man, aided by a guerrilla band of faithful and heroic followers. During his adolescence in Manchuria, Kim Il Sung had, according to official accounts, proved a precocious youth and a leading light in revolutionary circles. His most notable achievements were the founding, while he was still at school, of an organisation called the 'Down with Imperialism Union' and his brief imprisonment in Jilin Gaol on the orders of the Japanese, who had found his revolutionary activities too disruptive for comfort.

The legend recalls how, over the following years, he made himself a revolutionary pain in the neck to the Japanese along the Chinese–Korean border. In 1932 he founded the Korean People's Revolutionary Army, the forerunner of the Korean People's Army. On September 1st 1936, Kim Il Sung spent his first night back in his homeland after crossing the River Amnok at the head of a guerrilla army. Before long he had established his main base on Mount Paekdu, the extinct volcano on the Korean–Chinese border that is regarded as sacred by the entire Korean nation. With his still small band of men and women, he inflicted a series of defeats on the Japanese.

Military success was just one side of the coin. The other was the political training of his soldiers and the people in the areas they liberated, and beyond. Revolutionary bases were set up across the northern part of Korea and political work teams were dispatched further south to parts of the country still occupied by the Japanese, to prepare the people for the day of national liberation.

At the height of the resistance to the Japanese, a son was born to Kim Il Sung and his fellow guerrilla Kim Jong Suk in the KPRA's secret camp. On February 16th 1942 a star rose over Mount Paekdu, signalling to the faithful guerrillas and the whole Korean nation the birth of a great general who would take up his father's mantle and lead them ever on to victory.

Kim Jong Il's birthplace is a rough log cabin in a forest on the mountainside. In Christmas card-like depictions the cabin is seen covered in snow, a light shining at the window. Today, this humble abode is preserved as one of the most sacred sites of the revolution.

Thus the birth of Kim Jong Il can be traced back to the field of battle. His father would continue the fight against the Japanese occupation for the next three and a half years, until the day of the country's liberation.

The Arch of Triumph stands close to Kim Il Sung Stadium, on the site of which, on October 14th 1945, Kim Il Sung made a historic speech following his triumphal return home after achieving the ambition he had declared as a 13-year-old boy.

'Ah, yes,' I said for Mr Choe to translate for the guide who was telling me about the Arch. 'That would be when he set out on the 3000-*li* Journey for National Liberation.'

Mr Choe, as I had hoped he would be, was impressed. It was time, I had decided, that I chalked up a few plus points. Given how much effort I was putting in to my work, it seemed unfair that he still saw me as a lazy, irreverent, pleasure-seeking capitalist. He made no bones about telling me he regularly checked with the cooks that I was having breakfast – the insinuation being that, having failed to get up on time on my first morning in the country, I had, ever since, regularly been starting work late. Even though he grudgingly admitted that he was told I only missed breakfast on Sundays, he still made a show of inquiring how long I slept after lunch, and appeared unconvinced when I said I didn't.

Despite my fierce resentment over the diary incident, I was determined to create a good impression. Striving to be irreproach-able was my instinctive reaction to a situation in which everyone around me was seeking to provoke me and find fault. Getting by in Pyongyang, I had decided, was a matter of scoring plus points to offset the unintentional mistakes.

My resolve to be a model worker was never tested more than during the regular sessions at the publishing house in which I discussed with the translators the corrections I had made to their work. 'In French we call this *confrontation*,' Madame Beatrice told me.

Because of the urgency of *On the Art of the Cinema* it was some time before I received my first summons. I was, despite Madame

Beatrice's dark hint, looking forward to a welcome break from sitting at my desk at home. And so that first visit proved to be. A car was waiting in the courtyard downstairs to take me to the publishing house, which turned out to be an innocuous-looking premises ten minutes' drive away. It was a long grey building of five storeys with a taller section stuck on one end.

There was an armed guard at the gate, just as there was outside every official-looking building I'd seen in the capital. Ours was a young lady, dressed in baggy green uniform and Mao cap. She pressed a foot pedal at the approach of our car, thus lowering the thick metal chain that stretched at just below bumper height across the entrance.

Mr Choe had already told me why such guards were necessary. They were there to protect key institutions from the US imperialists when they attacked. I wondered, as our car turned onto the driveway that arched up in front of the publishing house's main entrance, what would be the US forces' main target, if and when their mighty armies succeeded in overpowering the little girl on the gate. Would they go for the weekly *Pyongyang Times*, or perhaps the offices of the magazines? I concluded smugly that they would surely head straight for my own Section. After all, we were responsible for the words of the great leader himself.

A small delegation was waiting on the steps to greet me, including Mr Choe. He introduced me to the two other men, translators from the English Works Section, and then ushered the three of us inside. The interior had a cold and gloomy, grey feel about it, although some colour was added by a life-size portrait of Kim Il Sung and Kim Jong Il standing side by side on the wall opposite the main entrance. Mr Choe led us to the right and up some stairs to the first floor, where he held a door open so that I could pass into a vast room with a green carpet covering the whole floor. Both long walls had lined against them a row of armchairs of white wood and padded green seat and back. In front of each pair was a coffee table. Mr Choe told me I was in Number One Meeting Room, and left.

In truth, we didn't do much work. The two men were far too interested in me and my circumstances, and in telling me about their country. Korea, they informed me, had four distinct seasons: spring, summer, autumn and winter. What about England? The best scenery was to be found in the mountains; Kumgangsan[11] was known as the most beautiful mountain in the world. Had I heard of it? Not to worry. I must ask to be taken there. Also I should go to Panmunjom on the 38th Parallel, where the US aggressor army stood in direct confrontation with the glorious Korean People's Army. The situation was unstable, but a visit would be memorable.

Then they asked my age and my response of 25 provoked a lengthy exchange between the two of them in Korean. Did English people normally marry so young, they wondered. But if, as I said, I wasn't married, my fiancée must be waiting for me. Perhaps she might join me later in Pyongyang.

Baffled by their line of reasoning I told them that I didn't have a fiancée. I added gallantly that there was always the chance I might fall for a Korean girl.

This was the worst thing I could have said, so Philippe explained when I sought clarification of the strange conversation. The translators would have assumed that someone would have been

[11] Diamond Mountains; the suffix *san* indicates a hill or mountain.

hired who was already attached, because he or she would be seen as safer, in other words more likely to stay quietly at home in the evenings, rather than going out and causing trouble by drinking and chasing the opposite sex. I'd really blundered with my light-hearted reference to an interest in Korean girls, for whom liaisons with foreigners were absolutely forbidden, and by no less a person than Kim Il Sung himself. The translators would feel obliged to report what I had said to Mr Choe.

I wondered why, if they were so concerned about relationships developing, they had brought me and Philippe to the country. Surely it would have been wiser to stick to hiring more elderly and less troublesome employees, like Madame Beatrice.

I was already feeling woebegone because of the many mistakes that I had, in Philippe's view, committed. Pak the Spanish interpreter didn't like me, so Philippe informed me, because he considered me too much of a capitalist. This completely took me aback. I thought I'd been getting along fine with Pak, and although I racked my brains I couldn't think of what I might have said or done to offend him, unless it was something to do with the very weak joke I'd made in the car when I'd nervously gone with him to our local department store, the Rakwon, which Pak explained meant 'Paradise'.

'It would be paradise if I didn't have to pay for anything there,' I'd said.

Pak had been taking me to the Rakwon Department Store to help me buy a short-wave radio with money I'd saved from my first few months' salary. I'd anticipated being able to do this much earlier, but I'd had a shock when my salary had first been discussed; the sum on offer was far less than what I'd been promised. I would get the full amount, Mr Choe had promised me, after six months. As a result it had taken me longer than I'd expected to save up for a radio.

I'd needed Pak's help as an interpreter, but I was feeling extremely uncomfortable about his presence. For one thing, I was aware that the sum of money he was about to see me spend represented more than a mere fortune to him; it was hard currency, unobtainable to an ordinary translator such as himself. On top of that, I was wondering nervously if I was forcing him to aid and abet me in a crime.

I'd been devastated to learn from Philippe soon after my arrival that I would not be able to listen to the BBC World Service, for the simple reason that it was not permitted. Anyone who bought – or brought into the country – a radio capable of receiving anything other than North Korean broadcasts was obliged to take it to the police, who would make an adjustment to the tuning mechanism and render it incapable of picking up dangerous and harmful propaganda.

I'd asked Mr Choe and Pak, together and separately, if I would have to have any radio I bought doctored in this way. There seemed no point in buying one if I did. Neither had given me a direct answer, although Mr Choe had surprised me by observing that he thought the BBC was quite good.

All I got out of them was a promise that Pak would go along to the shop with me to interpret. But even in the car on the way to the Rakwon, he refused to say anything about taking the radio to the police. In fact, nothing was ever said; I'd simply breathed a sigh of relief as we headed directly home with my new purchase.

I was relieved also to find that reception of the BBC was good. For a few weeks I was careful to turn the radio off every time I heard someone coming to visit, but eventually I stopped bothering. Clearly, although no-one would take the responsibility of saying so, foreigners were not subject to the restriction on listening to foreign radio broadcasts. If that had not been the case, I reasoned with the benefit of hindsight, the radios would be doctored before they went on sale.

Our hosts liked to keep us up to date with developments in the news, so every weekday we would be given a copy of the bulletin produced by the Korean Central News Agency which, along with the Foreign Languages Publishing House and Radio Pyongyang, was a main engine of the country's foreign-language propaganda machine. I always held out the hope that the bulletin might contain some interesting item of news. Sadly it rarely, if ever, did. But at least keeping abreast of local events was an excuse for taking a break from work every morning to settle down with a cup of coffee and my bulletin.

Just as with all the country's other media, the KCNA bulletin opened with reports on who the great leader had met, where in the country he had been giving on-the-spot guidance, and who had been recent beneficiaries of his wisdom. There would be a list of the countries and leaders from whom he had received gifts of late and the details of any foreign ambassadors who had called on him during the previous day, either to hand over their accreditation or to bid him farewell. The KCNA bulletin might then devote a few pages to a few more newsy items, such as atrocities in South Korea, and would wind up with details of the latest violations of North Korean airspace committed by the US air force.

The Pyongyang Times, the English-language weekly produced by the Foreign Languages Publishing House, had the unenviable task of condensing all this into something informative. Presumably to make life easier for the editor, it adopted a fairly rigid formula in doing so. As a result, the front page would almost always carry a photograph of the great leader in the company of some visiting foreign delegation or other. The attention-grabbing headline, which cleverly would not refer directly to the picture but to an event of perhaps even greater importance, would read something along the lines of 'Great Leader President Kim Il Sung greets Secretary General of WXYZ' – WXYZ being some obscure revolutionary organisation in a little-known African country that was inexcusably ignored by the rest of the world's media.

The remainder of the front page would be filled with revelations along the lines of the great or dear leader receiving a gift from such and such a delegation visiting Pyongyang, although the reporters in my view always failed in their journalistic duty by not revealing what the gifts were. It would, I thought, have livened things up to compare, in value and prestige terms, the pair of tusks that might have come from the African head of state to the porcelain vase that could have been the gift of the visiting Chinese military delegation.

In a particularly good week for news, Kim Il Sung or Kim Jong Il might have been awarded a medal by some revolutionary group in Latin America, or an honorary doctorate by a university somewhere in the Pacific Ocean, or the freedom of a small Belgian town with a left-wing mayor. A kindergarten in Eastern Europe or a street in southern Africa might have been named after either Kim Il Sung or Kim Jong Il. And if all else failed, there was bound to be some group somewhere in the Third World that was studying, or some publishing house that had proved its impeccable revolutionary credentials by printing, a volume of the thoughts of the great leader or the dear leader.

I tended to skip the inside pages of *The Pyongyang Times*, which covered such domestic news as the latest agricultural production figures – invariably outstanding – and the completion of a new fertiliser factory or revolutionary opera, and turn directly to the international news on the back page. Not that I would read the articles, mind; the headlines provided all the interest I was ever likely to extract from what was an extremely blinkered view of world events.

Although there wasn't much digression from a pretty straight editorial line, the writers and translators always managed to come up with headlines to liven things up, presumably designed to bring to the boil the reader's simmering outrage. 'Provocative War Plan' might refer to some statement made by a US official about the North. A background piece on the South Korean president could go under 'Top Illicit Money Grabber'. As for the territory he governed, things weren't looking too good, to judge by 'South Korea Engulfed in Gunsmoke' and 'Land of Death: South Korea'.

But all South Korea's troubles could not be laid at the door of the president. 'The US: Wirepuller of Man-slaughtering', I felt, gave a nice hint as to what exactly might be going on. Japan, too, might find itself cast in a negative light, hence: 'Japanese Reactionaries' Arrogant Behaviour' was the response to some perceived slight. And if, as frequently happened, the US and Japan ganged up against the North, then among the rather neat headlines that might fit the bill were 'Monstrous Acts', 'Unpardonable Atrocities' and 'Fascism on the Rampage'.

I supposed that Philippe must have been right and Pak was harbouring a grudge against me for what he saw as my capitalist sympathies; that's the only explanation I could come up with for his outburst at the hospital.

Mosquitoes were quite a problem in Pyongyang, especially for us at the Ansan Guest House, which lay beside the River Potong.

That first summer in Pyongyang I reacted badly to the mosquito bites and my arms were covered with large, irritating red swellings.

Mr Choe told me I should go to the hospital. It had become something of a joke, his suggestion that we should rush off to see a doctor at the slightest sign of a health problem. A sneeze or signs of a temperature, and Mr Choe would be telling the driver he should get ready to go to the foreigners' hospital.

His concern for our health was, I'm sure, genuine, but there was also an element of wanting to show off the country's free medical care. The foreigners' hospital, which our elevated position entitled us to attend, was one of Pyongyang's finest medical facilities, located in the diplomatic quarter of town.

On this occasion I agreed to go and see a doctor, and Pak and I took a car and headed off across the River Taedong. There was nothing to worry about, the doctor told me, but I should apply some ointment he would prescribe.

It was after the hospital's pharmacy had filled a small plastic bottle with sufficient of the liquid for three days – I could get more after that, if I needed it – that my argument with Pak broke out. Proudly he handed me the little bottle and said, 'Now you see how good is our socialist system because you do not have to pay for your medicine.'

Even at the time I knew I should just smile and say, 'Thank you.' But I didn't. 'As a matter of fact,' I actually replied, 'we have free medical care in the UK.' Which hadn't been completely true for a while, but I'd wanted to bring him down a peg or two since he'd been far too smug for my liking.

Pak was furious. I'd always found his eyes quite fierce and now they were positively blazing as he almost screamed at me, 'You are lying!' Oblivious to the medical staff stopping to take in this scene, he went on, 'You are from a capitalist country. There is no free medical care in a capitalist country.'

Downstairs at the Koryo, my new friend was always pleased to see me. I'd discovered she was studying English, although she was making slow progress and relied on her English–Korean phrasebook to tell me about herself.

Through our awkward but nevertheless charming conversations I learned that she lived with her mother, father and brother in a four-room apartment on Chollima Street. She liked her work. On her days off she loved to walk on Moran Hill.

The bar was a quiet place where there were few interruptions. When other people occasionally did come in, I was happy to watch her at work, chattering and smiling.

In my haven, as I was now thinking of it, I reflected on Pak's naked hostility and the culture of dishonesty that meant he could assume so readily that I was prepared to lie in defence of my own country. And I thought about Mr Choe who, I was now convinced, was a master of manipulation and deception.

When I looked back on everything that had gone wrong so far – the violation of my suitcase, Pak's inexplicable animosity, Ali's alienation – all could be explained if I accepted that, despite his apparently genuine insistence that he only had my best interests at heart, Mr Choe was scheming against me behind the scenes. My thoughts had been taking me in this direction ever since Philippe had confronted me with the accusation that I'd told Mr Choe about the secret telephone calls he received at the Potonggang Hotel. So convincing had Mr Choe apparently made his lie sound that it had been only with the greatest difficulty that I'd managed to persuade Philippe that I was innocent.

I had no idea what Mr Choe might have told Ali to set him against me and Philippe. But now I had no doubt that he was sufficiently devious to want and be able to sow discord among the foreigners in his charge.

But what was the point? The answer was that Mr Choe wanted to leave me vulnerable and without any friends, apart from himself. Following this line of reasoning, I began to wonder about some of the confidences he conveyed to me in private. Mr Choe, it now seemed to me, hoped, by sharing supposed secrets with me, to gain my trust so that I, in turn, would confide in him. But now I came to question whether the purpose of his weekly visits to the foreign ministry, for instance, was quite as sinister as he made out. He had told me it was part of his duties to report on us foreigners. I didn't doubt this, but were the security people really so interested in everything we'd said, where we'd been and at what time, and who we'd met? What were they spending their time doing if they had to rely on Mr Choe for all this information?

It was an argument that, when I followed it through, made some sense of why he dropped hints about the hidden microphones in my room. From time to time he would tap the wall in a couple of places and put his finger to his lips, presumably to indicate the presence of a listening device or two. To my sceptical new way of thinking, the performance probably meant our rooms weren't bugged at all.

Perhaps I was being harsh on a perfectly innocent man. But I doubted it. The safest thing to do, I concluded, was simply to assume that everything he told me was a lie and, for my part, not tell him anything that might incriminate either myself or anyone else. Unfortunately, since he was effectively in charge at the guest house and because of his hold over Director Kim at the publishing house, I was very much at his mercy. All I could do was carry on being the model worker; my Section seemed to appreciate my efforts, and that no doubt counted in my favour.

As for Pak, he appeared to be enjoying the extended stay he had been promised at the guest house and it occurred to me that if Mr Choe had the influence to help people like that, he could probably also cause them a great deal of trouble. I wondered if there was any point having a quiet chat with Pak, to explain that he'd been turned against me by a manipulative boss. But I was pretty sure it wasn't the Korean thing to do. Come to think of it, Pak was presumably very happy with the situation. It looked as though I would just have to grin and bear any more outbursts such as the one at the hospital.

But going back to Mr Choe, perhaps it was time to make a stand. He'd shown, through his lying, his manipulation and the violation of my diary – for which, now more than ever, I was convinced he had been responsible – that he had only contempt for me and no regard for my efforts to respect his country. So, if the opportunity presented itself, I thought, I might just show him that he couldn't take my acquiescence for granted. But the question was, how? Mr Choe's genius was that he had so blurred the boundary between reality and the narrow world of restriction and deception he had created for the foreigners in his charge that I had no understanding of where I would be overstepping the mark, and with what consequences.

My main concern was that others might suffer as a result of my ignorance; or perhaps out of their own ignorance, they might overstep the mark.

I was worried when my friend said she had told her colleagues in the Koryo that I came to see her often. I thought I had misunderstood. But no. She knew I went to the hotel's upstairs 'counters', as she called them, and she instisted that she had talked to the other girls about her foreign friend.

She was happy because she knew what work I was doing and I would stay a long time. She said the words slowly in Korean and I recognised 'Foreign Languages Publishing House' and 'Works of the great leader Comrade Kim Il Sung'.

I said I wondered if it was a good idea to be telling the other girls about her foreign friend. She didn't understand. I supposed she knew what she was doing.

'It is because you are English,' Mr Choe told me, sadly, when soldiers arrived to man the guardhouse at the gate of our compound, which had previously been deserted. 'It is not my doing.' The inference was that, although he personally trusted me, there were those at a higher level who thought the Westerners needed closer watching.

But then Mr Choe found out about our new, very important neighbour – a vice-minister had moved in next door – and he cheered up. He told me to ignore the guards; they were not for the foreigners. He would criticise them if they stopped me on my way in or out. Of course I was free to come and go as I pleased. The guards were there to keep an eye on the other two buildings in the compound.

Thus, within two days Mr Choe told me, with utter conviction and an apparently compelling concern for my welfare, two wholly contradictory stories. I was right, I felt, not to believe a thing he said.

Despite my doubts, shared by Philippe, about whether our rooms really were bugged, we decided that to be on the safe side we should act as if they were, especially when doing something as illicit as listening to South Korean music. Philippe had bought himself a small, battery-operated radio and after lunch each day we would lock the front door and sit in the corridor that linked our flats – the safest place from prying ears – and listen to a pop music programme.

The tunes were a welcome alternative to the stuff played *ad nauseam* in Pyongyang. North Korean music consisted chiefly of film scores, revolutionary operas, folk songs and some light pieces. Although the melodies tended to be quite pleasant, there was no great variance of style and the perfection of the voices tended to become irritating. To make matters worse, a new song would be played to death on the radio and television and in the shops, restaurants and hotels.

What we heard on the South Korean radio was, by contrast, a mixture of well-known Western songs and some domestic productions. The Beatles seemed to be quite a hit in South Korea, as did Simon and Garfunkel. As for the South Korean songs, despite a clear Western influence they sounded highly original; innovative combinations of traditional and modern musical styles. So impressed was Philippe that he resolved that, the next time he went to China, he would try and buy some South Korean music and smuggle it back into the country.

There was an engineer staying at the Koryo – he was French I think – who had come up with a brilliant plan. He wanted to get rid of his 'minders', as he called them – an assortment of driver, interpreter and company official – but he had discovered that if he wanted to complain about them, the only person he could approach was the company official himself and, as he spoke only

Korean, the services of the interpreter would be required. No doubt the driver would also listen in.

Having learned that the hotel's bars were almost certainly bugged, the engineer decided to air his grievances directly with the internal security. So night after night he would sit at a bar, drinking beer, talking into the air and, he fondly imagined, a microphone, about what the driver, interpreter and company official had got up to that day. His main complaint was that they were scroungers on a scale way beyond the odd beer or packet of cigarettes that was normally passed on quite cheerfully by visiting foreigners to those working with them.

Not surprisingly, the scheme failed and the engineer continued to be pestered throughout the whole of his stay by the same driver, interpreter and company official attempting to extort, so he said, bottles of alcohol, meals, clothes, even money. What he had failed to appreciate was that, even assuming the authorities had found something wrong with the Koreans' behaviour, they couldn't have done anything about it, since by taking action they would have been tacitly admitting that the hotel's bars were bugged, which of course they weren't, if the official line was to be believed. The other flaw in the plan was that it was scarcely likely that anyone would take seriously the comments of a lunatic who spent every night drinking and talking to himself.

Our plan was to penetrate the secretive heart of Pyongyang. We'd studied a map and done our surveillance and we'd decided that, if caught, we could reasonably plead ignorance.

Maps of Pyongyang showed Changgwang-*gori*, the Restaurant Street that ran across the front of the Koryo Hotel, continuing northwards after it crossed Haebangsan Street into an area of green. Inside this area of green the street was met by a lesser road, which opened on to Chollima Street near the Changgwangsan Hotel. On the Koryo Hotel side entry was restricted by a heavily guarded, automatically extending and retracting gate that opened, apparently on a previously passed signal, to allow cars with darkened windows to sweep through. No-one ever seemed to enter or leave on foot. But on the Changgwangsan Hotel side there appeared to be no such security. Access was along a narrow street, which neither cars nor pedestrians ever seemed to use.

It was widely known that the central part of Pyongyang housed the offices and homes of the most senior Party and Government officials. Philippe had suggested that we see for ourselves what kind of houses they lived in, what sort of cars they drove – or rather, were driven in – and generally how the elite really lived.

We waited in the coffee shop of the Changgwangsan Hotel for night to fall. I drank beer to calm my nerves, as did Philippe, unusually for him. I knew that what I was about to do was foolish, but this was my way of rebelling against the injustice of my treatment. Of course, the authorities were unlikely to sympathise with my motive, and we had decided that, if we were caught, we would claim that we thought we were taking a short cut to the Koryo Hotel. We could hardly be condemned for getting lost.

The sky grew darker and we judged it was safe to set off. We crossed Chollima Street and entered the pitch darkness of the anonymous alley. It was completely deserted. There was no sentry post and, as we took a first few tentative steps, no challenge.

We'd only gone some 20 metres from the main road when the watchers declared themselves. A powerful spotlight suddenly came on. We stood like frightened rabbits in its bright glare. A voice spoke from the heart of the light; not unkindly, I thought with surprise. I didn't understand the words. I decided anyway that the game was up. But Philippe carried on regardless, even as I was taking a few hesitant steps out of the spotlight back in the direction we had come from.

The voice came out of the darkness again, more forceful and less pleasant, and Philippe decided it was time to go. But the main road didn't offer the expected sanctuary. Just as we stepped out onto Chollima Street a car pulled slowly out behind us. I noticed a hoop antenna on its roof and several other aerials sticking up from its front and rear. As we walked, it followed just behind, matching our pace. We hurried, and imperceptibly the car speeded up; we slowed, and it maintained precisely the same distance behind us.

On reflection, our plan seemed hopelessly naïve. After all the time we'd spent in Pyongyang who would we ever convince that we'd been looking for a short cut? We were going to be thrown out of the country. It would mean a moment of fame back home. But all I could think about were the uncomfortable days and weeks of shame, the humiliating questioning and the snickering at our stupidity, that I would have to endure before I was put on an aeroplane out of North Korea.

Still we headed for the Koryo, as if that had been our original destination, all the time with the menace of that dark, bristling Mercedes tracking us; until, that is, we reached an area where the street lamps were brighter. There, without our being aware of exactly how or where, the car vanished.

We heard nothing about our night-time adventure. Mr Choe never said a word. But to my way of thinking this didn't mean he hadn't been informed. It seemed logical to assume that, like telling lies, withholding information was a means of creating an atmosphere of uncertainty and deception around us.

But Philippe did get into trouble, although for an entirely unconnected offence, one that was serious enough for the man developing photographs at the Rakwon Department Store to decide that an impromptu public criticism was warranted.

Philippe's crime was to have taken a photograph in his room that showed just part of the great leader's portrait on his wall. If he'd shown the whole of the portrait or no portrait at all, there would have been no problem. But chopping him in half was considered an insult to the great leader's person. After a lecture that was stern and forceful enough to gather a sizable crowd, the self-righteous developer of photographs told Philippe he could take the rest of the prints away with him, but not the offending item, and he should be more careful in the future or the matter would have to be reported.

In retelling this episode I solved the mystery of why Kim Il Sung's portrait did not appear on the country's banknotes, if the story told me by a Soviet diplomat was to be believed. For a time it had, but disrespectful foreigners had been guilty of carelessly folding the notes in half, creasing the image of the great leader. Even intervention by the foreign ministry, which sent officials to the various embassies to explain how the banknotes should be folded carefully in three with the two ends meeting in the middle over the portrait, failed to remedy the situation and the notes were withdrawn.

Madame Beatrice was most impressed that I would be going to the 38th Parallel, since it was very rare for one of our number to be taken on this most sensitive of excursions so soon after their arrival.

Not wanting to disillusion Madame Beatrice, I didn't tell her that I suspected the choice of trip was in fact related to one of the more serious blunders I'd been guilty of, dating all the way back to the welcoming banquet arranged for me at the guest house.

A vice-director of the publishing house had attended, and he had taken the opportunity to stress that the Korean people did not hold me personally responsible for the crime committed against them nearly 40 years earlier. My government, acting on the orders of the US, was to blame for Britain's involvement in the Korean War, not the ordinary British people.

I stopped short of openly contradicting him, and although I made only a mild comment to the effect that our history books tended to tell a somewhat different story, I was aware that I had spoken out of turn. The vice-director's response was a gentle suggestion that during the time I spent in his country I could learn the truth of history.

The border village of Panmunjom lay five miles south-east of Kaesong, the ancient capital of Koryo, which was the first unified state on the Korean peninsula. I liked Kaesong; it had suffered little during the war and much remained there of historical interest. It had ancient temples, a Confucian College, a large traditional city gate and the site of an ancient palace. There was also a large statue of Kim Il Sung in the centre of the city.

My favourite sight in Kaesong lay within 100 metres of our hotel. A narrow stream was crossed by a bridge which, Mr Choe told me, was called Sonjuk Bridge. Here many centuries before a loyal servant of the Koryo Dynasty, Chong Mong Ju, had been murdered on the orders of Li Song Gye, the first king of the Li Dynasty. Soon after his death a bamboo tree, the symbol of faithfulness, had appeared on the spot and the bridge's name had been changed to Sonjuk, meaning 'blood-soaked bamboo'.

Subsequent kings sought to atone for the crime of their predecessor and next to Sonjuk Bridge there was a pavilion housing the Loyalty Monuments. These were two stone tablets honouring Chong Mong Ju, each standing on the back of a carved tortoise, that had been placed there by the Li Dynasty monarchs Yongjo in the eighteenth century and Kojong in the nineteenth century.

My overriding impression of Kaesong, though, was of the people staring. In Pyongyang I was always made uncomfortable by the bold appraisal I was subjected to by strangers in the street. But in Kaesong it was far worse. People would stop as they saw me approach with Mr Choe; they would interrupt conversations and nudge one another and point at the foreigner. And they would continue staring long after I had passed, as I discovered whenever I looked back.

Mr Choe explained that the people of Kaesong had to be extra vigilant, living as they did so close to the 38th Parallel and the US imperialist army massed on the other side, just a short distance away. I said nothing, but I did wonder if the people of Kaesong seriously thought that the Americans would be daft enough to send, as part of an advance unit of their invasion force, someone who stuck out like such an extremely sore thumb and who, were they to address him, they would discover had a command of their language that entailed little more than an ability to order beer and tell a barmaid her dress was pretty.

I was having to rethink my plan for learning Korean. My original idea had been to absorb the language by listening to people speaking around me. I would soon be hearing the same words repeated quite often, I reasoned, and if I couldn't work out for myself what they meant, I could always ask someone. Before long I would be able to make out the gist of conversations and from there it would be plain sailing to fluency.

Still, I'd decided to buy a book to help me along and one day I'd set off for the Potonggang Hotel and its large bookshop. There, among the familiar volumes of the president's works, the pamphlets of ideology produced by his son, biographies of the two men written by admirers both domestic and foreign, albums containing spectacular photographs of spectacular scenery, music tapes of revolutionary operas and calendars filled with the beaming, chubby faces of children living happily in the leader's warm embrace, I'd found just what I was looking for – a small, slim volume called *Speak in Korean*.[12]

By its size, it suggested that learning the language wouldn't take long, or much effort for that matter. Now that was just what I wanted! So I'd bought my copy and headed home to get my teeth into Lesson One, 'Modes of Address'.

Mistakenly, I decided to skip the first 30 pages, which dealt with grammar and the alphabet, thinking all this would take care of itself as I made progress with the vocabulary. It wasn't many weeks before I'd realised my error and gone back to tackle the matter of word order and the construction of characters, the former being highly complex, the latter quite simple once one has discovered, as I did by reading cigarette packets, that written Korean consisted of characters that were formed according to logical rules by simple letters.

I was ignorant of all this as I carefully repeated to myself from Lesson One, 'Excuse me, Comrade Guide!' It was an interesting start to my studying, I thought, but I was disappointed by the

[12] *Speak in Korean*. Published by the Foreign Languages Books Publishing House, Pyongyang, 1975.

rather mundane contents of the next few chapters. 'Let's have a little walk' was far too commonplace and likely to get me into trouble, anyway. But then I got to Part 2, which was called 'Everyday Conversation'. 'What building is that?' seemed a perfectly reasonable thing for the new arrival to be asking on the way to the hotel. Soon, however, the friendly chit-chat turned to, 'Let's mutilate US imperialism!'

As interesting as 'On the Way to the Hotel' was I felt that the book didn't really get into its stride until its closing chapters. 'At the Hotel' seemed almost a waste of paper, since I couldn't envisage any circumstances where a foreigner would not have the services of an interpreter to take care of such chores as checking in and out. It was under the unlikely heading, 'Farewell Talk', that I found some of the book's true gems.

'The US imperialists should quit South Korea' was right up there among the likes of 'I've enjoyed my stay here' as a favourite form of saying goodbye, as was 'The Pak Jung Hi clique is the dual lackey of US and Japanese imperialism'.

Then I came to the appendix, 'Our Foreign Friends Say', and here I began to speculate what a boon this little book must be to the foreign visitor who'd been scouring less helpful volumes in search of just how to say, 'Marshall Kim Il Sung is the sun of the oppressed and exploited people the world over'. And what a relief it must have been to the overawed and tongue-tied visitor to find just the right thing to impress his Korean hosts: 'Juche Idea is the great idea that announces the downfall of the twentieth century's imperialism'.

I'd tried a few of these phrases out on the guest house's waitresses when they paid their daily visit to my office to replenish my supplies of biscuits, fruit, bottled water and cigarettes. I never knew if they'd giggled because of what I'd said or the way I'd said it.

Mr Choe had ensured that I was quite worried by the time we were being driven from our hotel in Kaesong to the demilitarised zone. I'd noticed that the number plates on our car had been removed and that a red flag had been attached to the roof. 'Security,' Mr Choe explained. He made no bones about the fact that the situation was very tense, entirely the fault of the US imperialists, who were in the habit of violating North Korean territory at will. I was, he insisted, entering real danger.

He told me the story of how, a few years earlier, there had been a particularly gruesome incident in the border village itself, when two American officers had been axed to death by peace-loving Korean guards who had objected to a tree being cut down.[13]

We drove some way south, past barbed wire fences and large concrete constructions that Mr Choe said were tank traps. We stopped at a solitary building in this no-man's land. Here we were greeted by a military officer. Although he bore no insignia of rank on his uniform, Mr Choe told me he was a major. He painstakingly studied my documents. Then he joined us in our car and we drove on.

Apparently there was more for me to see at Panmunjom than there was for those visiting from the southern side. I was taken to the low building where the Armistice was signed in 1953 ending the Korean War. It was significant that the ceremony was held on the North's territory, so the major told me, as this indicated that the DPRK had made territorial gains. Also significant were

[13] In 1976, American soldiers in the Joint Security Area at Panmunjom attempted to cut down a tree that was obscuring their view. A confrontation ensued with North Korean soldiers and two American officers were killed with their own axe.

the photographs of the American generals being driven to the signing ceremony, since their cars displayed white flags, which suggested they were surrendering.

I was nervous as I emerged onto the steps of the Reunification Pavilion that overlooked the main border area at Panmunjom from the northern side. I saw a number of huts painted light blue, lying across the line of raised concrete that was the 38th Parallel. Between the middle two huts stood three North Korean soldiers on our side, two slightly behind one who stood at the apex of the triangle, his toes right up against the line. Normally, Mr Choe explained, three US soldiers would have been opposing them in perfect symmetry. But alerted to our visit, he went on, and ashamed of their illegal presence at a post that should, according to the Armistice, have been occupied by United Nations forces, they had just left.

He touched my arm. 'Look,' he said, pointing up at an observation platform on the southern side of the divide. 'The US imperialist is taking your photograph.'

My legs were a little unsteady as we descended the steps and entered one of the huts. Here, the major explained, the Armistice talks had taken place and meetings between the North Korean and US imperialist militaries were regularly held. A green baize-covered table divided the room. On each side of the table were seats and down its middle was arranged a row of microphones, their cables, so the officer told me, lying exactly along the 38th Parallel. He invited me to cross to the other side of the table. 'Now you are in South Korea,' he said with a smile that brought the first welcome relief from the tension.

I sat on the far side of what I now thought resembled an elongated card table. Mr Choe was looking away to my right and I followed his gaze. I saw a helmeted US soldier with his face pressed against a side window.

'Now the US bastards, they will never let you into their country,' Mr Choe told me, impassively.

In the afternoon we visited an observation post in the dimilitarised zone to the east of Panmunjom, where another officer told me about the concrete wall built by the South Koreans to divide the country across its entire width, about the minefields they had laid, about the daily aerial violations of North Korean airspace by US aircraft, and about the regular incidents of shots being fired from the southern side of the DMZ.[14]

I gazed across the wide green space and saw nothing but beautiful, unspoilt countryside: rolling fields, scrub, bushes and trees. The officer lent me his binoculars, but still in the hazy distance I could not see a wall or any enemy. But I had no reason to doubt that they existed, just as the landmines must surely lie beneath the carpet of grass, and I wondered how anyone could possibly hope to make it across. In particular I thought of the four American soldiers Philippe had told me about who had apparently done just that, coming from the South to the North. He had heard about them from some African students who had run into them in the Rakwon.

They claimed they'd been in Pyongyang for a number of years. So why had no-one heard of them before? If they were being kept in hiding, as would probably be the case, then what had they been doing in so public a place as the Rakwon?

The students had insisted that the four had made no secret of who they were. But it seemed more likely that this was one of those sensational stories that were grist to the Pyongyang rumour mill; four new arrivals in town had perhaps been trying to pull a few legs. There said to be any number of Americans in Pyongyang: prisoners of war who had declined

[14] Demilitarised Zone.

the offer of, or had been prevented from, returning home in the 1950s; soldiers kidnapped from the US army in South Korea; deserters who had made the hazardous journey across the 38th Parallel.

It would be several years before I got to the bottom of the matter. By the time I did, Pyongyang's community of GI deserters numbered just three.

We spent the day following our visit to Panmunjom in the hills outside Kaesong, where we had a very pleasant picnic beside a waterfall. We also visited the ancient tomb of King Kongmin, not far from the city, where two burial mounds – of the king and his good lady wife – were attended by perfectly preserved statues of various courtiers, soldiers and ministers; all originals, Mr Choe assured me, and as such in marvellous condition considering the centuries that had passed since they were erected. But my lasting memory of that day is of Mr Choe's reaction to my comment that I was disappointed by the absence of bicycles in Pyongyang; in Kaesong, by contrast, it was a popular means of transport and I told him I enjoyed cycling. Mr Choe's response was to stop the car on a deserted stretch of dusty road and hail a boy, probably no older than ten, who happened to be cycling in the opposite direction. 'You ride,' he told me as the boy timidly offered me his bicycle. I did, for all of a minute before handing the bicycle back to the anxious and overawed lad.

That trip outside Pyongyang was probably my happiest memory of Mr Choe. He seemed more relaxed, especially after the visit to Panmunjom, and I wondered if he'd feared I might speak out of turn. I'd been tempted. I'd found the claims about the US surrender absurd and the description of my own country as a US 'satellite' insulting. The constant references to the Fatherland Liberation War, rather than the Korean War, had been ludicrous. However, I'd learned my lesson about speaking out on this most sensitive of subjects, but I did wonder – wasn't calling it a 'war of liberation' in fact a tacit admission that you started it?

Evidently not. The Americans not only had started the last war but were also likely at any moment to start another one, and the North Korean authorities never missed an opportunity to remind the people to be constantly on their guard.

When a South Korean airliner was blown out of the sky off the coast of Burma in November 1987, killing 115 people, the finger of suspicion was turned unhesitatingly on North Korea. With its history of terrorist attacks against targets in the South, and given its resentment over the attention the South was expected to attract as the host of the 1988 Olympics, Pyongyang appeared to have the means, the motive and the lack of scruple for undertaking such an outrage.

International condemnation swiftly followed, with the US and South Korea threatening sanctions against Pyongyang. The attack heralded the end of a period of détente between the two Koreas, in which the possibility of co-hosting the Olympics was being discussed. Clearly optimistic about the talks' success, Pyongyang had undertaken a massive building programme that would see the construction of three new stadiums, an entire sports village and several international-class hotels.

Even before the airliner's destruction, though, there had been strong concerns in South Korea about the North's intentions regarding the Olympics, should the talks on co-hosting fail. US experts had been called in to advise on security, including strengthening the defences around Seoul's Kimpo Airport to guard against possible missile attack. Worries were also expressed about the construction of a dam just north of the 38th Parallel which, if breached, could flood vast areas of South Korea, with the devastation possibly reaching as far as Seoul.

North Korea was no stranger to accusations of terrorist activity. It was believed to have been behind the October 1983 attack on a visiting South Korean government delegation in Rangoon that left 17 people, including four cabinet ministers, dead. South Korean president Chun Doo Hwan, the presumed target, was lucky to escape with his life. In 1968, North Korean agents had infiltrated as far as the presidential palace in Seoul in a previous assassination attempt on a South Korean president. In the subsequent two decades a number of tunnels were discovered beneath the 38th Parallel separating the two Koreas. These were intended, it was assumed, to facilitate an invasion of the South by the North.

The official North Korean media carried no immediate reports of the bombing of the airliner or of the accusations levelled against Pyongyang. Even so, there was a climate of heightened tension in the North Korean capital as the possibility loomed of a US reprisal attack.

My improved relationship with Mr Choe didn't survive the return to Pyongyang, and by the end of the year his suspicion of me had driven him to accuse me openly of spying. I suspected all was not well when Pak came to summon me. Mr Choe liked to run a relaxed ship, at least as far as protocol was concerned, and would drop in whenever he had something to discuss. So when a very serious Pak came to my room and told me that Mr Choe was waiting for me in his office, I was immediately on my guard. Pak and I had maintained an uneasy, somewhat cool relationship since the visit to the hospital, but now he was glaring at me with undisguised animosity.

Had they found out about the expeditions with Philippe, I wondered. But if that was so, Philippe would surely have some inkling and would have mentioned it. Or had I made some terrible mistake in my work, putting wholly inappropriate words into the great leader's mouth? If that was the case, then my response was obvious: since the translators made changes to my work after I'd edited and discussed it, it was almost certainly their error.

Mr Choe was sitting on the low windowsill in his office, facing the door. Pak went to sit on a chair to one side. I was left standing in the middle of the carpet as Mr Choe addressed me.

He didn't exactly get straight to the point. He asked me some blunt questions about my feelings for North Korea. I told him that I liked the country and its people very much, and in response to his next question, insisted that I would very much like to stay longer. I told him I really wanted to understand more about a place that had made such a positive impression on me. His face was impassive; there was not a flicker of the smile that was his usual reaction to such flattery.

It was Pak's turn to speak. He wanted to know, if that was the case, why I'd betrayed them.

'I don't know what you're talking about,' I retorted, thoroughly disconcerted by now.

They had found out that I had secret dealings with South Korea.
'No I don't,' I said.

So, when did the contacts with South Korea begin?

'Never,' I said, desperately casting about in my mind for a hint of what they might have got hold of. Oh, no! They must know about the radio. Had they already talked to Philippe? If so, what had he told them?

Mr Choe took over. They had found proof of my connections with South Korea in my clothes. My raincoat revealed that I was a spy.

I couldn't make head or tail of this. I knew they were paranoid, but surely not to the extent that a foreigner wearing a long raincoat must inevitably be a spy. Was it possible that they'd seen someone in a photograph in South Korea wearing a similar coat, who looked like me?

The explanation, when it came, was even more ludicrous. Pak had noticed the label in my mackintosh: Made in the Republic of Korea. Was this some sort of revenge for the hospital incident, I wondered.

I said there really was no need to fetch it so he could show me. I hadn't been aware that my raincoat was made in South Korea, but if they said so, I saw no reason to doubt them. But in my defence, I said there was a perfectly innocent explanation. We couldn't get away from the fact that my country and South Korea were trading partners and considerable quantities of South Korean goods, clothes included, were exported to the UK. It was an important source of income for the South Korean workers.

I like to think that it was this reference to the poor South Korean workers that allowed Mr Choe to bow with some sort of dignity out of what even he must now admit was an absurd situation. Still, he had to save face. He understood me, but others might make the mistake of thinking I was a spy.

'You pire the coat,' he instructed me. 'You must put pire to your laincoat.'

Chapter 3

I still wonder what would have been Kim Il Sung's reaction if he had been aware of the extent to which the special treatment he ordained for the foreigners in his country made them unhappy, resentful and ultimately antagonistic, rather than filling them with admiration for what his people were achieving. I am of course making the assumption that he didn't know. Perhaps he did, but I'm inclined to believe that he was largely kept in the dark about the negative effects of the policies he enforced.

A tale I remember appearing more than once in the great leader's writings is that of a Japanese woman who had settled in the country, having accompanied her Korean husband back to his homeland. The lady's friends and relatives in Japan were concerned about her and she would regularly receive parcels from them. One day a small package arrived containing a strange metal object and she had no idea what it was. The neighbours came round to examine it, but no-one could be sure of its purpose. It was, in fact, a complicated lock for her front door.

The moral of the tale is that locks and keys are not necessary in North Korea. Such is the harmony prevailing throughout society that it would never cross anyone's mind to break into someone else's house and deprive them of their belongings. Given the great leader's frequent references to the absence of crime in his country, I can only assume that he believed that such social harmony truly existed. The cynic, though, in the unlikely event that he or she could be convinced that there really was no crime, would surely point out that in a perfectly egalitarian society, in which one member is just as well-off as the next, no-one should have anything that you haven't and it frankly isn't worth the risk of being caught just to get a bit more.

CHAPTER THREE

State of Delusion

It was my contention, which in a rare open moment I shared with our new colleague Whitney, that the worst thing the North Koreans could do was invite a committed socialist to their country. Where was the propaganda percentage in a committed socialist going away still a committed socialist? But think of the damage if he were to be so horrified by the grotesque reality in which his ideals were applied that he went off shouting from the rooftops that he was no longer a committed socialist! As bad, if not worse, was the scenario of him denying that what he had witnessed in North Korea was true socialism at all.

On the other hand, if they were to bring in a real capitalist, someone with a genuine commitment to the exploitation of the toiling masses, to the ideals of imperialism and to the benefits of colonialism, a true supporter of the United States and all her foreign policy ways, there was always the chance, however remote, that he or she might just be surprised by North Korea and see something they liked. They might even, in the most glorious of events, become a convert to the cause. Now this was the stuff that propaganda dreams were made of! And this was precisely the sort of stuff – implausible tales of foreign converts that slipped neatly into the propaganda mainstream of local heroics – that Whitney had to work on.

Whitney's given name was Edward, but Edward being a little tricky for Koreans to pronounce, they called him Whitney. He was a socialist, although his motives for coming to Pyongyang were not ideological. It seemed that having spent 40 years living a blameless and mundane life he had decided, just for once, to do something reckless. So he had given up his career to come to Pyongyang for a year, which suggested to me that Philippe might well be right. He had to be planning to do something to earn some money after he returned home, such as write a book.

Apart from being a socialist, Whitney was also very British. He had a slightly aloof air about him and looked slightly down, albeit benignly, on the world through metal-rimmed glasses. His hair was greying and his face was pale. To the astonishment of the Koreans, he wore an earring – a way of showing, I imagined, that there was a rebel in there somewhere.

Little did he know that, by the very normality of my appearance, I had established myself with our hosts as the non-conformist. Nowhere, not even in an ear, was my body pierced and I'd caused some consternation by not having green hair. The girls working at the guest house had explained soon after my arrival that they'd seen a programme on television about Britain in which all the people had spiky green hair and pins through their noses. The punk revolution had long departed British shores, I thought, but one corner of the world remained ignorant of the fact.

Whitney was the second British person ever to live in North Korea and by the time of his arrival, the first was feeling pretty lonely and sorry for himself. In five months all I seemed to have succeeded in doing was isolate myself in the world's most isolated country. I was tiring of the secretiveness of the guest house circle, I had little to do with Pyongyang's tiny foreign community and I wasn't allowed to socialise with Koreans. Whitney could, I suppose, have become someone I could confide in, except that he was probably writing his book.

Whitney had come encumbered with financial commitments back home and had been incensed to discover, as I had, that the promised salary would not be forthcoming. And just as I had done, when Messrs Choe and Kim arrived in my room to explain that a translator's error meant I'd been led to expect almost double the amount actually on offer, Whitney also told them to put him on the next flight home. Clearly his threat was taken more seriously and he began receiving the full amount almost immediately, although he was not to tell me or Philippe.

He didn't. What he did tell us was that he wasn't to tell us something about the salary, which was very good of him, except that he hadn't really helped because, by complaining about our pay, we would be revealing that he had told us something. It was a dilemma that was soon resolved, however, and in unexpected circumstances.

In the meantime a decent man who might have been sympathetic to the socialist cause was set to work on a task that would push his tolerance to the limit, editing the effusive and uncompromising propaganda of a newspaper and magazines that would be sent to Pyongyang's foreign embassies and hotels and to DPRK diplomatic missions and sympathetic foreigners around the world. Like *The Pyongyang Times*, the publishing house's two monthlies, *Korea Today* and the lavish pictorial *Korea*, would follow a pretty rigid formula. There would be a page or two, sometimes more, bringing readers up to date, in words and pictures, with the latest meetings and preachings of the great leader and the dear leader. This would be followed by a section on the successes on the construction site, at the workplace or down on the farm of the working masses, examples of the self-sacrificing spirit of individuals, and interviews with a Labour Hero or two. Details of further achievements would follow, relating to scientific breakthroughs, to archaeological discoveries revealing the glories and length of Korean history, and to sporting triumphs, mainly table tennis and wrestling, in the international arena.

The magazines would find space for the thoughts of foreign friends, either praising to the heavens the great leader, the dear leader, the glorious Workers' Party of Korea, the Government of the Republic and the progress made by socialist Korea under the wise guidance of the great leader, or damning to hell the US imperialists, the Japanese militarists and the South Korean puppet clique. In other world news the Non-Aligned Movement might get a mention for its efforts to combat imperialism. The last few pages of the newspaper or magazine would be devoted to articles and photographs describing the latest horrors inflicted on the South Korean people.

For once, a speech by Kim Il Sung lived up to the billing of historic. In his New Year Address for 1988, the great leader proposed that high-level contacts be held between the governments of the northern and southern halves of the Korean peninsula, to discuss reunification.

The offer appeared to be a response to recent developments on the political scene in South Korea. Chun Doo Hwan, the latest in a line of military dictators, had agreed to hand over power and in direct elections, which had gone ahead late in 1987, the people had chosen as his successor Roh Tae Woo, who was due to take office in February. The nomination of Roh to take over from Chun was initially greeted with derision by the North Korean media, which produced a long list of charges against him. In particular, he was accused of using bribery to persuade the International Olympic Committee to award the 1988 Games to Seoul, which 'delighted his US masters', who hoped the Olympics would 'give colonial south Korea the semblance of an independent state'.[1] Roh's ultimate reward was to be installed by the US as Chun's number two.

There was some let-up in the verbal onslaught during the months leading up to Roh's assumption of power. Clearly, though, considerable obstacles remained to be overcome before any contacts between the two governments could be held. But for the tens of thousands of Korean families separated since the Korean War, the proposal held out the hope, however remote, of being reunited with relatives they had not seen or heard from for 35 years or more.

But it would have been foolish to be too optimistic. Tensions stayed high after the bombing of the South Korean airliner in November, with North Korea eventually vehemently denying any involvement. In a predictable attempt to turn the tables, Pyongyang accused the South of hatching a plot to discredit it and thus have a pretext for undermining efforts aimed at giving the North a number of Olympic events to host.

Still, Kim Il Sung's proposal was a clear signal of where Pyongyang saw its priorities lying. There had been speculation that a visit by the North Korean leader to Beijing in the middle

[1] *Korea Today*, 1987, 11.

of the previous year might herald the adoption of Chinese-style economic and social reforms. Comments he made at the time, stressing that the successes achieved in building socialism were suited to Chinese characteristics, were subsequently shown to indicate that no such thought had crossed his mind. Instead, it had become apparent, closer cooperation with Seoul was Pyongyang's preferred road ahead.[2]

Quite how the South might react to the great leader's overtures remained to be seen. The basis of North Korea's approach to reunification was the founding of the Democratic Confederal Republic of Koryo,[3] under which the two halves of the peninsula would retain their existing systems of government. Few in South Korea would doubt, however, that the North's ultimate aim was to bring its neighbour under communist rule.

To read North Korean propaganda was to realise that the South Korean people, dreaming of the day when they would be reunited with their brothers and sisters in the North in the great leader's embrace, stood permanently on the brink of revolt against the puppet regime that ruled them in accordance with the orders of the Americans. The regular students' demonstrations provided the proof – and ample video and photographic material for North Korean propaganda purposes – of the people's yearning for a brighter future.

[2] A report on Kim Il Sung's visit to China is carried in *Korea Today*, 1987, 8.

[3] The formula for Korean reunification under the Democratic Confederal Republic of Koryo was presented by Kim Il Sung in 'Report to the Sixth Congress of the Workers Party of Korea on the Work of the Central Committee, October 10th 1980'. In *Kim Il Sung: Works*, vol. 35, January–December, 1980. Foreign Languages Publishing House, Pyongyang, 1989.

Sadly, students were from time to time killed, succumbing perhaps to the tear gas or batons of the police or perhaps they might commit suicide in futile acts of defiance. To people north of the 38th Parallel they would become heroes; their images would be plastered on the television screens and in the newspapers; mass meetings might be held to honour their names; condolences would pour southwards.

If North Korean propaganda was to be believed, it was small wonder, I thought wryly, that the students would take to the streets to protest so frequently, in such numbers and with such violence, given the horrors to which they and the population at large were routinely subjected. As young people themselves they were conscious of the plight of the many who were denied any education at all and who were instead forced in their droves into begging and petty crime. The streets of Seoul were littered with the homeless, living among the filth and the rats. The country was plagued with pollution, poverty was rife and disease was rampant. Millions were unemployed. Inevitably, hundreds of thousands of young women were forced into prostitution.

South Korea had the highest incidence of AIDS in the world, *Korea Today* reported, going on to reveal why this was so. It had been discovered that the US army had established a special unit of servicemen suffering from AIDS, some of whom had been dispatched to South Korea with orders to infect as many people as possible. It was part of an experiment on the use of the condition as a weapon of war. The same project involved the US exporting AIDS-contaminated blood to South Korea.

To back up claims that were, by any standard, incredible, the magazine pointed out that there was historical precedent. As the world knew, the US had a history of dabbling in bacteriological warfare; there was plenty of evidence that it had dropped bombs bearing the micro-organisms of various diseases during the Korean War. Spreading AIDS would doubtless be a key strategy of the next attack on the North by the US imperialists. What else could be expected of 'bloodsuckers and butchers of humanity who are trying to force the AIDS disaster as well as a nuclear holocaust upon mankind'?[4]

It was hardly surprising that, as he laboured to give sense and reason to such hysteria, Whitney quickly became disillusioned with socialism, North Korean style.

Within a few months of Whitney's arrival Mr Choe left us quite suddenly to go back and work at the publishing house. He was replaced at the guest house by Kim Song Il, a young speaker of French who was the third member, along with Director Kim and Mr Choe, of the publishing house's foreign affairs office. The new arrangement at the guest house, however, did not suit Whitney; French and Spanish interpreters were no help to a man who only spoke English.

Song Il was a very amiable young man, highly intelligent – Philippe warned me he was 'tricky' but in my previous dealings with him I had found him far more straightforward than Mr Choe – and from a very good family. His father was an old comrade-in-arms of Kim Il Sung's from his anti-Japanese guerrilla days and was now a general, which meant that Song Il had enjoyed certain privileges while growing up, including the distinction of Party membership in his early 20s.

He was very relaxed and self-confident, so I was immediately put on my guard by how nervous he seemed when he informed me that the new general director of the publishing house wanted

---

[4] The claims were carried in *Korea Today*, 1987, 10.

to see me. He would come the following day. Did I want an English interpreter, or would I manage in French? Since the matter to be discussed was serious, he suggested someone should be sent from my Section.

My imagination, which normally I managed to keep in check even as I tried to make some sense of the secrecy and lies, now threatened to drag me over the edge into panic. I was fearful that I was to be called to account for some misdemeanour; the attempt by Philippe and me to break into the heart of Pyongyang sprang to mind, but that had been months before. To put my mind at rest, I asked Song Il why the general director was coming. It was a simple enough question. But Song Il couldn't seem to grasp what I was driving at and all I could make out from what he said was that it was because he was the new general director.

When he arrived he was accompanied by Hong Man Do from the English Works Section, and a stranger. It was this gentleman the general director had brought to see me. He was Director Kim's successor, Mr Li. He would be the new head of the foreign affairs department, with Song Il as his deputy, replacing Mr Choe.

We drank tea and the general director and Director Li told me they'd heard good things about my work. They hoped I would stay longer in their country, and then they left to visit the other guest house residents.

I wasn't sorry to see the back of Mr Choe. Philippe soon found out what had happened to him. He had been dispatched to Africa, to an office of the publishing house there. As for Director Kim, I was genuinely sorry about the departure of this courteous and gentle man. Philippe claimed several weeks later that he had chanced upon him in the street, looking tired, thin and nervous.

The obvious conclusion was that the two men had stepped out of line. Friends in high places had protected Mr Choe, while Mr Kim might be undergoing re-education through labour, a harmless enough procedure to judge by the official descriptions, rather like returning to school for a lengthy detention. The emphasis was very much on ideological education, since the root cause of most counter-revolutionary activity – there was no crime in North Korea – could be traced to an inadequate grasp of the Party's teachings.

But it would have been terribly naïve to assume that the punishment was quite as benign as it sounded, considering how sinister was the labelling of miscreants. It was the duty of everyone in society to report on those who showed signs of ideological impurity, even members of their own family. In order to encourage this, I had learned from some of the foreign diplomats, there was the implicit threat that a whole family could be held to account for the misdemeanours of a single member. There were dark tales of lorries that appeared in the middle of the night to spirit away whole families to a fate that would remain unknown, since they would never be heard from again.

Within a week of the general director's visit, Director Li and Song Il came to discuss my salary. Director Li told me that he personally had convinced the publishing house to pay me more. He named what he thought might be a reasonable salary, and since it was the amount I'd originally been promised before I left the UK and the amount Whitney was receiving, I thought it was reasonable, too.

Amid great fanfare it was announced that a 200-day battle was to be launched, one designed to give a boost to production. What this meant was that the workers and farmers were expected to redouble their efforts – suggesting that they had already doubled them – to mark with glorious feats of labour the 40th anniversary of the founding of the Republic, which would fall on September 9th.

For my Korean colleagues at the publishing house this did not mean they had to churn out more books and magazines; they were expected instead to spend more time on building sites lending a helping hand. It was already the practice every Friday for office employees to go and temper themselves at sites of socialist construction. In other words, those who spent the rest of the week exercising nothing more than their brains were packed off to put their backs into a spot of building.

How grateful the regular builders were for this help, I had no way of knowing. It occurred to me that a bit of machinery might be of far more use. I saw on a daily basis, as I walked guiltily from the guest house across the nearby site where a bridge was being built, on my way to the Potonggang Hotel for a beer, that there was already plenty of manpower.

Machinery appeared only so often. But with the odd mechanical digger or bulldozer at the workers' disposal on a permanent basis, there would surely have been no need for a 200-day campaign. Efficiency was hardly the watchword in a process that involved three men – or more probably women – using a single spade to shift the soil, one holding the handle and the other two pulling at strings attached to the blade to bring it forward. A fourth person would then enter the fray to carry the soil away in a sack on her back.

I also speculated that the process could have been speeded up, had not the men been so dedicated to the principle of sexual equality. They spent long periods of the working day sitting around and watching the women proving they were their male colleagues' equal in doing back-breaking labour. Then again, if the workers were to cut down on their siestas and various other breaks, they might well finish things a lot quicker. And perhaps if they weren't constantly being interrupted by the mobile propaganda units that turned up in speaker vans, blaring out loud music and hysterical entreaties to step up their efforts, they would really have been able to get a move on.

The Revolutionary Martyrs' Cemetery commands a lovely view of Pyongyang from the top of Mount Taesong, which rises a few miles to the north-east of the city. I was taken there by Paek Chol Man, the young English translator who had, much to Whitney's relief, replaced Pak at the guest house as resident interpreter. Strangely, after his departure Pak would give the impression, whenever I met him at the publishing house, that we were the best of friends, and I was happy to assume that he, too, had realised that our animosity had been a creation of Mr Choe's. He knew Paek Chol Man well, Pak told me, and he was confident I would get on with him.

Built originally in 1975 and extended a decade later on the orders of Kim Jong Il, the Revolutionary Martyrs' Cemetery is the final resting place of his mother, the indomitable woman revolutionary fighter Kim Jong Suk. She occupies the central plot at the raised far end of the cemetery. Before her, in row upon row of graves marked by bronze busts on marble plinths, lie her former comrades-in-arms from the anti-Japanese struggle, many of them still in their teens when they perished. Alongside them are the most prominent casualties of the Korean War and others who died in later years, having earned heroic status for their outstanding contributions to the revolution.

These were the heroes whose self-sacrificing spirit the workers toiling away in the 200-day battle were being exhorted to emulate.

The legend relates how, in his speech at the October 1945 Pyongyang rally to welcome him home after the liberation, Kim Il Sung called on people from all sections of society to unite in building a new, democratic Korea. 'Let those with strength give strength; let those with knowledge give knowledge; let those with money give money,' he said, 'and all people who truly love their country, their nation and democracy must unite closely and build an independent and sovereign democratic state.'[5]

The priorities were building the Party, the state and the army. The Party would come first, since it would play the leading role, and on October 10th 1945, the Workers' Party of Korea, a Party of and for the masses of the working people, was founded.

The official accounts relate how the weeks, months and years following liberation was a time of great hope and optimism, at least for those Koreans in the Party's embrace. The land north of the 38th Parallel seethed in a frenzy of construction, with towns, cities and factories springing up like mushrooms after the rain. The great leader was always at the forefront, tireless and utterly devoted to the cause of building a new country. A famous monument stands at a fork in a road leading to his birthplace at Mangyongdae, where on his return to Pyongyang the leader stopped and deliberated for a moment: should he go and greet his grandparents, whom he hadn't seen for all those years, or should he continue to the local steelworks and give guidance to the workers there? Naturally, the steelworkers won.

The only shadow was that cast by the Americans, who in August 1945 had occupied the southern half of the peninsula. That there were Soviet forces in the North is mentioned only in reference to the demand of the Korean people for the simultaneous withdrawal of the Soviet and US armies from Korea, which would leave the Korean people free to set their own house in

---

[5] 'Every Effort for the Building of a New, Democratic Korea; Speech Delivered at the Pyongyang Mass Rally of Welcome, October 14th 1945'. In *Kim Il Sung: Works*, vol. 1, January 1932–December 1945. Foreign Languages Publishing House, Pyongyang, 1989.

order. But the US authorities rejected this plea and instead, so North Koreans are told, set about rigging elections in the South so that their lackey Syngman Rhee could take power. This prompted immediate action from the great leader in the North and, at a conference of leaders of political parties and social organisations of North and South Korea in Pyongyang in June 1948, he proposed that the Democratic People's Republic of Korea should be founded without delay. On August 25th elections were held and a fortnight later the first Supreme People's Assembly convened in Pyongyang. On September 9th 1948, the founding of the Democratic People's Republic of Korea was announced, with Kim Il Sung elected Premier of the Cabinet and Head of State.

The country-building continued unabated, with the new Premier always leading the way, criss-crossing the country to offer advice and support wherever it was needed – in the factories, on the farms, in the offices of provincial and district committees and at army bases. Everywhere he went, workers, farmers, officials, technicians and soldiers would rise up in response to his call and perform heroic feats for their new country. It was in those heady days that he established the system of leadership that would be known as 'on-the-spot guidance', where the leader travels constantly to direct operations in person, wherever in the country he might be needed.

'Their new life was full of joy and song,' the story goes. 'The new democratic Korea prospered and developed and was moving dynamically forward towards a bright future in accordance with the magnificent plan unfolded by the fatherly leader.

'Factory chimneys towering high into the blue sky were belching smoke and the vast expanses of fields were full of golden waves of ripe ears of crops.

'Lovely sons and daughters of workers and peasants with satchels dangling from their shoulders were streaming into schools. In the evening every home was overflowing with merry laughter.

'The young people of this land competed with each other to join the glorious Korean People's Army, solemnly pledging themselves before the folks of their native places, before their motherland, not to allow the enemy to deprive them of this life and this happiness.

'The deep-blue and red of the flag of the Republic was fluttering, and the resourceful working people were doing above their assignments under the national economic plan in high spirits.

'Just as everything comes back to life in springtime, in new Korea, under the wise guidance of General Kim Il Sung, new blossoms were budding and branches were spreading luxuriantly in all the political, economic, military and cultural fields. Now the motherland was entering the time of prosperity.'[6]

But two devastating blows would suddenly shatter the optimism of those early years of the Republic. First there was the personal tragedy for Kim Il Sung of the loss of his wife, the indomitable revolutionary fighter Kim Jong Suk, on September 22nd 1949. And nine months later, war broke out.

In the early morning of June 25th 1950, so Pyongyang's version of events has it, South Korean forces acting on the orders of the US military command in Seoul launched a surprise attack on the North all along the 38th Parallel. Despite being taken

---

[6] *Kim Jong Il: The People's Leader*, vol. 1, by Choe In Su. Foreign Languages Publishing House, Pyongyang, Korea, 1983, pp. 48–49 (original Japanese version published by the Yuzankaku Publishing Co., Japan).

completely by surprise, the northern forces immediately went over to a counter-offensive.

Within three days the heroic officers and men of the Korean People's Army, under the brilliant leadership of the great General Kim Il Sung, had liberated Seoul. From there they headed south, rolling all – both South Koreans and Americans – before them.

The North Korean army quickly managed to occupy the whole peninsula apart from its south-eastern-most tip, and this was where the US brought in an army, after tricking the United Nations Security Council into approving the use of force against the Communists.[7] Having secured military support from 15 satellite countries, the US then conducted a landing at Inchon, to the west of Seoul. Crucially, their advance was held up by the heroic defenders of Wolmi Island who, although hopelessly outnumbered and outgunned, put up stern resistance.

In the meantime, the ever-victorious, iron-willed, brilliant commander, faced with this reversal in the fortunes of his army, hit upon the perfect solution – a temporary strategic retreat. Having led the Americans almost up to the Chinese border, the Korean People's Army then received some help, when the Chinese Volunteers Army came to the assistance of their fraternal Korean allies. Thanks to their intervention, the Americans could be pushed back to the 38th Parallel, where for more than two years futile attack and fruitless counter-attack took the lives of hundreds of thousands of soldiers and civilians.

[7] The Soviet Union was at the time boycotting the United Nations Security Council.

Early every year the United States would give North Koreans a powerful reminder of its military might when its forces in South Korea staged a huge military exercise called 'Team Spirit'. Each time the exercise was held, Pyongyang would describe Team Spirit as a war game, a preparation for another invasion, and whip its people up into an anti-American frenzy through denunciations and rallies. To bring home how real the threat was, there would be a blackout.

My only concession the first time I experienced a blackout was to visit the Potonggang Hotel more than the Koryo in the evenings, for no other reason than it was nearer. I would, however, take a circuitous route in order to avoid the building site, which was too dangerous in the pitch dark.

On one such excursion I was walking down a short street in front of a block of flats when suddenly a spotlight came on, capturing me right at the heart of its bright white glare.

I waited for a shouted order, the sound of a rifle being cocked. Instead I heard a giggle, and then another. I squinted, and just about made out two female forms, dressed in baggy military uniforms and soft Mao caps.

'*Annyonghasimnika?*'[8] I greeted them, smiling.

'*Annyonghasimnika?*' they said, and giggled again. I walked on.

One benefit for me of the 200-day battle was that, with my publishing house colleagues toiling away on building sites, there was less chance of being summoned for a *confrontation*. As Madame Beatrice had hinted, these were excruciating ordeals: the indecipherable pages of my editing would be laid before me

---

[8] 'How do you do?'

and I would be asked to explain every single change I had made. In particular I'd come to dread a call from Mr Ma, one of the senior translators with the English Works Section and a real stickler for detail.

Whether a comma was necessary in a certain place could be the cause of a half-hour debate. Terminology I'd been able to make no sense of would be explained to me in the minutest detail. I admitted quite frankly that it was because I was not an expert on fishing, agriculture or the weaving of cloth that I'd struggled over the explanation of how to mend a fishing net; I'd been unaware of precisely how the plastic sheeting should be erected to cover transplanted rice seedlings; and no matter in how much detail he drew that particular type of weaving machine on the back of the translated page, I still wouldn't know its name.

Exasperated, Mr Ma would shake his head and then describe to me all three processes in their entirety, clearly thinking that my education was lacking. He also seemed to think that my education was lacking with regard to English grammar, and it wasn't long before I was thinking that I agreed with him. Far too often I would find myself nodding and apologising for the over-sight that had the great leader saying 'I shall' when he should really have been using 'I will'. Silly me, I would reprimand myself, when Mr Ma pointed out that I'd failed to correct 'one another' for 'each other'.

I'd got into the habit of nodding sagely in an attempt to give the impression that I was guilty of an oversight rather than a lack of knowledge, when Mr Ma gave me one of his lectures because I'd come to recognise that, while my command of English was that of a native speaker with only a basic grasp of the grammar rules, he knew his stuff – in theory. Although he had no flair for English, his translations were always, so I was told, exact to the Korean and the English was invariably correct, with the result that they sounded nothing like natural English at all. My opinion was that if he showed me the same respect that I had learned to pay him, then with a few more of my ideas taken on board we might come up with something pretty good, accurate but at the same time fluent.

Madame Beatrice and my East German colleague Gerhard shared my frustrations at the nit-picking attention to detail that led to a poor final translation of the president's speeches. While thus reassuring me that my own complaints did not reveal my inexperience – they were professional language editors while I was a novice – they did warn me not to get too upset when I read the published text and found that a word, construction or sentence I thought I had convinced the translators to accept had been changed back to what they had decided was better English.

I was given to understand that this was particularly likely to happen in speeches in which the president explained his theory of revolution. I had to admit that Mr Ma had already ruthlessly exposed my communist credentials for what they were – non-existent – and I'd quickly learned to hold up my hands and admit to ignorance, as a capitalist born and bred, rather than put my foot in it yet again by describing as laughable some terminology that for decades had been the bedrock of socialist ideology. Worse still was to risk deriding some home-spun usage of the great leader's own making.

So once I'd acknowledged that the two fortresses of communism – ideological and material – were the object of an ongoing struggle, it was only a matter of discussing whether they had to be seized or taken. Since people were being remoulded anyway, however painful it might sound, then I supposed it made little difference whether it was being done on or along communist lines. If it really was impossible to talk about the US without adding imperialists at every mention, well, so be it.

And yes, decadent bourgeois culture did sound a little hysterical, but if that's what the man said, who was I to argue?

I did, however, draw the line at 'workingclassization'. Gerhard was a great comfort after one particularly strident argument in which Mr Ma had accused me of knowing nothing about socialism and not understanding the terminology because I came from a capitalist country. I had insisted that 'workingclassization' did not exist in English. Mr Ma had disagreed, saying that obviously it would not appear in a capitalist dictionary, but in socialist – and hence proper – English dictionaries it would doubtless be found. Unfortunately, the publishing house, being forced to rely on *Oxford*, had no such dictionaries he could consult to prove his point.

When I recounted this episode to Gerhard I was hugely relieved that he rolled his eyes skywards and told me that he had, on numerous occasions, had precisely the same argument with his own colleagues, and had still failed to convince them that the word did not exist in German, either – not even in the GDR's finest dictionaries.

While the workers and peasants struggled through their 200-day campaign, Whitney was embarking on a personal battle, one for survival. By the mid-point of his stay he was thoroughly fed up. He hated the work; Pyongyang's normally limited social scene had been non-existent during the winter; and he hated the food.

So every morning he turned up at breakfast to announce how many days remained until his departure. Breakfast was the only meal he could stomach, since they couldn't really go wrong with eggs, toast and coffee. He couldn't stand the rest of the food and he didn't thank me for telling him how much better and more plentiful it had been until shortly before his arrival.

In fact, I'd eventually complained, although it seemed callous under the circumstances. The propaganda consistently claimed that the populace had sufficient to eat, but it was quite clear that food was in short supply, and if that was the case in Pyongyang, one dreaded to think what the situation was in more remote parts. The Korean diet was basic, little more than rice and pickled cabbage; meat was only available on special occasions. So I felt acutely embarrassed to be complaining that I didn't have enough.

When I'd first arrived at the guest house I had been astonished at the richness of what we were served, in terms of both the quality and the quantity. Suddenly and dramatically, however, the amounts we were given declined. This happened at a time when several cars would, after dark once every week or so, pull up outside the guest house. The East Germans and Cubans, who normally ate in the dining room next door, would be ushered in to have their dinner with us. Naturally we decided to peek into the room where they normally ate and there we saw the table laid out for a banquet and a group of strangers being hosted by the guest house manager, Mrs Kim.

As much as anything else, it was the injustice that caused me to complain. I was having to go out and spend my money in restaurants, just so Mrs Kim could entertain her guests who, Song Il explained, were her bosses from the organisation in charge of Party guest houses.

I tried to be tactful when Director Li came to discuss the problem. I said I was grateful for the care the publishing house took of me, but I wondered if they were aware that, in the matter of food, there had been a marked reduction in the amounts we were served. Of course, if there were food problems in the country, I was quite prepared to tighten my belt, just like everyone else.

Director Li said no, there wasn't a problem and he promised to look into my complaint, and within a short time of his visit Mrs Kim herself, an elderly, hard-faced woman who tried unsuccessfully to cultivate the image of a kindly grandmother, came to see me. After the usual platitudes about how good my work was – although I couldn't see what that had to do with her – and how the guest house staff liked me, she addressed, albeit obliquely, the matter at hand, saying I was young and rather large – this uttered with a smile – and she understood that I probably needed more to eat than did the average person.

Anyway, she said, the solution was clear. The waitresses would be instructed to give me more rice. I protested, insisting that we were simply being served less meat, fish and vegetables than before. Mrs Kim then pointed out, with a sly glance at Song Il, who was interpreting, that I understood the country quite well. The food situation, she explained, was sometimes difficult.

As I told Whitney, in a way we should be thankful to Mrs Kim and her bosses for easing our moral dilemma. At least, thanks to us, some Koreans weren't going hungry and we could count ourselves among the ranks of the starving masses, rather than of the privileged foreigners.

It took a while, but North Korea finally managed to cobble together some sort of defence against accusations that it had been responsible for the blowing up of the South Korean airliner in November 1987.

No less a person than a former South Korean prime minister came forward with testimony that the whole terrorist outrage had been cooked up by Seoul and Washington as a way of discrediting the North. Kim Jong Ryol issued a declaration of conscience that made its way onto the pages of *The Pyongyang Times* in May. The newspaper reported that Kim had expressed a wish to apologise 'for at least some of my grave mistakes to the aggrieved souls who departed this world while crying out for democratization'.[9]

He explained that he was 'bringing into the open my ignominious record' mainly relating to the elections that had brought Roh Tae Woo to power, which he said were rigged in a 'computerised production' by the US, Japan and the South Korean regime. But then Kim mentioned 'Mayumi', the Japanese name used by a woman arrested for the bombing of KAL flight 858. 'The woman who went by the name of Mayumi,' he said, 'was a character in a plot jointly planned by the United States, Japan and the south Korean[10] regime,' which involved a plan to assassinate opposition leader Kim Dae Jung during the election campaign. The ultimate aim, Kim Jong Ryol said, was to ensure that Roh Tae Woo succeeded his mentor and predecessor Chun Doo Hwan.

Unfortunately, *The Pyongyang Times* article failed to provide any clear explanation as to how the airliner incident and the plan to kill Kim Dae Jung were linked. The US, Kim Jong Ryol said, intervened in order to prevent the assassination, and one could only assume that the success in discrediting Pyongyang and highlighting the ever-present threat from the North by blowing up the plane had been deemed to have done enough to persuade South Korean voters of the wisdom of backing the

---

[9] A version of Kim Jong Ryol's article, originally entitled 'White Paper to the People', appeared in the May 28th 1988 edition of *The Pyongyang Times*.

[10] North Korean publications use lower-case 's' and 'n' for the south and the north of Korea, in order to avoid the suggestion that the two are independent countries.

military leaders they knew, rather than the more liberal, and perhaps more pro-North, Kim Dae Jung.

The statement, it would seem safe to think, came as a relief to the North Korean authorities, whose defence against accusations of being behind the airliner's destruction had amounted to some weak claims concerning the self-confessed North Korean agent who had admitted responsibility. Apparently she had delivered her confession in a manner of speaking that proved she was from the South, and no school records could be found in the North of anyone with the name she said was really hers.

Kim Jong Ryol's article was, according to *The Pyongyang Times*, originally published in 'a Koreans' newspaper under the influence of Mindan ('ROK Residents Association in Japan')'. Although the fact that it didn't appear originally in a pro-North publication gave some credence to his claims, the failure in the logic and the rather haphazard nature of the allegations merely fuelled the inevitable suspicions about how much tampering had taken place during the translation process.

The failure to resolve the food situation rather blotted Director Li's copybook, as far as I was concerned. He'd got off to a flying start by raising my salary and expectations – mine at least – were high that his appointment and the easygoing Song Il's move to the guest house might usher in a more relaxed regime. But such hopes were quickly dashed.

Orders filtered down that Philippe should reduce the frequency of his trips to Beijing. The Koryo Hotel should be considered out of bounds, and we should take a car instead of the metro if we wanted to travel across the city. There was also rather too much fraternising between the guest house staff and the foreigners, presumably referring to Philippe and myself, who often shared a beer or two with the cooks.

Before long, however, the suggestion filtered up that we should not take these instructions too seriously. Clearly Director Li wanted to make his presence felt. But in this I thought he was guilty of one of the criticisms most often levelled at officials by the great leader – behaving like a petty bureaucrat or, as I thought of it, chucking his weight about. Although still struggling with the technicalities of rice transplanting, I could quote quite handily what Kim Il Sung had to say about officials and I often wondered what would be the reaction of, say, Director Li or Mrs Kim if I were to throw the great leader's words in their faces.

In surprisingly blunt and sometimes quite personal terms he would upbraid members of the Administration Council – the Cabinet – for their failings. For example, they didn't act decisively to solve problems and they didn't visit the grassroots and mingle with the masses as often as they should. Such criticisms would extend in general terms to more junior officials at factories and enterprises, among whose number I was confident Director Li should be counted.

If he'd mingled with me a bit more after my food complaint, he would have realised that the remedy of a couple of extra spoonfuls of rice had fallen well short of the president's call for bold solutions. Come to think of it, he was supposed to help his subordinates by displaying kindness and understanding; yet he still hadn't organised a trip to Mount Paekdu, even after I'd asked on numerous occasions. If he'd managed just that kindness, I might have forgiven him all his other faults.

Admittedly the charges were rather weak. But put together they certainly were sufficient to lay at Director Li's door one of the most persistent criticisms made by the great leader about officials: that they failed to follow his instructions absolutely and to the letter. Looked at another way, the same charges also indicated he was guilty of another failing often cited by the great leader; that officials didn't show enough initiative.

By this time I had a whole host of problems that needed solving boldly, not that Director Li could have done much about most of them, I had to admit. I'd had no news from home for ages and the cost of international telephone calls was prohibitive. I was lonely, I was bored, I was sleeping badly. Surrounded as I was by minders, I was struggling to keep a grasp on reality; in a situation where everyone around me seemed to be lying, it was a challenge even to know what that reality was.

To cap it all, my television set didn't work properly. Amid much fanfare Director Li summoned Mrs Kim, who brought in Mr O, the repair man. After a week of regular visits from Mr O, the television still didn't work. There was nothing worth watching, anyway.

It is not in the nature of Koreans to seek confrontation and so I never tackled Director Li about his failure to follow the great leader's teachings. It would have been a pretty extreme course to take anyway; much more reasonable would have been the argument that if Director Li wanted me to go out less in the evenings he should ensure I was given enough food, and if he wanted me to take a car he should do something about the drivers' behaviour.

What the guest house did give me without fail was my daily packet of *Paek Ma* (White Horse) cigarettes. I suspected that Mrs Kim was scrupulous in this because she knew that most of us foreigners never smoked them – they were too loosely packed and had a bitter taste – and instead passed them on to our drivers and interpreters, who would be quick to complain if supplies dried up.

I had no problem with handing over small gifts such as cigarettes to people who were, after all, providing a service for me. But I did object to the scrounging that some drivers were guilty of, when they followed me into a shop and made it quite obvious that they wanted something from me, probably foreign cigarettes, and not just a packet, but an entire carton.

To be honest, I was glad of the excuse for not taking a car, since I preferred to walk to the Koryo Hotel, my regular evening haunt, or take the metro. Once there, I would spend my evenings sitting on my own; most of the Koreans I saw in the bars were presumably frightened to be seen talking to a foreigner. From time to time a brave soul might ask what was my name, my country and my age, and I would cheerfully answer, drawing the line at revealing my salary. In return I would be left wondering who it was I had been talking to, since even names, professions and marital status seemed to be state secrets.

Philippe and I would often compare notes on whom we had met at the Koryo and spend many a coffee break discussing such mysteries as whether the Mr Pak from the trade company Philippe had run into, who said he knew me, was one and the same as the Mr Kim from the national tourist agency I had met, who said he knew Philippe. The descriptions sounded similar: tall by Korean standards, cheerful and flirtatious with the barmaids. Mr Pak, Philippe told me, had boasted of his beautiful wife. Mr Kim was single, I said. Mr Pak was a good friend of Song, the Spanish speaker who often hung out in the billiard bar. Would Song be Li, the Spanish speaker who didn't smoke, I wondered? Come to think of it, Song didn't smoke, Philippe would say. Now, that was a real giveaway in a country where almost every male was addicted to cigarettes. So by a process of deduction, if Song and

Li were one and the same, it was a safe bet that Pak and Kim were, too, although we were still none the wiser about what his real name was, what he did or whether he was married.

Identifying mutual acquaintances was further complicated by the large number of plain-clothes security people who mixed freely with the clientele in all the major hotels. At first I wasn't aware of their presence and I'd been disbelieving early on in my stay when Philippe had told me I'd been playing pool with someone high up in security at the Koryo. The man had said he was a businessman, but then he was hardly likely to tell me what he really did, Philippe pointed out.

The bar staff, of course, knew who they were, since hotel security covered ensuring that a proper distance was maintained between the staff and foreign customers. One of the tell-tale signs when a security officer came into a bar was that the barmaid might become a little more tense and less friendly. Another giveaway was that, as hotel staff, they could run up a tab, a privilege that was never granted to customers.

I was fearful of slipping into the world of subterfuge, half-truths and deceit I found in the hotels and I determined early on to be a model of honesty. So it was all the more galling to be accused to my face of lying when I told Koreans what I was doing in their country. No-one so young could possibly be doing such an important job, would be the common retort when I said I was revising the great leader's *Works*.

Slowly people began to open up a little, but then a new problem emerged. It was at first very flattering that an interpreter for another delegation would introduce himself and join me at the bar, saying he'd always wanted to sit and have a chat. Of course, it seemed natural to offer him a beer, sometimes two, when it became obvious that he had none of the foreign currency that was all that was accepted in the hotels.

But then there might be an innocent request for a packet of cigarettes. Oh, and did I know Mr Kang the driver? my new acquaintance might ask. He'd been with us at the Ansan Guest House until recently and was now working with his delegation. Perhaps I wouldn't mind buying a packet of cigarettes for him. I knew that for someone in my wealthy position it was the thing to do to be generous, but still it irked me that people I barely knew could ask me for favours on behalf of people I no longer had anything to do with.

There were times when I would excuse myself and head to another bar, or even home after refusing such a request. Having said no, it wasn't a lot of fun drinking beer under a cloud of righteous indignation. 'How much does my government pay you?' asked a certain Mr Cho I met occasionally in the Koryo. I pointed out to him that whatever the amount of my salary, his government didn't pay it so that I could buy him packets of Rothmans. It was like water off a duck's back. What sort of impression did I think I was giving of my country and countrymen? Did I want Koreans to think that all English people were mean? He'd had hopes that I might be different from all the other Englishmen, less of a capitalist interested only in money. He was very disappointed in me.

I was acutely aware of my comparative wealth, but there had to be limits on my generosity, particularly when the scrounging became downright underhand. I remember getting into a tearful row with a barmaid after I refused to settle the largish bill of an interpreter who had ostentatiously said hello to me and had then, rather than joining me at the bar, sat at a table and ordered beer and dried fish for himself and a number of his friends. They had quite a jolly time of it over several rounds of drinks. Only after the interpreter had ostentatiously said goodbye did the girl present me with his bill. But he is your friend, was her incredulous response when I declined to pay up.

Whitney told me that quite often, when he found himself rejecting requests to provide beer or cigarettes, the interpreter, only mildly affronted, might well say, 'But Michael always invites me.'

The attitude seemed to be that, having been around for a while, I could conveniently be assumed to understand the country. Thus I should be more sympathetic to the dilemma facing the Koreans who, to be fair, are by nature very generous when circumstances allow them to be. So when I rejected pleas for beer and cigarettes I appeared to be guilty of the most callous disregard for their situation; Whitney, of course, could be excused because he'd been there a much shorter time and would be leaving soon, anyway.

At the root of the problem was North Korea's complicated system of currencies. There were three versions of the *won* in circulation. The regular currency was to all intents and purposes worthless, a fact that was, in a roundabout way, acknowledged in the propaganda. The great leader himself boasted that his was the only country where there was no need for money. The Utopian goal towards which they were all working – to build a society founded on the principle of 'from each according to his abilities, to each according to his needs' – apparently ruled out the need for any form of currency, other than selfless sacrifice.

The leader and the Party were the great providers, with work units acting as the channels for their munificence. Thus the people – all of whom had a job – were provided with their food, clothing, housing and other basic necessities. At major holidays, principally the birthdays of the great leader and the dear leader, there was an increase in the flow of bounty, bringing perhaps a little meat to the table, a new suit, and some school things for the children.

Most of the time Pyongyang's shops were deserted. The doors to the grocery stores in particular were more often than not barred to customers, since nothing in them was for sale. When the staff did bother to turn up, their duties seemed to entail little more than overseeing the pyramids of canned food arranged in the window or on a shelf across the back wall.

The only regular outlets that attracted a steady stream of customers were those that provided a service. The barbers and the hairdressers, who needed only a pair of scissors to ply their trade, were kept busy. The restaurants also seemed to thrive, but patrons first had to obtain the necessary coupons. The tailors and dressmakers did a good business, too, although customers normally had to provide their own fabric – more often than not *vinalon*, a shiny material the invention of which was a proud boast of the propaganda machine, since it was produced from the country's abundant anthracite resources. I never really took to it; the men and women dressed in suits made from it looked vaguely like characters in science fiction films as they glistened beneath the sun or the artificial lights of a restaurant or bar. None of the well-to-do people I met would ever be seen dressed in the stuff – more wools and cottons imported from Japan or the UK for them.

For all of the services, people had to pay. But that wasn't a problem, because cash they had in plenty. The fact was there was next to nothing tangible for them to spend their money on.

Unless, that is, they had hard currency. Then a whole new world of hotel boutiques, expensive restaurants and department stores selling imported goods was opened up. The very few who had access to hard currency were the ones who smoked foreign cigarettes – Dunhill, Rothmans and Mild Seven being the fashionable brands. They were the ones who invited family and friends to a Japanese restaurant for *sushi* and whisky. And the tiny number of private cars on Pyongyang's streets were owned either by foreigners or by this wealthy elite.

Mostly those with access to hard currency were high-ranking officials and their offspring, and businessmen. But even the very few ordinary citizens who were lucky enough to travel abroad – diplomats and their families, students, and members of sports teams and official delegations – could be expected to save some of the money they were given for their trip and use it in ostentatious displays of generosity back home. Buying goods abroad that were unobtainable in Pyongyang was a risk, since the customs officers might confiscate them.

One interpreter I ran into from time to time was very proud of his girlfriend. She worked at the Rakwon Department Store and was paid part of her salary in hard currency. He made no bones about the fact that this was her chief – and in all probability only – attraction. I learned soon afterwards that the Rakwon had been stopped from paying its staff in dollars and I wondered if this had put an end to a beautiful romance.

I was established firmly among the richest of the rich. In simple Korean *won* terms I was earning something in the region of ten times a decent salary. What was far more significant was that I was paid entirely in dollars. These I changed for special banknotes bearing a red stamp, indicating they had been exchanged for hard currency. And it was these that I spent freely in the hotel bars, the restaurants and the department stores.

Not so lucky were my foreign colleagues at the guest house from socialist countries. They were paid less anyway and in a sort of halfway currency that was not as useless as the regular money, but not as powerful as the almighty red *won*. Their notes carried a blue stamp and although they could be used in the hotels, restaurants and shops, there were two drawbacks: the price of most goods was several times higher, and sometimes a salesgirl would refuse to take the blue *won*, presumably in the hope that the more desirable red-stamped notes might be forthcoming.

It was the price of *Pyongyang sul*, a clear spirit deemed an acceptable vodka substitute, that rankled with my Soviet colleague, Boris, who had to pay three times more for a bottle than I did. 'We supply them with all this aid,' he would fume, 'and when we're here they treat us like second-class citizens.'

Even though I was in a state of panic, I felt quite sorry for Mr Ma on the day I was sent to the publishing house to discuss nothing at all. Song Il had apologised after knocking on my door, but I had to leave my room immediately; no, we couldn't telephone to make sure there wasn't some mistake, not even if I was certain there was no outstanding work to discuss.

Clearly someone wanted me out of the way and obviously that meant they planned to search my flat. So I made sure I took one particular item with me – the music tape, the South Korean one I assumed they would be looking for.

Philippe had brought it back from Beijing, as promised. It was pop music, written and performed, he had assured me, by Koreans living in China. It was undoubtedly risky for us to listen to it, since it came from overseas Koreans, but whatever danger was involved was as nothing compared to that of listening to actual South Korean music. Unfortunately, that's precisely what it had proved to be.

And I had been so stupid as to let a North Korean listen to it; not only that, I'd made a copy for him. He was a young man, one of the bolder English speakers who would share a beer with me when his work brought him to the Koryo Hotel. He'd seen me coming in listening to my Walkman and had followed me to the bar so that he could examine it and listen to some English music.

I'd said no, he wouldn't like the music. He'd persisted. It was not music he was permitted to listen to, I'd said. He'd insisted and I'd agreed, swearing him to secrecy. He had listened, had loved it and had wanted his own copy. What was it? I'd told him about it being music performed by Koreans in China. And once again he'd asked if I would make him a copy.

All right, I'd said, and I had. I'd given it to him and two weeks later he'd pretended he hadn't seen me in the Koryo's foyer. Nervously and hurriedly, when I'd bumped into him just outside the men's toilets on the first floor, he'd told me he wouldn't be seeing me around. No, of course he wasn't in trouble. I'd asked him about the tape. What about it? he'd snapped back. It was lost.

Perhaps I'd been imagining it, but after that people had seemed to be more circumspect near me. I'd been for a *confrontation* and the translators had been so focused on the work there hadn't been any time for the casual chat and the cigarettes that usually took up most of our time. A driver who normally, in the safety of his car, asked if I had a tape of English music he could play while we drove had seemed very pointedly already to have had a revolutionary opera blasting out when I got into his car. The staff at the Koryo had seemed very unfriendly.

Mr Ma was apologetic. He wanted to discuss a book, the latest novel the translators had been given to read as a way of improving their English. He was very sorry to call me away from my work, but he knew I could spare the time. The book was *Gone with the Wind*. There were certain words, expressions and passages Mr Ma didn't quite understand; probably it was because his English was a little old-fashioned.

We endured about an hour of him pointing randomly at words and sentences and me providing half-hearted explanations, and then Mrs Min, the lady from the foreign affairs office who always made us tea, put her head round the door and said something. It was time to go. My driver was waiting to take me back to the guest house.

I found no evidence that anyone had been in my flat while I'd been away. But I hadn't expected to. I'd taken what they were looking for with me, and anyway I could hardly imagine, given how elaborate had been the scheme to get me out of my house, that anyone would have been so clumsy as to leave evidence behind. If I was in trouble, I realised, the clues would be much more subtle.

She had been told she must go, she said.

So it had happened again. Like the interpreter I'd given the tape to, like Director Kim, like Mr Choe, someone I had come into contact with was to disappear. I felt diseased.

I asked where she would go. She didn't know. But she thought it would be somewhere in the hotel. I would come and find her, wouldn't I?

I told her I would think about it and she got angry.

If only people could be more open, I thought. If someone had said to me, 'You're becoming too friendly with that girl,' I would have stopped seeing her and felt sad. But no-one ever said anything and I was left worried and frustrated, wondering whether she was being punished because of me. And she was angry in her ignorance of my concerns.

In the case of Mr Choe and Director Kim, perhaps they had been 'moved to other employment'. But the person who told me this had, before Whitney's arrival, informed the foreign affairs department that I had refused to edit *The Pyongyang Times*, even though I'd volunteered to do the job. The end, he reasoned, justified the means; I was too busy on the president's *Works*. So despite what he said about 'other employment' I'd been left thinking that the two men had been removed.

It was a culture of deceit and secrecy that fed on itself to produce the darkest speculation. For all I knew, Mr Choe and Director Kim were considered model officials and I had an unblemished record in North Korea. But there had been repercussions over the music tape, I was sure of it, even though no-one had admitted as much to me. I was pretty sure something had happened to the friend I had given it to. But there would be only denials if I was ever to broach the subject. Thus I was robbed of the power to do anything about it.

I told her that probably I would not see her again. I tried to explain that it was safer for her if I did not follow her. People would talk. But she didn't understand.

Eventually she asked, 'So you leave my country?'

I thought about it. There didn't seem any reason to deny it.

Anti-American feelings, normally pretty fervent, reached hysterical levels at least twice annually. In the early part of every year there was the hullabaloo over Team Spirit and then from June 25th to July 27th, the dates when the Korean War started in 1950 and ended in 1953, there was the annual month of anti-imperialist solidarity.

Both exercises presented a handy opportunity for the authorities to press home the message that invasion could come at any time, and rallies and meetings were held and air raid drills and blackouts were imposed to raise the people's awareness of just how imminent the threat was.

I'd treated the excitement over Team Spirit and my encounter with the girl soldiers as just another anecdote to add to the fund of stories I would have to tell upon my return home. But by June I was seething with resentment at what would be just one more bizarre excuse for placing restrictions on foreigners. My experience of the previous year's month of anti-imperialist solidarity told me there would be more than the usual insistence on us taking the car rather than going out on foot. It was also generally accepted among the foreign community that the already slim chances of getting any post would, for the best part of a month, be nil.

Like the rest of us, Whitney was receiving letters from home only intermittently and he could not be sure that those he was sending arrived. The staff at the international post office didn't help matters; rather than being sympathetic to the foreigners who made the trek in search of news from their loved ones, they seemed more irritated at having to interrupt a conversation among themselves and head off to our post office box. On one occasion they refused even to do that, after one seemingly important lady informed me there were no letters that day for any foreigners at all.

But there was some good news for Whitney: the treatment of other foreigners showed that, as the date of their departure approached, they could expect a sudden upsurge in the amount of post they were permitted to receive.

As for the June 25th commemoration, I told Whitney what he could expect. We would be shipped to a mass rally in Kim Il Sung Square to mark the commencement of the heightened xenophobia. There we would listen to hysterical speeches, with the crowd responding with raised fists and cries that sounded like 'Hoo-a! Hoo-a! Hoo-a!'. I was sure that, like me, he would react with bemusement and horror.

Even in my more congenial frame of mind a year before, I'd questioned what I was doing there, standing in Kim Il Sung Square listening to senior leaders of the Party and Government denouncing the US for its past crimes, its present duplicity and its future intent. I'd found myself wondering if I was the only person among the hundreds of thousands gathered there who found the exercise wholly irresponsible. The entire population had been brainwashed into believing that the US had instigated the South Koreans to start the Korean War. There must be some in the leadership who knew what had really happened. But they couldn't admit it, because the triumph over the Americans with the great leader at the forefront was an essential element of the modern history the regime had written in order to give itself legitimacy.

As it happened, Whitney and I were out of the capital on a postponed trip on the day the mass rally was held. It was probably just as well, considering how fed up we both were; not the best frame of mind for listening impassively while hundreds of thousands of misguided and ignorant people condemned your country, by implication as an ally of the leading culprit, for its role in a conflict that had left their own country devastated and millions of their fellow people dead.

Whitney was extremely scornful of the North Korean claims. He had read somewhere that the man in command on the communist side had, in fact, been the Chinese general, Peng Dehuai. He was also under the impression that the apparently trifling support from the Chinese had amounted to perhaps as many as two million men. Of these, tens of thousands had lost their lives, including a son of Mao Zedong. Given his belief that the North had started the war, and given the huge losses of military and civilian life, Whitney also wondered whether it could really be deemed as having ended in victory for North Korea.

In quiet conversation with no Koreans present, he questioned other aspects of the official legend. As Whitney related the story, the man later to be known as Kim Il Sung had been an officer in the Soviet army and had been nowhere near Mount Paekdu, let alone any Japanese, for most of the Second World War. In fact, at the time of Kim Jong Il's birth he had been in Khabarovsk. The official story of the glorious anti-Japanese struggle was, apparently, an exaggeration. Most notably, the victorious Battle of Pochonbo, when the youthful Kim Il Sung had supposedly led his gallant troops in a major triumph over the Japanese, was in reality little more than a minor raid on a small guard post.

Neither was the popular description of Kim Il Sung entering Pyongyang in triumph back in 1945 entirely in line with Whitney's version of historical reality. Official portraits depict the conquering hero, still in his early 30s, with a broad and engaging smile on his face as he waves to the adoring crowds. Whitney's version of events had him imposed on the Koreans in the North by the occupying Soviet forces. Taking the name of the well-known guerrilla fighter Kim Il Sung had seemed expedient as a way of convincing the population at large to accept him as their leader.

I'd had enough of trailing around revolutionary sites making polite noises about unlikely and probably downright untrue claims. So I was inclined to decline when the publishing house proposed a visit to a military college outside the city that the dear leader had attended as a young man. But it was a weekday and the trip meant a welcome break from work.

There was nothing of any great interest at the college. It was a very ordinary group of single-storey buildings that were distinguished only by their immaculate state. Inside there was the inevitable desk where the youthful Kim Jong Il had sat and the school things he had used, preserved in glass cases. Behind the building we were also shown the well from which he had drawn water, just like the other students.

Whitewashed stones marked the borders of flower-filled gardens, and perfectly manicured lawns stretched away to the foot of a hill a little way off. Indicating the hill, the guide informed me that there the dear leader Comrade Kim Jong Il, though still a student, had given important instructions to his teachers and fellow students.

I told my interpreter from the publishing house, Song Tae Bok, to ask the guide whether it was possible to climb and see the spot where the dear leader had imparted his wisdom. I was sure there must be a monument there to commemorate the event. Indeed there was, the guide responded. People flocked there to view it.

'So, let's go,' I said.

But it seemed that a visit for us would be impossible.

'Why?' I demanded.

This was a mistake. I'd long ago learned that a query beginning 'Why?' would not get a response from a North Korean. It occurred to me, as I observed the guide's confusion, that answering such a question necessitated a thought process involving an ability to reason that most North Koreans had never acquired. Or perhaps it was simply that they were not used to giving or receiving explanations; they were told, and told others, what to do. Questions along the lines of 'How many ... ?' or 'What ... ?' generally required quite straightforward answers. So people I met in the hotels would ask me specific and intrusive questions about my age, how much I earned, what I was doing in their country and how long I expected to stay. No-one, as far as I could remember, had ever asked me why I was there.

So I rephrased my question to the guide: 'What is the problem?'

First of all, she said, the weather had made it too dangerous to climb. Even Song Tae Bok laughed at this; it had been fine and sunny for weeks. He told the guide that he, too, would like to see the spot and before she could stop herself, she said that would be no problem. I knew enough of the language to understand this and I seized on it, demanding to know why he could go, but not me. Eventually the guide told me the climb was too difficult for foreigners.

It was useless to argue. I did anyway, pointing out that not only had she lied to me, but also she had insulted me by suggesting that I was not capable of climbing a hill that any Korean could manage. I was still fuming as we left and for the first time I refused to sign a visitors' book.

I told my friend Im about the incident. He was a diplomat's son who had spent most of his childhood in Eastern Europe and could often be found around the hotel bars, since he regularly worked as an interpreter for foreign delegations. He couldn't understand why I was so angry. It was a military college. So he guessed there was some army stuff they didn't want foreigners to see.

It made sense, but still I was angry. 'Why on earth didn't she just say so?' I said.

Throughout my time among Koreans I didn't come across a single one who appreciated just how infuriating being lied to could be. Im was no exception. His attitude was that the guide couldn't let me go up the hill because of what I might see, and telling me that the climb was too difficult for foreigners was a diplomatic way of explaining the situation to me.

'Come on, Michael,' Im said. 'You understand our country now.'

Precisely! If people thought I understood, then wasn't it time they started being more open and honest with me? What was the point of staying any longer if I was to carry on being treated as just another foreigner?

It must be devastating to discover that you have hardly any friends in the world. So by the summer of 1988 North Korea would have been feeling quite lonely after only three countries, Cuba, Ethiopia and Nicaragua, had agreed to back the call for a boycott of the Seoul Olympics. It was Pyongyang's attempt to spoil the party after receiving no invitation from the South to co-host the event.

Only Cuba's support for the boycott was significant in terms of the potential medal winners who would miss the Olympics. Still, the gesture was just as futile as was Pyongyang's insistence that it had a right to be a co-host. What the North Koreans chose not to recognise was that the Olympics were awarded to a city – in this case Seoul – and the original offer by South Korea to consider sharing the event was a generous gesture of reconciliation, if ultimately doomed to failure.

Although no doubt grateful for the support of its three revolutionary friends, Pyongyang must surely have been disappointed by the slap in the face it received from its allies in the socialist bloc. Even its fellow members of the Non-Aligned Movement, the vast grouping of poorer, mainly Third World countries in which Pyongyang aspired to be a leading light, largely failed to stand up and be counted.

Whitney, having completed his personal 365-day battle, left North Korea precisely one year after he had arrived. So determined was he to get out at the earliest possible moment that he declined even to stay for the extra couple of weeks that would allow him to witness the fruits of the workers' 200-day battle and the celebrations of the 40th anniversary of the founding of the Democratic People's Republic of Korea. He also missed the meeting of heroes.

Not that we foreigners had anything to do with it, of course, except admire the exploits of the models of socialist diligence and dedication. Those who attended the Conference of Heroes were men and women, mainly old but some young, from across the country whose chests were so plastered with medals that, as I watched on television, I silently pleaded with the cameraman to show them from behind so that we could see if there was any overflow onto their backs.

The point of the meeting was clear. Kim Jong Il himself had paved the way for it in a speech earlier in the year, *Let Us All Live and Struggle Like Heroes*. Here were the model workers whose example the toiling masses were expected to emulate, even as they might have contemplated putting their feet up for a while at the end of the exhausting, hard slog of the 200-day campaign. But true revolutionaries never rest on their laurels and the meeting adopted a 'Letter of Appeal to the Entire People' that called for another 200-day campaign, to start with immediate effect. If the workers thought they were hard done by, then there was a hint that they had, in fact, been let off lightly, with the letter suggesting that a 2000-, and even a 20,000-, day campaign would be what the true heroes they were all striving to become should be prepared to undertake.

Having missed out on the meeting of heroes, I found myself once again enjoying guest of honour status at an official function, this time the celebrations of the 40th anniversary of the founding of the Democratic People's Republic of Korea. The highlight was the march-past in Kim Il Sung Square which, I was assured, involved one million people. I didn't count, so I can't say for sure that a million people strutted and danced and shouted and sang and waved their way below me that morning as I stood on the steps that were my usual place for such occasions. As far as I was concerned there could well have been a million people, give or take the odd suited worker or uniformed soldier, green-clad university student or traditionally attired woman, considering the awfully long time it took for them all to pass. Undoubtedly it was an impressive spectacle, but as I stood with growing discomfort on one foot and then the other, constantly made aware by the television cameras pointing at me that I was really just a part of the spectacle, I did wish they would get a move on. But at least I could use the time to reflect on the speech made by the great leader the previous afternoon.

I suppose I should have been warned by its title. *Let Us Accomplish the Cause of Socialism and Communism under the Revolutionary Banner of Juche* is hardly designed to give credence to thoughts of reform and opening.

During 18 months in Pyongyang I'd never been addressed by the great leader before. I'd edited English translations of countless other speeches he'd made and it was with a certain amount of anticipation that I took my place among the crowd that packed the auditorium at the February 8 House of Culture. True, I cut an anonymous figure, but then Kim Il Sung, sitting on the stage flanked by senior leaders of the Party and Government, spoke to me directly. 'Comrades,' he began, 'Esteemed Heads of State from many countries and other guests from foreign lands.'

Of course, he could have just meant the foreigners in town for the celebrations. Then again, there might yet be a few words about opening up that might have repercussions for us foreign residents.

There weren't. The great leader wasn't far into his speech before it dawned on me there would be no hint or suggestion of a more tolerant attitude towards foreigners in North Korea. So, as the long discourse continued, I found myself concentrating less on the words and more on not clearing my throat. The great leader had a guttural voice, so much so that it seemed he must stop from time to time for a discreet cough. Since he didn't, he left me wanting to do it for him.

The speech was a rambling repetition of ideological theory and revolutionary back-slapping, of calls for international solidarity and denunciations of imperialism. There was no indication of change to come. It was a review of past glories and the only commitment was to more of the same. There was no mention of economic reform and thoughts of social change were knocked on the head, too. Nature, men and social relations, it seemed, still needed to be transformed along communist lines.

There was nothing by way of concession offered in the international arena, either. Foreign policy would continue to focus on strengthening solidarity with the international revolutionary forces; the victory of the world revolution was still the aim.

There was mention of 'top level' talks between North and South Korea. But this was the only suggestion of progress.[11]

Admittedly it was fun that evening, in the bar at the Koryo Hotel, to say to the crowd of foreigners that yes, the barmaid was saying she'd seen me on television. It was just some meeting I'd been to; you know, the one where the great leader had made his speech.

But, there was no getting away from it; there would be no opening up. For however much time remained to me in North Korea, I would have to grit my teeth and expect more of the petty restrictions, the monitoring of my movements, official invasions of my room and the ban on mixing with locals.

[11] 'Let Us Accomplish the Cause of Socialism and Communism under the Revolutionary Banner of Juche; Report Delivered at the Meeting to Celebrate the 40th Anniversary of the Foundation of the Democratic People's Republic of Korea', September 8 1988. *Korea Today*, 1988, 10.

PART 2

*T*he Paekdu Star could never eclipse the Sun of the East.

The peerless great man had passed away. The ever-victorious, iron-willed brilliant commander had fought his last battle. The world had lost the lodestar of human liberation. The socialist cause was without the master of ideology and theory. Korea had lost its greatest patriot.

For three years the star that had risen over Mount Paekdu more than half a century before had lost its light. But in Juche 86 it could be seen again and by the summer of Juche 89 it was shining brighter than ever to guide the people. The son that had grown up on two bloody battlefields had shown himself before the whole Korean nation to be the model of filial devotion, the true heir of his father and of the Juche cause. Like his father he believed in the people as in Heaven and thus he demonstrated his noble personality and his outstanding leadership ability. Under his benevolent and all-embracing leadership, in the summer of Juche 89 the whole society was living in single-hearted unity.[1]

The legend of the son was still in the making just over a decade earlier, and as 1989 dawned he remained in his father's shadow. There were three men in the highest positions of power back then: the father, the son and the defence minister. These were the members of the Presidium of the Political Bureau of the Central Committee of the Workers' Party of Korea. But there were whispers that the son, whom the people called their dear leader, was already the real power in the land.

---

[1] A compilation by the author of North Korea's more enduring propaganda claims. A taste of the eulogies for Kim Jong Il is *Many poems and songs created in Korea*, which appears on the Korean Central News Agency (kcna.co.jp) website for February 15th 2000.

CHAPTER FOUR

Different Ways

A year North Korea hoped would be a good one had got off to a bad start. Budapest had provoked Pyongyang's outrage by opening a diplomatic mission in Seoul at the end of the previous year, 1988. The North Korean media had responded with accusations of selling out the cause of socialism for short-term economic gain, of capitulation to imperialism and of the betrayal of socialism.[1]

It was a foreign policy coup for the South Korean government that threatened to tip the diplomatic balance on the Korean peninsula decisively in its favour; doubtless other Eastern bloc countries would follow Hungary's example. But the move struck at the very heart of North Korean foreign policy. Pyongyang had long insisted that there should be no 'cross-recognition' of either of the two Koreas by the allies of the other, the argument being that it

---

[1] See *Vantage Point*, October, 1989.

would give legitimacy to the division of the peninsula. For the same reason Pyongyang had consistently rejected any suggestion that the two Koreas should gain separate admittance to the United Nations.

'What North Korea has to face up to is that the world is changing,' was the unsympathetic view of Stu, an adviser on agriculture who had been persuaded to spend a year in Pyongyang only by a contract that promised him vast riches upon his return home to Canada. There was no denying that he was right. The fact was that the world was changing; Gorbachev had started the ball rolling. North Korea, Stu insisted, was already in dire economic straits and it needed outside help; to get that help it needed to shape up and introduce democracy.

Stu stayed at the Potonggang Hotel which, because it was little more than 200 metres from my guest house, I called my local. We would meet up quite regularly in its lounge bar, a green-carpeted clearing with wooden tables and armchairs amid an artificially bucolic setting of plastic trees with glaringly bright green leaves. The barmaid might be persuaded, if we promised not to laugh, to enhance the rural atmosphere by playing a tape of birdsong she kept behind the bar.

You couldn't blame Hungary, was Stu's argument. The government was only trying to improve the standard of living of the people through an alliance with capitalism, which was where the wealth was. The South Koreans were doing very nicely, thank you. They were free; they had democracy. Thanks to the Americans the economy had prospered. It was a technologically advanced country where people enjoyed a high standard of living.

Just compare that to the North, where the economy was in a state of collapse. Yet the propaganda kept churning out stories about the triumphs of industry and technology, all put down to the heroic efforts of the country's workers under the wise guidance of their two leaders. What about the rumours of unrest among the miners in the provinces? The foreign diplomats said industry was stagnating. The plant was outdated and poorly maintained. True, the country had vast mineral resources. But the North Koreans had mined just about as much as they could get their hands on with the low-level technology that was all they had. The economy was in a vicious cycle of collapse. For example, the more inaccessible coal resources that were left could not be mined without more advanced equipment; without more coal the power plants could not generate electricity for the factories to produce the machinery. Industry simply couldn't operate effectively under the conditions of frequent power cuts; in fact, machines were damaged. As for the stated desire to increase exports, there wasn't a market for goods whose delivery and quality were so unreliable.

They needed new and modern technology, but they weren't going to get it. Massive foreign investment would have to be obtained to update existing equipment. But they wouldn't be given any more money because North Korea was a bad debt risk. The country had driven Western banks to distraction by refusing even to discuss settling, let alone actually repay, any of the principal or interest on loans it had been granted in the early 1970s. And guess what they'd borrowed that money for! Right, to update plant and machinery! It was precisely this plant and machinery that were now in such urgent need of replacement.

The propaganda claims about the thriving economy were bad enough. But then there was this talk of regular bumper harvests. People must be wondering why they were starving. It was an open secret that in the provinces people were forced to eat tree bark and grass to survive. Any expert would tell you that collective farming had destroyed the countryside. They were using dangerous pesticides that could do long-term damage to the soil. They were growing the wrong crops. It was unbelievable, given the resultant food shortages, that there was no widespread revolt. It would come in time, once people had the courage to stand up to the reign of terror. It would come. Stu was certain of that. Not even North Koreans could fail to speak out when they didn't have enough food for their children.

Mark, an Australian journalist based in Seoul, could not dispute Stu's conclusions. But what he would say in North Korea's favour – and he had no particular reason for supporting Pyongyang – was that the situation on the Korean peninsula wasn't all black and white. North Korean claims about the situation in the South, though admittedly somewhat hysterical, were largely based on fact. The economic miracle hid the reality of a vast social underclass that felt betrayed and disowned by the rest of society. There was strong resentment in some quarters against the presence of US troops. For someone used to life in Seoul it was refreshing to visit Pyongyang, where there were no beggars pestering you, no prostitutes touting for trade. Of course one might have serious misgivings about the system in the North, but it could be just as hard to accept the situation in the South and the great gulf there between the haves and the have-nots.

Mark, whom I first met in the Potonggang Hotel when he was writing on the preparations for the World Festival of Youth and Students, was interested in my observation that North Korea seemed to be opening ever so slightly. Not to the extent that we could speak freely to Western journalists, I joked, and he insisted we were off the record. So I told him the local people had suddenly seemed much more relaxed around foreigners. I'd recently been out to dinner with two Korean friends. It wasn't much in itself, of course, I said, but since such fraternising had previously been unheard of, it gave substance to my belief that there was a subtle shift in attitudes.

Of course I didn't want to make too much of it. There had been no official announcements and it was only dinner, after all. But considering that just a year earlier such Koreans – these were two of the interpreters that I ran into regularly in the Koryo Hotel – wouldn't even have given me the time of day, it represented a small triumph, at least on a personal level.

I wondered whether their invitation to join them for dinner might have been the outcome of a decision that had filtered down, to allow more openness towards foreigners. More likely it was a reflection that I personally had earned a certain amount of trust. Perhaps it was a combination of the two and mixing with certain foreigners was to be tolerated. It sounded rather silly to talk about official policy when all that had happened was that I'd been to a restaurant. But I couldn't help wondering.

Another thing was, they'd offered to pay. I'd been resigned to the fact that I would be expected to pick up the bill. It had left me feeling vaguely uncomfortable throughout the evening, the thought that I'd only been invited along so that they could enjoy a free meal. So I'd been genuinely delighted when the two of them had brought out their wallets and handed over some precious red *won*. They'd refused to take any money from me, agreeing instead that we could meet again some time so that I could treat them.

This added substance to an impression that had been forming at the back of my mind, that there wasn't so much scrounging going on in the hotels. For a time it had been quite a problem, I told Mark. Possibly I'd learnt how to handle things better. Anyway, the nice thing was that I could actually relax in a hotel bar and talk to local people.

Stu and Mark, who were sent by overseas employers and who came and went, were on the fringes of Pyongyang's foreign community. Stu, although on a year's contract with an international agricultural organisation, was in and out of Pyongyang, making the most of any opportunity to travel to Beijing or home to Canada. Mark, by contrast, would have liked to stay longer, but his newspaper needed him in Seoul.

Pyongyang's more permanent foreign community was tiny, and far from permanent anyway. A stay of two years, which was the milestone I was approaching at the beginning of 1989, could be matched only by a handful of reluctant diplomats, a dozen or so unhappy students, the other stalwart language advisers at the Foreign Languages Publishing House, and an indeterminate number of shadowy figures, presumed defectors or kidnap victims, whispered about but living in a different orbit.

I got the impression that most of the diplomats were unhappy with life in Pyongyang and sulked in their embassies; one of the few I ran into regularly, mainly in the Koryo Hotel's coffee shop, was Arti from a North African country, who I was sure wanted to get himself expelled, even though it would mean a black mark on his diplomatic record. He made no bones about it; he was fed up with having no proper social life, and he was bored. So he drank too much and got a bit loud.

Things might have been a lot better if he could have had a proper girlfriend, he said. But that wasn't going to happen. It wasn't just a matter of sex, he insisted; it was a matter of being free to go for a walk on a Sunday afternoon along the river with a pretty Korean girl on his arm, of being allowed to take her to a restaurant for dinner. He missed the companionship.

In fact, he couldn't even have proper male Korean friends. Of course there were the interpreters and drivers he worked with, but they were colleagues. There were also those elite types he ran into in the hotel bars, but they weren't particularly interesting. They were frightened to say anything too revealing and so conversations tended to be very limited. In short, he had little opportunity of meeting locals and even less of socialising with them in any normal fashion.

So what could he do with his free time, apart from drinking? The theatre and cinema were out; they had nothing to offer except domestically-produced stuff, just stiflingly correct revolutionary classics. There was the golf course, but at 100 dollars a round it was a real rip-off.

I suggested, jokingly, that he could always watch television. It wasn't up to much in the evenings, but there was Mansudae, the third channel, at the weekends. It had foreign films, dubbed. So what if they were Chinese classics and ancient black-and-white stuff from Eastern Europe? He could watch and maybe learn some Korean in the process, I suggested.

Arti was horrified at the very idea of learning the language. If his embassy thought that he could even say 'hello' in Korean they would label him an expert on the country and put him down for an extended stay. And as for Mansudae, he'd been watching it the other day and had been absolutely disgusted. First there was the international news; strikes in the UK, murders in the US and environmental disasters anywhere in the world; and of course the little groups of people in Africa studying the Juche idea.

But he'd had to turn it off during the programme about the pygmies. There was a tribe of them living possibly in New Guinea; he wasn't sure. They were like animals, always naked, fighting over raw meat to eat and smearing themselves with mud. The only thing that made them different from animals was that they pierced their bodies, causing horrible disfigurements. Whatever the patronising Korean commentator had been saying, it was clear what the message was – look how people live in other parts of the world. It was just the Koreans' way, Arti was convinced, of conning their own people into thinking they were well off.

I'd seen the programme and had been just as disquieted about it as had Arti. But talking to Mark had convinced me that North Korea wanted to come out of its shell. As the country became more open, there would be no place for such distasteful propaganda or, indeed, terrorist outrages. There had been genuine fear in Seoul, Mark told me, that North Korea would launch some kind of attack during the Olympics. It hadn't happened, which could be taken as an indication of Pyongyang's desire to join the international mainstream. Look at the excitement over the Youth Festival they were hosting in July, he told me. Maybe it could be called orchestrated hysteria, but there was no denying that the enthusiasm among the population at large was getting quite infectious as the opening approached. On a global scale the Festival would doubtless be quickly forgotten, if not ignored altogether, but such a vast friendly foreign invasion was bound to have an impact on the local scene, and might possibly be used by the authorities to test the waters for a more liberal attitude towards those foreigners living in the country.

The man in overall charge of the Festival preparations, Mark pointed out, was none other than the dear leader himself who, foreign diplomats he had spoken to suggested, was now in charge of the day-to-day running of the country, while his father Kim Il Sung was kept largely in the dark about the country's difficulties. Quite what role the third power in the land, Marshal O Jin U, had no-one seemed to know, except that he was Defence Minister, an old comrade-in-arms of the great leader and a supporter of Kim Jong Il's succession. His must have been an interesting position at the meetings of the Party presidium, Mark speculated, if ever the other two members, father and son, fell out.

But back to Kim Jong Il; he seemed intent on doing something about the country's economic situation. One project with which the dear leader had been closely associated was the construction of the Sangwon Cement Complex, costing hundreds of millions of dollars. Commissioning it from a West German company appeared to represent a departure, albeit it minor, from the great leader's teaching of economic self-reliance. The dear leader was also linked with other projects that tapped into the country's extremely strained foreign currency reserves, aimed at bringing the country into the modern technological era. One such project was the brand new international telecommunications centre, with its direct telephone and fax lines to the outside world. Its construction was an interesting departure, considering that previously contact with the rest of the world had hardly been a priority.

While it would of course be foolish, and almost certainly misguided, to try and identify any policy differences between Kim Il Sung and his son and heir – such a suggestion could at best be described as groundless speculation – there was just a hint that Kim Jong Il was a little more liberal when it came to foreign influence.

As I sat listening to Mark beneath the artificial leaves of the Potonggang Hotel's lounge bar it seemed as though by North Korean standards there might yet be interesting times ahead. If nothing else, the 13th World Festival of Youth and Students would, because of the very numbers of visitors coming to the country, represent an unprecedented opportunity for ordinary members of the local population to mix with foreigners. For once there would be no possibility of the usual restrictions being imposed.

But Stu simply could not believe what he was hearing when he joined us in such conversations. As far as he was concerned, there was nothing good that could be said about North Korea. Take that airliner, which the North Korean agent had confessed to blowing up. But, I countered, hadn't she as a result been granted a presidential pardon and allowed to live in anonymity in South Korea? Try, I said, reversing the situation. Imagine your reaction if a self-confessed South Korean agent had said, under interrogation in Pyongyang, that she had blown up a North Korean plane on the direct orders of a senior figure in the Seoul government. You wouldn't believe a word of it, because you'd be convinced that she'd have done anything to avoid the death penalty.

No, I wasn't saying she hadn't done it, I insisted. I was simply pointing out that we shouldn't always take explanations at face value, just because they coincided neatly with our own views. Believe me, I told him, I had plenty of personal reasons for condemning North Korea. But that didn't mean it was always in the wrong. North and South Korea, as Mark had said, weren't black and white.

The trouble with Stu, I thought, was that like many other foreigners, when faced with the absolute conviction of North Koreans in the greatness of their leader, the righteousness of their cause and the superiority of their nation, he was inflexible in his condemnation. The Cold War, although diminishing in intensity elsewhere, still raged in North Korea, where ideological prejudice was fuelled by ignorance. In my own case, in two years, I realised, I had managed only to reinforce the negative perception of North Korea, but there was clearly more to the country than the little I had managed to learn about it.

I was probably deluding myself into thinking there would be some sort of opening, but if there was I wanted to be there. I was living in an interesting place in interesting times. All of which made me think I hadn't been wrong to tell the publishing house I would like to stay for another year and see what 1989 had in store.

Chapter 5

*N*orth Koreans are under constant pressure to maintain the highest standards of personal behaviour. The exhortation carried on their televisions screens every night, in the newspapers they read every day, in the speeches of the president they study every week, is that they should be true revolutionaries who are boundlessly faithful to the Party and the leader; heroic, self-sacrificing and devoting their all to their comrades and the revolution, even at the cost of their lives.

The celebrities in the films they watch and the books they read are people who observe the highest standards of communist ethics. A trait of a true revolutionary that conveniently coincides with traditional Korean values is beautiful socialist morality. This convergence of principles is highlighted in *The Tale of Chun Hyang*, a traditional story of the triumph of a pure heart over the brutality of a corrupt society. Leaving aside the socio-political considerations that seem to creep in to every aspect of North Korean life, there is a charming naïveté in the aspiration to encourage the highest standard of personal behaviour.

Chun Hyang is beautiful, but as the daughter of a *kisaeng*, a female entertainer, she is planted firmly at the foot of the social ladder. Her mother, though, is determined that Chun Hyang should not follow in her own footsteps, and she ensures that she receives an education befitting a young lady of high rank.

And so Chun Hyang grows in beauty and accomplishment until she reaches young adulthood. One fateful festival day she goes out and is seen by Mong Ryong, the son of the local nobleman, who falls head over heels in love. Later that day and for several evenings following, Mong Ryong visits her house to pay court. Initially Chun Hyang's mother opposes any idea of romance between the two young people, but she is eventually won over by the suitor's sincerity.

Then disaster strikes! Mong Ryong's father is summoned to the imperial court in Seoul, and the lovers must separate.

Without telling his parents, who would be bound to object to his relationship with a girl of such low birth, Mong Ryong is betrothed to Chun Hyang on the night before his departure. He promises to return for her when he has completed the imperial examination.

The years pass and Chun Hyang remains faithful to her departed fiancé, despite the attentions of the new local official. He is a corrupt libertine who learns of the young woman's beauty and status and determines that she should be brought to serve him. When she resists his advances, he has her thrown into prison and beaten.

Finally, her beloved Mong Ryong returns as a royal inspector charged with rooting out corruption in the provinces. He swiftly dispatches the corrupt local official, restores order to the county, releases Chun Hyang from prison and marries his faithful lover. They all live happily ever after.[1]

It's a pretty hard act to follow for the Korean women of today.

---

[1] *The Tale of Chun Hyang*, rewritten by Cho Ryong Chul. Foreign Languages Publishing House, Pyongyang, 1991.

CHAPTER FIVE

First Lessons

*T*he students at the publishing house had politely asked if I might find some time once a week to give them an English lesson, Director Li told me. They would welcome the rare opportunity of being taught by a native speaker. The publishing house had its own school, which attracted the country's brightest and best linguistic talents to train as translators of the great leader's works. In normal circumstances teaching didn't appeal to me, but it struck me that getting to know a group of young people might be an interesting exercise. Philippe treated his lessons as a conversation class, and this seemed to be all that was required. If I could, like Philippe, gain the confidence of my class in the course of improving their English, I might just persuade them to open up a little. I had to admit that I was struggling to make sense of the country, to reconcile the propaganda claims with the dim view of the reality I had gained in two years, to find common ground between the rest of the world's view of North Korea and North Korea's view of itself. So the more contact I had with North Koreans, especially the younger and presumably more open ones, the better for my understanding of their country.

So I prepared for my first lesson. I needed some texts to work with as the basis for conversation. My search through Philippe's collection of old *International Herald Tribune*'s yielded a few suitable pieces; not much, since of course I had to steer clear of politically sensitive subjects. Anything that fell short of out-and-out condemnation of United States foreign policy couldn't be used. There could, of course, be no mention of South Korea – that was far too sensitive. It was a pity. I would have liked to find out what the students really thought of the plight of their oppressed brothers and sisters. But, I reasoned, with time the occasion might present itself. Anyway, I shouldn't lose sight of the fact that I was there to teach them, and not the other way round.

A Western journalist – I think she was British – once wrote of how she escaped the attentions of her minders in North Korea for an evening. Out in what was apparently the restaurant street in front of the Koryo Hotel she was propositioned by a young local who, despite speaking no English, managed to convey the message that he would give her his gold watch in exchange for, well, one can only speculate. She declined his offer, but indicated that she might be interested in his Kim Il Sung badge. Horrified, the young man beat a hasty retreat.

The story conveniently fitted preconceived notions about North Korea: men who saw foreign women as easy prey; wealth casually discarded by a small elite; constant fear of the authorities; and the all-pervading presence of the great leader who seemed even to become involved when boy met girl. Given such ill-conceived reporting it was small wonder that Pyongyang had such an uneasy relationship with the foreign media.

For long periods journalists wouldn't be permitted into the country, unless the applicant was a tried and trusted friend. From time to time, though, for example when the country wanted the world to witness one of its periodic triumphs, such as the 13th World Festival of Youth and Students, the ban would be lifted. But inevitably something would be reported that would displease the authorities and once again North Korea would retreat into its shell. To make matters worse, in between times the odd antagonistic journalist would sneak into the country in the guise of a tourist.

On a personal level, bumping into a Western journalist, especially a British one, presented me with quite a dilemma. I was naturally inclined to have a chat; foreign visitors normally being quite rare, it was always nice to share at least a few words. I also felt I should make some effort, if only to reassure myself, to dispel the notion that long-term residents were too frightened or were forbidden to talk to reporters. Even so, always at the back of my mind was the fear that an ignorant reporter might misquote me or mention my name in a negative article. However obscure the publication, I knew there would be some North Korean in some embassy somewhere in the world scouring the entirety of the local media in search of every mention of his country, for use back home for propaganda purposes if the comments were positive, and for who knew what recriminations if the country was cast in a negative light.

Madame Beatrice had told me of a Latin American employed by the Foreign Languages Publishing House some years before my arrival, who had been somewhat outspoken about the propaganda – with a view to helping them improve things – and had wound up in prison for his trouble. As far as I could ascertain, he had made his comments only to his colleagues, and had never done anything so foolish as to convey his views to a reporter. So it was with horror that I found myself quoted in one British newspaper talking critically about the use of 'capitalist running dogs' in North Korean propaganda.

On reading the story – a British friend had brought the newspaper back with him from a trip home – my only comfort was that I had never seen 'capitalist running dogs' in any of the work I had done. So I couldn't imagine having mentioned it in a conversation with the journalist, who I did remember meeting and who must have thought he was in China where, I seemed to recall, the phrase had been used by Chairman Mao. Still, the report caused me a nervous few weeks, as I contemplated quite how the authorities would deal with such a betrayal of their trust by someone who was, after all, employed to present the country in a positive light. In the meantime I made a point of saying some strong things to any Korean who would listen, particularly my publishing house colleagues, about lying and manipulative foreign reporters. I don't know if this made any difference, but nothing was ever said about 'capitalist running dogs', although I could have sworn I heard the phrase whispered among colleagues a couple of times when I was at the publishing house. Probably it was just my imagination becoming over-active under the stress.

Without doubt, some reports were unsound in their depictions of North Korea. But it was the conclusion drawn by an elderly, Western, male journalist that beggared belief. He, like the lady reporter, had managed to escape his minders, although in his case he had had to get up early in the morning in order to do so. He had found himself in a park where he espied a girl sitting on a bench, studying. He approached and sat next to her, and was, he said, shocked when, rather than engage in friendly conversation, she got up fearfully and walked away. The conclusion? That even in a deserted park ordinary North Koreans were so afraid of who might be watching that they dared not be seen talking to a foreigner. On reading the story I was left wondering what female students in New York or Montreal or Sydney or London or wherever he was from did, when they were approached by strange, elderly men in deserted places who attempted to talk to them in a foreign language.

The visit to Pyongyang by a South Korean dissident at the end of March 1989 suggested that there were some, albeit a minority, south of the 38th Parallel who were prepared to respond to a summons from the great leader to discuss reunification.

The Reverend Moon Ik Hwan, described as an adviser to *Chonminryon*, the National Alliance of the Movements for the Nation and Democracy, flew into Pyongyang and was greeted with near-hysteria by the North Korean press as an ambassador of reunification. He held a series of meetings with representatives of such unlikely sounding organisations as the Central Committee of the Korean Christians Federation and the Committee for the Peaceful Reunification of the Fatherland. He also enjoyed the privilege of two audiences with the great leader himself, at which the main topic of conversation was, not surprisingly, reunification.[2]

Just as predictable was the good pastor's arrest upon his arrival back in Seoul, described thus in *Korea Today*:

> More than 4,000 police troops were unleashed at the airport. Civilians were banned from entering the airport, so

---

[2] An account of Rev. Moon Ik Hwan's visit to Pyongyang is found in *Korea Today*, 1989, 5.

that a peaceable function to welcome Rev. Moon Ik Hwan was 'blockaded in advance'. This repression is a most illegal barbarity that can be perpetrated only by the traitorous military blackguards of south Korea.

The *Korea Today* article went on to pour scorn on the claims of the South Korean president and his 'fascist blackguards' to champion the reunification cause. Their promises to promote exchange between fellow countrymen, including politicians, businessmen, religious people, scholars and students, and to open the door to free travel between North and South were proved by the arrest of Reverend Moon to be 'a mere trick to hoodwink the south Korean people and world opinion'.

Reverend Moon visited Pyongyang in response to an invitation issued by Kim Il Sung to the presidents of four political parties and a number of other prominent figures in South Korea, with the pastor named among the latter. What *Korea Today* failed to point out was that the South Korean president was being invited only as the leader of his party, on an equal footing with the three other leaders, and thus somewhat below the great leader in standing. Seoul also had cause to quibble with the wide-ranging representation from the two sides, since the diverse political parties and dissidents from the South could be expected to present a broad range of views that would no doubt be overwhelmed by the united front of the representatives from the North, who were unlikely to deviate from Kim Il Sung's vision of how things should be done.

But there were two sides to the argument, and despite the omissions and the rather colourful language, *Korea Today* undoubtedly had a point; what did the South Korean authorities hope to achieve by the pastor's arrest? Pyongyang had repeatedly called for the National Security Law, under which unofficial contact with the North was banned, to be repealed, and it remained hard to see how its continued enforcement could be reconciled with the South's stated desire for reunification.

Whitney's departure had heralded a change in interpreter at the guest house. The French-speaking Song Il remained with us as the representative of the publishing house's foreign affairs office, but the previous autumn the English-speaking interpreter, Paek Chol Man, had, at the gentle insistence of my Cuban colleagues, been replaced by another Spanish speaker.

Cho Jang Yop was a pleasantly open and easy-going young man. He was in his mid-20s, I guessed, and single. His usual dress of brown loafers, light-coloured trousers and zip-up windcheater jacket was markedly casual by comparison with the severe grey, dark blue and black trousers and jackets of his publishing house colleagues.

Cho confided to me that he was in love with one of the waitresses at the Potonggang Hotel and asked me to go there with him from time to time to see her, since he wasn't allowed in the hotel on his own. I confided to him that I didn't know what to teach my students, and he offered to help, since he himself had studied at the publishing house's school, in the Spanish department.

For my first lesson with my students my censorship of the *International Herald Tribune*, with Cho Jang Yop's help, had left me with a collection of lifestyle pieces, a gardening hint or two and something about the Channel Tunnel. All perfectly harmless and consequently, I realised, of absolutely no interest to students, probably not even to North Korean students, which Cho confirmed, although he did reassure me by saying that my class would just be delighted to meet a native speaker of English.

And at least I wouldn't upset the teacher who, I was certain, would be sitting in to make sure I didn't step out of line.

The best way to get the students to open up, I thought, was to encourage free and open conversation by answering quite frankly whatever questions they put to me. I imagined that as a rule the North Korean learning experience must be stiflingly dull. So my lessons would offer something a bit different; a chance for conversation, rather than the learning by rote that was the normal method of language learning.

As I'd anticipated, the teacher was there. He was a venerable old man, thin and a little stooped with a shining dome of a head. He greeted me very courteously at the door of the school that was literally attached to the publishing house. He showed me to the classroom and, as the students stood up to greet me, went and took up his position at the back of the room.

The dozen students were standing straight-backed at their desks, looking at me with dull curiosity as I nervously took my place behind a wooden lectern at the front of the room. Here, I imagined them to be thinking, is a real foreigner. We've not seen one of them before; and this one is a native speaker of English. I took a deep breath and said, 'Do please sit down.'

I looked over the class. There were a couple of girls; the rest were boys, and all were aged around 20, I guessed, and dressed in navy blue jackets – apart, that was, from a strange figure lounging at the back of the room. He looked a little older than the others, his collar-length hair was quite untidy compared to the short back and sides of the other boys, and he wore an open-necked dark shirt and white suit.

I made a little speech introducing myself. 'Er, is there anything else you'd like to know about me?' I asked at the end. I looked down at a dozen faces, all impassive. Their eyes were fixed ahead; no-one met my glance.

'Perhaps you'd like to introduce yourselves now,' I said.

Silence. Fortunately I had a list of the students' names. 'Would Song Gwang Sun please stand up and tell me about himself?'

A titter. A girl stood up. 'My name is Song Gwang Sun,' she said robotically and sat down.

I was smarting at my self-inflicted wound, but I was determined not to let them see. So I went back on the offensive. 'So, how do you spend your time?' I asked.

She stood up again. 'I study English,' she said impassively and sat down again.

This was getting me nowhere. The lesson was scheduled for an hour. With this level of cooperation we'd be done within ten minutes.

'What are your interests, Miss Song?' I asked.

She stood up again. 'I am interested in my studies.' I was ready with my next question and fired it off before she could sit down again. 'What do you hope to do in the future?'

She looked puzzled. 'I will be a translator of the *Works* of the great leader Comrade Kim Il Sung,' she said and sat down.

I went round the whole class, to discover that they were all studying English and would all become translators of the *Works* of the great leader Comrade Kim Il Sung. I thought that a little explanation might help.

'What I hope to do,' I said, 'is to encourage conversation. I'd like to know what your interests are so that we can just talk. Your teachers here can teach you about grammar and so on. What I can do is give you the opportunity – and the confidence, which is important – to talk to a native speaker of English.'

I took a breath. 'So, is there anything you would like to talk about?'

The student in the white suit stood up at the back. 'Please Sir,' he said. 'What is your opinion of current United States policy towards South Africa, specifically relating to the issue of sanctions against the apartheid regime?'

I swallowed. The teacher caught my eye. He was furiously shaking his head and making rapid scything gestures with his two hands. The poor chap will do himself an injury, I thought. But if these lessons were going to work and I was going to encourage conversation, I couldn't refuse to answer the first question put to me, even if I had been set up. So, pretending I hadn't noticed the teacher, I soldiered on.

I made some noises about the injustice of apartheid and the lack of principle in US foreign policy, and the conversation moved on to safer ground. One of the girls wanted to know about the British royal family. I started to talk about the legacy of history, the contemporary symbolic role the royals played and the limited political powers of the Queen as head of state. The students seemed more interested in Princess Diana. I suggested that I would find some articles from the newspapers about her for the next lesson.

'I know Philippe, of course,' the young Korean sitting at the bar said. Actually, the barmaid had just told him she used to see Philippe and me quite often together, but not so much now. By the way, the barmaid was asking if I knew Kris the student. He came in quite often. He spoke good Korean. Philippe did, too.

It was a familiar scene with a familiar dialogue. The setting this time was the small bar on the left, just inside the entrance to the Underground Restaurant by the Koryo Hotel. But it could have been any of a dozen other places with a cast made up of any of a dozen other young English speakers enjoying a drink and any of a dozen barmaids.

From the disco at the Potonggang Hotel that belted out revolutionary music to a deserted dance floor, to the dingy bar adjoining the diplomats shop, from the expensive coffee shop at the Changgwangsan Hotel where you were brought iced water and a wet towel as soon as you sat down, to the Taedonggang Restaurant where I always ordered *yukaejang* spicy beef soup, everyone knew Philippe and Kris. In the Pyongyang Hotel opposite the Grand Theatre there was a fairly shabby place where, just for show, Kris kept a bottle of whisky behind the bar, Japanese fashion, although he never drank from it. Philippe was well known in the Taedonggang Hotel's coffee shop and billiard bar, but Kris was known to Kum Suk and Myong Ok, the respective barmaids, too. Hye Ran in the first-floor billiards bar in the Diplomats' Club was impressed by how well Kris spoke Korean; she knew Philippe, too, although she said he rarely went there. Downstairs in the restaurant where they served excellent Chinese food the girls said they saw quite a bit of Philippe during the week, while Kris came mainly at weekends. Both were regulars at the Koryo, of course, in its ground-floor coffee shop and first-floor billiard bar, and at the Changgwangsan Hotel, in the small bar upstairs on the right, where Kris was well known to the regulars, Yun Ae the barmaid knew all about Philippe, even though he'd never set foot in the place. But then, her best friend worked at the Koryo.

One evening after work I went to the Ansan Club, an extended walled and fenced complex of shops, restaurants and guest rooms that lay at the bottom of the long, tree-lined drive leading to the Potonggang Hotel. A place of quiet seclusion by day, in the evenings the Ansan Club presented a quite delightful spectacle of floodlit pools and gardens and low, pastel-coloured buildings with porthole windows. The sense of pastoral tranquillity was enhanced by its proximity to the river, and there was little more to hear than the lapping of the water against the banks, the occasional cry of a bird and the rustle of leaves in the breeze.

The main building of the Ansan Club housed three restaurants: a Japanese *sushi* bar, a traditional Korean *pulgogi* restaurant, and a cheaper place serving Pyongyang cold noodles. Amazingly, in none of these restaurants had anyone heard of Kris; Philippe dropped by occasionally, but he would just eat his noodles and leave.

I decided I liked the Ansan Club and became a regular customer.

The ubiquitous Kris was from Malta. Quite what he was studying in Pyongyang, I didn't know. What I did know was that, whatever it was, it took an awful lot of studying because he appeared to have been around for many years.

While other foreign residents, lulled into lethargy by the lack of excitement on the Pyongyang social circuit, struggled to venture far or too often from their hotel or embassy, Kris bounced from one side of town to the other, exuding bonhomie and sociability. He evidently kept in good shape and took care of his appearance; his moustache was impeccably groomed, his teeth were a brilliant white and he wore his ostentatious jewellery with confidence. He appeared to have little interest in politics and was simply trying to forge the best social life possible for himself in what most visitors considered to be the gloomiest of backwaters.

Kris was set apart from the other foreign students because he had money. He came from a wealthy family, he said. He could even afford to run a car, and every evening he embarked on a grand tour of the few watering holes that Pyongyang had to offer. A naturally friendly person, he would pick up on all the local gossip and keep tabs on who was in town.

I must confess that I initially found his pretence of knowing everyone very irritating. Whenever he arrived in a bar he would go through a ritual of greeting every member of staff by name; he would say hello to all the guests, whether he knew them or not; and then he would pick up the telephone and call someone. Whatever hotel we were in, he claimed he had a friend there, although not once when I was with him did any of these friends respond to the call by appearing. But this, I realised over time, after I'd become convinced that his pleasure on meeting me was genuine, was just Kris being his natural, ebullient self.

One problem of being a long-term foreign resident was that you became the target of a two-pronged media assault, from North Korea and from abroad. Generally I'd learnt how to defend myself from the local attack and in this I had an able ally in Song Il, who had impressed me early on in his stay at the guest house by telling me he routinely rejected requests from the publishing house's publications for a quotation from a handy foreigner. I liked to think of myself as a cooperative employee but, as Song Il pointed out, what I actually said would in all likelihood bear little or no resemblance to what was finally published.

Not that he put it quite this bluntly. He suggested that the accuracy of the translation might leave something to be desired. It seemed that whatever I said would have to be translated into Korean and then back into English, as well as into the various other foreign languages. Reading between the lines, this seemed to allow plenty of scope for improvisation by a propagandist dedicated to the principle that ideas were best reinforced by constant repetition, which explained how it was that so many foreigners, most of whom would conveniently have left the country by the time their views were published, lapsed into North Korea-speak – 'greatest man who ever lived', 'beautiful Korea advancing under the unfurled banner of socialism', 'South

Korean puppet clique' – in adding their voices either to the chorus of praise for the country, the system and its leaders or to the cacophony of condemnation of the South Korean regime, the US, and imperialists in general.

I was quite surprised when the call came the following week, inviting me for a second lesson with the students. The teacher, I thought, must have appreciated my efforts to avoid controversy, although I decided it would be better not to push my luck; rather I should focus on more harmless subjects such as Princess Diana and the Channel Tunnel.

The teacher wasn't there to greet me. He's working in his office, the two students waiting at the school door told me. Probably he was worried his health wouldn't stand up to another of my lessons, I thought.

'Excuse me, Sir,' one of the two said to me as we walked up the stairs. 'My friend at the Foreign Languages University asked if he could come to your lesson. I hope you don't mind. He came with his colleague.'

'No, of course not,' I said.

'In that case,' said the other student, 'you won't mind that my friend came from Kim Il Sung University. With his friend.'

'No, no.'

The room was packed when we got there. My dozen students were sitting at their desks. But there were others two deep along the back and lining the side walls; there were even students squatting between desks.

'Excuse me, Sir,' said one of my girl students, standing up. 'My friend came ...'

'Yes, yes. No problem,' I said. 'For all of you. I hope you don't mind if I don't ask all the newcomers to introduce themselves.'

I was flattered. Word had got around. I wondered what Miles Everett, the professional teacher, would make of this when I told him. He was an American who had arrived in Pyongyang shortly after I did, to teach English at Kim Il Sung University.

We had a lively conversation, myself and the original students, about the royal family. It was as if they were showing off in front of their guests. They spoke quite airily about Princess Diana and one of them pointedly informed the class that the Queen, as head of state, played only a limited political role. But then one of the guests intervened and asked me a question.

'Hey, you!' said the student who had asked about South Africa and the United States. 'This is our lesson. You keep quiet.'

Which rather dampened the mood. Without any explanation, the following week and ever afterwards I was back to my dozen students, and no guests.

My students seemed to think it was high time, given my age, that I was tying the knot. One of the young men even suggested I should call my parents and ask if they'd found me a bride yet. He hinted that I would be quite within my rights to tear them off a strip for being so negligent of their parental responsibility if there wasn't some lucky young lady lined up for dispatch to Pyongyang for me to cast my eye over.

Conversation with the students was the basis for my research into courtship, Korean style, and I had been astonished by how casual the process was. Traditionally, two young people of marriageable age and who were considered a suitable match would be introduced, either by their families or by mutual friends.

The romance could well consist of nothing more than an evening stroll, before the couple realised they wanted to spend the rest of their lives together.

And so a proposal would be made, although not necessarily by the man himself. It was common for friends of the potential groom and bride to step in and do the proposing and accepting or rejecting; that rejection was a possibility I assumed to be the reason for this third-party business, since having the bad news broken to him gently could save the jilted suitor considerable embarrassment and loss of face in the event that, as was only too likely in my opinion, given the casual nature of a courtship, he had got the wrong end of the stick after a single stroll.

Song Il, I'd become aware, was to get married. His bride was to be Sun Ok, our waitress at the Ansan Guest House. There had been speculation among the foreigners that there was some sort of romance going on, ever since the two of them had been spotted taking a *sampo*, or evening stroll, together. That appeared to have been the entirety of the romance and effectively meant they were betrothed.

By Korean standards, Song Il and Sun Ok had got to know each other quite well prior to their wedding, in the course of working together at the guest house. They struck me as being the perfect couple. The well-connected Song Il could offer his wife and their future children a life of relative comfort, while the pretty Sun Ok had, as a trained waitress, already acquired many of the accomplishments – good service, cooking, sewing and so on – associated with wifely virtue.

Since they were both residents of Pyongyang, one major element of the matchmaking equation was removed, the desirability of residing in the capital, where the standard of living was significantly higher than elsewhere in the country. By tradition a new wife would travel to live with her husband in his home town, which was supposed to be one reason why the population of Pyongyang was expanding. Girls outside the capital were keen to find a husband there, while those already in Pyongyang were hardly likely to contemplate a marriage that would take them to a life of comparative poverty in the provinces.

It was a trend that the propagandists were attempting to reverse, with films and songs playing several variations on the theme of a city girl moving to the countryside to get married, the point being that it was honourable to give up a life of relative comfort to go and live among the farming communities.

All works of art and literature had a message, one that was revolutionary, inspiring and highly moral. This most definitely included films, in which the dear leader took a personal interest, as *On the Art of the Cinema*, now mercifully nothing more to me than an additional volume on my bookshelf,[3] had demonstrated. A case in point was *A Bellflower*, the big hit of 1987 and winner of the Gold Torch Prize at the First Pyongyang Film Festival of Non-aligned and Other Developing Countries.

It's the story of a young woman living in a remote mountain village who refuses to accompany her fiancé when he heads off to seek his fortune in the city. Years later, she becomes management board chairwoman and succeeds in making her small village prosperous. In the meantime he has learned to lament his decision to leave. The message here is clear: those living in remote places have an important and honourable job to do and should stay put.

[3] *On the Art of the Cinema* was published in English by the Foreign Languages Publishing House, Pyongyang, 1988.

North Korea's girls, apart from being urged to opt for a life in the countryside with a farmer husband, also found themselves pushed in certain other directions concerning the choice of a partner. They could expect to find themselves in the propaganda spotlight, for instance, if they were to marry a disabled soldier. Caring for a man wounded in the defence of the motherland was considered the height of socialist patriotism.

The impression was that girls were leaving the cities in their droves for the simple life in the countryside. Being disabled while on military service, which seemed to be a surprisingly frequent occurrence, appeared to promise soldiers the pick of the most desirable local lovelies. The men were expected to do their bit, too. There never seemed to be a shortage of young people eager to become the son or daughter – and hence live-in help – of childless elderly couples unable to look after themselves. And every winter a child or two could be guaranteed to fall through the ice on a river or pond somewhere, and someone, probably a soldier, would be on hand to pull them out.

Such were the tales of socialist morality that littered North Korean newspapers and magazines, radio and television broadcasts. I saw no reason to doubt that they were true, although my admiration was tempered by the unworthy thought that the models of socialist morality could anticipate some sort of material reward for their exemplary behaviour, in addition to their moment of fame. Still, I could see nothing essentially wrong with encouraging people to sacrifice themselves for the sake of their fellow man.

While *A Bellflower* was quite clearly encouraging a self-sacrificing spirit, I found the message of *Song of Memories* more elusive. A popular film as the World Festival of Youth and Students approached, *Song of Memories* offered an interpretation of events during the Korean War that might, by North Korean standards, have been described as controversial; except, of course, that it must have been approved at the highest level, by the dear leader himself.

What made the film unusual was that it hinted at a romance between a Korean girl and a foreigner. She is serving in the navy during the war and is ordered with her troop to accompany a foreign prisoner, a musician, back to headquarters. She and her companions are also musicians and on the great leader's birthday he witnesses them singing. He is won over by their sincerity and confidence in victory. He is released and shortly afterwards runs into the girl sailors at the World Festival of Youth and Students in Berlin,[4] where his feelings for her and the Korean people grow deeper. Many years later he returns to Pyongyang for the annual April Spring Friendship Art Festival, only to discover that the girl was killed later in the war. The *Song of Memories* of the film title is the piece he writes for the girl he has been dreaming of for all those years.

One of the most common questions put to me by the foreign journalists was: 'Have you ever visited a Korean's house?' By the spring of 1989 I could say that I had. I could also say that the living conditions were pretty good; the houses I'd visited were modern, adequately furnished and well maintained and easily big enough for the families that lived in them. What I chose not to say, since it would have been an unkind comment on what had been a thoroughly enjoyable experience, was that I was only allowed to see inside the best houses and even then the visit was carefully arranged to give a positive impression.

[4] Held in 1951.

It was more in a spirit of curiosity than of excitement that I accepted my first ever invitation to visit the home of a North Korean. It would hardly be the informal 'dropping by' I would have preferred and I tended, like Philippe, to be scathing after Director Li had visited all the publishing house's foreigners to explain the arrangements. We would be in two groups; while one group visited one of the publishing house's translators and his family, the other group would go to another and then we would swap. Still, I thought, never again would I be in the ridiculous situation of having to confess to outsiders that after two years I still wasn't friendly enough with any of the locals to have visited them in their homes. It was a relief also to know that no longer would I be forced to admit that my knowledge of the country didn't extend even to how the people lived.

So, having not set foot in any Korean's home for over two years, I visited two in the single afternoon of the great leader's 77th birthday. Thus I found myself, after a brief stop with the family of a Spanish translator I hardly knew, at the home of Song Tae Bok, who had accompanied me on the ill-fated trip to Kim Jong Il's military college.

Song Tae Bok's home was modern and clean. The walls were whitewashed and the layout functional and spacious. That the bath was filled with water tended to suggest that water supplies were intermittent. The kitchen, as far as I could see, had no cooking appliances, gas or electric. Hot meals, when people had them, were provided at their workplaces and schools. As for the furniture, it was convenient that traditionally Koreans sit and sleep on the floor, I thought cynically, since this cut down on household expenses.

The first thing I looked out for after we entered Song Tae Bok's house was a jar of instant coffee and I spotted it immediately, standing prominently on top of the television. In the previous house we'd visited I'd noticed a jar, also unopened, at eye level on the bookshelf in the main room, facing the door. Koreans, I'd been told, didn't particularly like coffee, and the jars seemed to confirm my suspicion that our visit was yet another stage-managed propaganda exercise, with props supplied.

I hadn't been in Song Tae Bok's home long before I realised how terribly uncharitable were such thoughts. Of course the food, some if not all, had been brought from our guest house; one of his daughters had clearly never seen a prawn before, since her mother had to stop her eating the thing whole, shell, feelers, eyes and all. But the family and all the neighbours who popped in were so genuinely pleased to see us and so thrilled by my attempts at their language that I found it impossible not to start enjoying myself, helped on my way by the liquor that Song Tae Bok had in plentiful quantities.

The two daughters sang and played the accordion. Their mother was the model of Korean female decorum and courtesy as she lifted food onto our plates. And Song Tae Bok was the genial host, filling his guests' tiny celadon cups with liquor while keeping us entertained with some amusing stories.

'Michael was so angry I couldn't believe it,' he said. Song Il and Director Li seemed quite impressed. The four of us – Ali, who was still not speaking to me, and Madame Beatrice had by this time occupied the room's two chairs and were enjoying more entertainment from the daughters – were sitting cross-legged at the low rectangular table that was in the centre of Song Tae Bok's living room, listening to him recounting the tale of our visit to the military college.

'Is it true?' Director Li said. 'Michael's always so calm, not like the other foreigners.'

I didn't suppose it mattered that he must already have known the story; surely Song Tae Bok had reported what had happened.

But maybe Director Li wasn't pretending he hadn't been told, perhaps he'd simply forgotten. Either way, I'd do better not to get my mind into a twist with such thoughts, especially when the conversation was turning to more personal matters.

Just what did Director Li mean when he asked me if I had any plans to settle down? Was he hinting at something? Did he know something?

I'd done what I could to make my visits downstairs seem completely innocent. I'd been to other bars too, and to other hotels. But I'd been spending a lot of time there and people gossiped.

She'd come to find me one night when I'd been upstairs in the hotel billiard bar, thinking I was protecting her by not going to see her. She had told me she hadn't been moved. There was nothing wrong with me visiting her.

So I'd gone back and I'd told her I wasn't leaving the country – not just yet. And just like old times, with the only noise the sound of water in the background, I'd had time to think.

The rules were being relaxed, but only slowly. Like Philippe with his friends from China, I was from time to time arranging to go out for dinner with Koreans – colleagues from work and English speakers I ran into in the hotels. They seemed unconcerned about being seen with a foreigner, so I ignored my own misgivings and allowed myself to be guided by them. Invariably my companions were male; the sight of a Korean girl alone with a foreign man would have excited far too much attention.

My favourite places for a rendezvous were the three so-called '50% restaurants' in the street outside the Koryo, which were called this because you could pay for food half in foreign currency and half in local money. This made it convenient for a foreigner and a Korean to split the bill.

Of course we had to assume we were being watched and listened to all the time. For this reason it seemed sensible to stay off the subjects of what life was really like for North Koreans, how poor and restricted they were by world standards, and what was really going on in the rest of the world. Unless they asked, of course; otherwise it seemed only polite to enjoy a few jokes, some beers, a bit of gossip. I was pretty sure they hadn't suggested dinner out of a desire to be interrogated.

The trouble was that, whoever I was talking to, I could not shake off my conviction that somewhere in the light-hearted banter my companions might be trying to tell me something, a vital hint at information good for my well-being that had to be passed on in the form of an innocent comment in case it should be picked up by listening ears.

'Korean girls only ever say "I love you" once in their lives,' an acquaintance told me in a bar one night, with his companion nodding sagely at his side. The companion was the interpreter I'd once given the tape to, looking a little thinner and a little older since I'd last seen him almost a year before. When I'd first run into him again he'd looked me in the eye and shaken his head, as if to tell me, 'Don't ask.'

'When do they say it?' I inquired, my mind assuming that here was a hint to help me on my romantic way.

'Just before the man asks them to marry him,' the friend who had raised the subject said.

'So now you know,' his companion told me. 'He's getting married. We need more beer to congratulate him.'

So better just laugh Director Li's comment off; have another little cup of liquor and not bother my head so much. Change the topic, yes that was the answer. Forget about me; what about Song Il? Did getting married automatically entitle him to become a higher form of comrade?

They laughed, and Song Il said, 'People must call me Excellency.'

One of the most difficult aspects of learning the Korean language was proving to be the complexity of the forms of address. Depending on how the speaker was related to the person he or she was addressing, there were any number of levels of courtesy, conveyed by combinations of personal pronoun and verb ending. Someone who was older should be talked to with greater respect, as should any adult who was a guest or in a position of authority. Getting married led to a more formal personal pronoun and a longer verb ending, in anticipation of attaining the elevated status of parent.

Communism, rather than being the great equaliser, had only added to the difficulty, since it turned out there were two levels of comrade. 'Dongmu' referred to younger comrades, probably unmarried. More elderly comrades and those entitled to due respect were called 'dongji'.

The difficulty was exacerbated because in Korean a person could not be addressed only by his or her name. It was always 'Comrade Song Il' or 'Professor Kim', and a foreigner blundering around in the language was both the source and the object of additional confusion. I was forever calling a dongji a dongmu and vice versa. My scheme to avoid causing offence by addressing everyone by the more exalted title backfired because it was considered universally insulting; those entitled to the higher form felt I was slighting them by using it on everyone, and those used to the lower form thought I was laughing at them.

I must have been an especially severe linguistic headache. I was still young and unmarried and therefore a prime candidate for *dongmu*. But then I was a guest and moreover one doing highly important work – probably no foreigner could be doing work more important – and so obviously I was a *dongji*. But then again, I was from a capitalist country and the reasoning must have gone that I might not want to be addressed as comrade. So how about *sonseng* – professor? Not bad for someone so young.

The afternoon at Song Tae Bok's house ended with Song Il and myself staggering downstairs to the car that was waiting outside. Fortunately we weren't drunk, because the great leader said there was no drunkenness in North Korea. But Song Il's face was red, which meant by his own reckoning that the time had come to stop drinking.

Someone once explained to me why it was that the Asian face could turn so quickly and violently red with drinking. Apparently it was because of the lack of an enzyme that treated the alcohol in their system. I wasn't too clear about the science of this, but I did know that Song Il invariably decided that once his face turned red, then he shouldn't drink any more.

The problem was that his metabolism was inconsistent and at times his face simply remained its normal colour, however much he drank. I'd been with him on several occasions, even in such public places as hotel bars, when he might exhibit all sorts of signs that he had had several over the eight – becoming somewhat loud, stumbling unsteadily on his way to the toilet and even falling off his stool – but as long as his face had not turned beetroot, he remained convinced that there could be no objection to having just one more '*pour la rue*' as our inept translation had it. All in all, I'd learnt that once it was time to go home, the best thing to do was tell him that his face was red and hope that he didn't head off to the toilet to check in the mirror.

On one of the rare occasions I judged it safe to allow myself to be trawled into the propaganda net, I briefly became a farmer. It was later in the summer when we – that is my foreign colleagues at the publishing house, along with an assortment of officials, interpreters and journalists – were driven off one morning in a minibus to a farm on the outskirts of Pyongyang. There, by the side of a road and with the chairman of the cooperative farm management board in attendance, we all stood for half an hour up to our knees in mud and made a complete mess of planting rice seedlings. 'Foreign friends helping with the planting' would no doubt be the photo caption for the article, although I was sure there would be no mention of the foreign friends heading off for a jolly good lunch afterwards, presumably while the poor farmers were undoing all our work and planting the rice seedlings properly.

Farming is thirsty work. But one thing the banquet lacked was cold beer. So I was looking forward to a couple of cans at the Potonggang Hotel as reward for my contribution to the advancement of socialism.

'I'm not serving you beer,' the girl working in the lounge bar said. 'You're drunk.'

'I haven't touched a drop all day,' I protested. 'I've been working on the farm.'

A likely story, was clearly what she was thinking. 'So why's your face red, then?'

Koreans, it seemed, didn't know about sunburn.

'Please feel free to call again anytime,' Song Tae Bok had said as we left his house. But I never thought for a moment that this was anything more than a form of words. Not so Kim Il Sung University's American professor, however. Miles had apparently seen things differently. A week or so after an official visit to the house of a senior professor of English, he did just what he had been invited to do, and 'dropped in' again one Sunday morning. 'He looked almost shocked when he answered the door,' Miles told me. The professor didn't even invite him in.

Given the anti-US propaganda, it must have been a North Korean's worse nightmare, a tale told to frighten a naughty child, to have an American turn up unannounced on your doorstep. A general ban was in force on US citizens entering the country. Still, Miles being there was a reminder that in North Korea there were powers at work making it possible to get round even openly-stated restrictions.

Miles was a Saturday night regular at the Changgwangsan Hotel disco. To Pyongyang's foreign community Saturday night at this, the only real disco in North Korea, was an institution. It was located on the top floor of one of the hotel's two towers and entrance was free to regulars. It stayed open and continued serving beer into the early hours of Sunday morning. This was one place where no-one had any objections to foreign music and the play-list would be an eclectic mix of Cuban sambas, Beatles favourites, African dance tracks with their heavy rhythms, forlorn Russian love songs and '80s disco.

No Koreans were ever allowed in to this scene of decadence, unless they were extremely well connected. Occasionally a few of the braver Chinese students might venture there, but generally it was the place for Pyongyang's foreign, mainly African, students to meet, along with diplomats from the Soviet and Eastern European embassies. A handful of younger Cubans would also show their faces. The clientele would be complemented by tourist groups and other visitors to Pyongyang who had heard about the disco. In most cases they would have heard about it from Kris.

He was well known at the reception desks of all Pyongyang's hotels and would keep himself informed of which 'delegations' were due in town. Any that sounded promising – in other words that were likely to contain young single women, Soviet tour groups being a particularly hot prospect – he would follow up on and he would happen to be around their hotel on a Saturday evening, so that he could pass on an invitation to the only real disco in North Korea.

I ran into him most Saturday nights in one or other hotel bar and he would always ask if I was coming to the Changgwangsan, and I would always say no. I was never much of a one for discos. Anyway, I wanted to resist being drawn into the foreigners' camp.

When Cho, the Spanish speaker who had helped me prepare my lessons and had, until a couple of months before, been the resident interpreter at the guest house, came to visit, I decided he might be able to make sense of a development that had me baffled.

He was looking fit and brown. He told me he'd been going after work every evening for several weeks to lend a hand on a building site on Kwangbok Street. It was hard work, he said, but spirits were high. He was on his way there and wondered if I might give him a bottle of something so that he could invite some new-found friends to a drink.

'No problem,' I said, and I asked him about his girlfriend at the Potonggang Hotel, the one we'd been to see together several times in the bar where she worked. He shrugged. She was getting married to someone else. No, he wasn't upset about it. All the time we'd been getting to know her – I remembered some fairly aimless chat about mutual friends – she'd been planning to marry someone else. He was lucky, was Cho's view; she was clearly rather fickle – an unfortunate trait of some more modern Korean girls – and not the type for him to marry.

Then I tackled the matter that had been nagging at the back of my mind. I asked him about the bonus the entire population was to receive of an extra month's pay. He said it was a very nice surprise, a thank-you to the people from the authorities for all the late nights and weekends on the building sites that had been put in to ensure that everything was ready for the World Festival of Youth and Students. Everyone, he said, was included.

Not quite everyone, I told him. Foreigners earning hard currency were not covered. I knew because I'd asked.

But this wasn't the point. What I'd been wondering was why everyone, from the waitresses and barmaids at the hotels, to our guest house staff, from our drivers to the publishing house's translators and students, was so delighted at the news. In a country where the shops didn't function as normal sales outlets and the state distributed everything, what could they spend the extra money on? They could only have so many haircuts.

I asked Cho if he had any plans for spending his bonus. No, he said. He would save it.

He had, he assured me, volunteered for the work; it was the sort of thing a young revolutionary did. He was enjoying the camaraderie and was very proud of the block of flats he and his publishing house colleagues were helping to build. He laughingly called me a capitalist when I suggested that he'd only volunteered because he knew there'd be a bonus. No, he insisted, he hadn't.

It was Mr Chang, the student who had asked about the US and South Africa and apartheid and had spent a year, he told me, studying English in Tanzania – which explained his worldly-wise air – who helped shed some light on the mystery.

When I began my lesson as usual by inquiring if anyone had any questions, Mr Chang raised his hand and asked, while the other students tittered, if I had ever visited one of the farmers' markets on the outskirts of Pyongyang. The what? I asked. Farmers' markets, one of the girls repeated. The students looked at me expectantly.

'I'm afraid not,' I said, to their evident disappointment.

I'd heard vaguely about farmers' markets. They were a form of capitalism that was tolerated by the great leader. Farmers and other workers, Mr Chang told me, were permitted to sell whatever they had produced above their quotas, such as extra vegetables or eggs, cooking oil or rice.

These, then, might be the places where people could spend their extra cash, and I asked the students what else might be for sale. But there was silence. The class, it seemed, had decided there had been enough discussion of such a controversial matter and wanted to return to the British aristocracy.

The workers from the building site next to the guest house had packed up and gone, having completed their bridge. I liked to think that they might be heading home for a few weeks of rest and relaxation, but I had to admit there was scant chance. It was far more likely that they had been dispatched to another site of socialist construction, to do more back-breaking labour. But perhaps that might be preferable to a return to the dangers of military service or to the rigours of scratching out a livelihood from a few hectares in some remote mountainous region.

Our bridge across the River Potong was a key link between central Pyongyang and Kwangbok Street, the brand new residential district of 20,000 apartments built initially for the delegates to the 13th World Festival of Youth and Students, and into which some of Pyongyang's luckier residents would later move. Adjoining Kwangbok Street was a newly constructed sports village featuring a dozen or so halls, built to prove that Pyongyang would have been capable of co-hosting the Olympics. Along with buildings for table tennis, wrestling, volleyball and several other sports there was also a 30,000-seat stadium. The village was served by three new hotels and on Kwangbok Street itself there was a new indoor circus and a sprawling 'schoolchildren's palace' where youngsters could pursue extra-curricular sporting, cultural and scientific activities. Then there were shops and other facilities to serve the families that would live there later, and there was even a brand new department store.

Elsewhere in Pyongyang there was the new telecommunications centre on the other side of the River Potong, not far from our guest house. It would now house the international post office, to which our letters were in theory sent. On Yanggak Island in the River Taedong there was another hotel and a stadium. But the jewel in the crown was on a different island in the Taedong. This was a 150,000-seat stadium, which would be the venue for the opening and closing ceremonies of the 13th World Festival of Youth and Students.

As July and the opening of the Festival drew near, excitement was mounting and it was difficult not to get caught up in it. The propaganda machine was in full cry and it seemed uncharitable to be cynical. The anticipation ahead of a great party was there, and what was the harm in it? Nothing, apart from the cost, of course. But then, in an economy such as North Korea's, what was the real cost? The materials were available, the labour was available, and everything that was built would still be standing afterwards for use by the local population.

Except that the country's creditors wouldn't see it like that. North Korea was reported to be some $4 billion in debt and seemed to have no intention of ever repaying the money. In the autumn of 1987, a consortium of Western banks had declared Pyongyang in default of debts totalling some $700 million. As Stu had delighted in telling me, most of the money had been borrowed in the early 1970s to fund an earlier ambitious building programme and the purchase of modern machinery from the West. The machinery was, nearly two decades later, largely out of date and the money spent on it had not been repaid.

Not that this seemed to concern anyone in North Korea.

The entire history of North Korea is marked by a series of bold and ambitious building programmes, and a monument to the greatest of these so-called 'upsurges in socialist construction' can be seen on the northern side of the popular beauty spot, Moran Hill. It is a tall pillar, on the top of which is a statue of a winged horse and its rider. The horse is Chollima, or 1000-*li* horse, which according to legend was able to fly 1000 *li* – some 400 kilometres – in a day. But nowhere could a rider be found with the skill to ride it. Until, the inference is, 1958.

The Korean War had devastated the country; its industry was in ruins and its already limited arable land had been laid to waste. To get a sense of the utter destruction one can look at photographs of the capital in the immediate aftermath of the war. The 280,000 bombs that were said to have been dropped on the capital had left nothing but rubble. The city, so the

Americans had apparently boasted, would not rise again for 100 years. How wrong they were!

In August 1953, within a month of the war's end, a plan was adopted that envisaged the restoration of the national economy to pre-war levels within three years. Heavy industry had naturally been a prime target of the American bombers, and its rehabilitation was identified as the focus of the reconstruction effort. Agriculture and light industry, though, were not to be neglected. The programme was apparently well coordinated, with the heavy industry plants that were rebuilt first providing the basic materials needed elsewhere. Steelworks in particular were brought back into operation as quickly as possible, to supply factories producing the machinery required by industry and agriculture.

The successful completion of the Three-year Plan meant that by 1957 a Five-year Plan could be launched. The main targets this time were to complete the socialist transformation of the relations of production, lay a basis for socialist industrialisation and basically ensure the supply of food, clothing and housing for the people.

Kim Il Sung, naturally, led the way. He called on the workers of Kangson near Pyongyang to produce 10,000 tons more steel and in response they turned out 120,000 tons from a blooming mill with a supposed capacity of only 60,000 tons. Thus they were credited with lighting the torch of what the great leader dubbed the 'Chollima Movement'.

Under the slogan 'Let us dash forward in the spirit of Chollima!' miracles were recorded in all areas of economic activity. The targets for industrial production under the Five-year Plan were met in just two-and-a-half years. As a result North Koreans could boast that their backward, colonial agrarian country had been transformed into a socialist industrial–agricultural state with the firm foundations of an independent national economy.

Nowhere was the miracle more evident than in Pyongyang, which rose again on the ashes as the glorious capital of the Revolution. Thus Chollima, the winged horse, was tamed by the workers of North Korea.[5]

While the rest of the world watched on their television screens the unfolding drama that led to the horror in Beijing's Tiananmen Square on June 4th 1989, in North Korea the events went unreported.

The crushing of the Chinese students' pro-democracy movement could hardly have been worse in terms of its timing for the leadership in Pyongyang, coming as it did just a month before the city was due to host the World Festival of Youth and Students. Certainly, Kim Il Sung would have been concerned by the potential for the pro-democracy demonstrations to spread to his country, with news perhaps brought by the hundreds of North Korean students in China. So it was no surprise that the crackdown by the authorities in Beijing not only went unreported but also won the support of North Korea's rulers.

Still, the Tiananmen Square massacre threatened to overshadow Pyongyang's moment in the spotlight. Among the 20,000 young people expected in the city, there were likely to be a few who would take the opportunity to show their solidarity with the Chinese students. Any such action could be guaranteed to earn

---

[5] There are many North Korean accounts of the economic development under the Chollima Movement. A brief description is found on the website of the Korean Central News Agency (www.kcna.co.jp) for June 8th 2000.

the disapproval of the Pyongyang authorities. The question was, how far would the guests go in expressing their views and how far would the authorities go to stop them?

It came as a shock to learn that our movements would be restricted for the duration of the Festival. Specifically, the city's hotels were to be off-limits, even to its foreign residents. This meant we would not be able to meet many of the Festival delegates. It was a huge disappointment, but Kris remained confident that all would be well.

He reasoned that he, Philippe and myself were so well known at all the hotels that no-one would deny us entry. It was obvious that the restriction on movements was aimed at the Festival delegates, whom the organisers didn't want wandering off, in case they got lost. It was nothing to do with us.

The problem was solved after Philippe made a fuss. Eventually those of us foreign residents who wanted one – Kris took one just in case – were issued with special passes that allowed us access to all the hotels and other Festival venues. I made a point of showing mine to the doorman at the Koryo the first time I went there after the Festival started. 'What have you got that for?' he asked, examining the pass with curiosity. 'Everybody knows you here, Michael. We don't need to see that.'

Predictably, Kris had the time of his life during the Festival. I saw very little of him for a month, but when I did occasionally run into him he would regale me with tales of singing and dancing in the daytime and evenings spent in the company of strangers who quickly became friends at an open-air food market on Kwangbok Street, and in hotel bars, taking part in impromptu concerts.

It's hard to conceive of a capital city transforming itself so completely as did Pyongyang for the month of July 1989. It wasn't just the physical changes embodied in the impressive new buildings; it was also the change in attitude demonstrated by an entire population who, for once, could show their natural warmth in welcoming foreigners into their midst.

Of course, there was a serious, political side to the proceedings. What else could be expected of an event that went under the banner 'For anti-imperialist solidarity, friendship and peace'? North Korea was keen to use the Festival to promote itself as both the champion of the socialist cause and the Workers' Paradise, and so enormous efforts and vast sums of money had been channelled into making Pyongyang a showcase.

The ideal Korea the Festival organisers portrayed was nothing if not bright. The scene was set by the overwhelming display of colour at the Festival's opening in the vast new 150,000-seat May Day Stadium, where marching bands in red and turquoise, dancers in robes of green and white, blue, crimson and yellow, delegates in traditional costumes that combined the bold mustards and browns and greens of Africa with the fabulous silks of Asia, strutted and whirled and leapt and cheered in an outpouring of exuberance.

After the excitement of the opening ceremony, delegates would spend a week or more sharing their time between demonstrations of internationalist solidarity and appreciation of the host country. So they were taken to the tomb of King Tongmyong, where a vast grassy expanse was at normal times a good place for a picnic. During the Festival it was the location for folk games, in which the more intrepid guests were invited by locals dressed in the traditional bright silks of the Korean peasant to take part in the wrestling and archery, the swinging and see-sawing. There was a traditional wedding ceremony, too, where visitors were offered snacks prepared for what was, it turned out, the real marriage of the swaggering, silk-coated groom and his painfully demure bride in her bright red wedding gown.

Wherever they went, the Festival guests could not have failed to be touched by the warmth of the welcome they received from people who were not normally encouraged to mix with foreigners. I'm sure I wasn't the only person witnessing this to wonder if the 13th World Festival of Youth and Students, undoubtedly a triumph for North Korea, might just have indicated to the country's government, and to the world at large, that it was high time that North Korea came out of its isolation.

A week or so after the Festival ended, Song Il and I found ourselves sitting on a bench in the middle of the deserted Kwangbok Street, after the last of the stalls from the food market had been dismantled to leave the pavements empty. It was a rather sad and desolate scene, I reflected, compared to the animation that had filled it so recently.

The first evening I'd gone there during the Festival, it had been at Song Il's insistence, and I'd never experienced anything like it in Pyongyang before. The crowds roaming the street were made up of Koreans and foreigners, mixing in a perfectly natural way. I ran into Koreans I knew, waiters and waitresses, barmaids, interpreters and drivers, friends and acquaintances, some of whom were such casual acquaintances I scarcely recognized them, people who at other times might not even have risked acknowledging me, but who now stopped and chatted and invited me to join them for a bite to eat or a drink; actually to sit with them in the open air, in public, and talk.

Song Il had been astonished. 'I didn't know you knew so many people,' he had said. And in truth, neither did I.

So I was sad on that last night, as I sat with Song Il on the bench in Kwangbok Street. It was as if an era had come to an end. It had been a magical time when normal human friendships had superseded politics. I wondered if I would ever experience the like again in North Korea.

An image of the 13th World Festival of Youth and Students that endured in North Korean minds long after its conclusion was of a pretty South Korean student, Rim Su Gyong. She was a delegate of *Chondaehyop*, a radical South Korean students' organisation, and she made her appearance at the Festival's opening ceremony, where she was treated to a special round of applause and even a wave from the great leader himself, who I'm sure would have been much less happy about another incident – the unveiling of a banner in support of the Tiananmen students. Actually, the great leader could well have missed this brief pro-democracy demonstration by a delegation I was told was from Scandinavia, so quickly was it dealt with by the plain-clothes security forces in the stadium. Subsequently there would be a small number of demonstrations against the Chinese government on the fringes of the Festival and even protests over North Korea's own human rights record, all of which were ignored by the North Korean media and were not, to my knowledge, allowed to detract from the party atmosphere.[6]

By attending the Festival, Rim Su Gyong had defied the South Korean authorities and the country's National Security Law, and for this she was the focus of adulation in the North. Everywhere she went during the Festival she was cheered and idolised, surrounded by smiling and adoring Koreans and, it has to be

[6] An account of the protests by foreign delegations at the 13th World Festival of Youth and Students is found in *Vantage Point*, December, 1989.

said, foreigners. She was dubbed the Flower of Reunification and it was impossible not to be captivated by the romantic appeal of this young and smiling woman, who faced certain imprisonment upon her return to Seoul.

With the Festival over, it was her declared intention to return home to South Korea through Panmunjom; a single step across a simple line – the 38th Parallel – but a highly symbolic gesture for national reunification. The North had no objection to her doing so and she was transported down to the truce village amid the full glare of the local media. On the other hand, South Korea, which strongly objected to having its hand forced in this way by someone who had broken the law, refused to grant permission for her to take the historic step back home.

There was speculation among the foreigners in Pyongyang that there might be enormous propaganda potential in the Flower of Reunification settling in the North, if it came to that. Those of us who worked at the publishing house, and believed we had developed a nose for the best propaganda angles, could see the possibilities in describing how her joy at staying in the North was tinged with misery at being separated from her parents and sweetheart by the evil machinations of the anti-reunification forces in South Korea. No doubt footage would soon become available of her weeping family in Seoul, wondering why she was being kept from them. It's not our fault, the North would say with a sad shrug. We did all we could to ensure that we got her home safely, even taking her to within inches of the South, but the authorities there refused to let her in. Then parallels could be drawn between the plight of Rim Su Gong unable to rejoin her loved ones, and the millions of other Korean families torn apart because of the national division, and the North could explain yet again how all its efforts to achieve reunification had been thwarted by the South.

No doubt the girl herself could be induced to add to the pathos. She might well find it necessary to denounce South Korean society, and would probably make regular appearances on television, dabbing at her eyes as she spoke about her family and friends back home and explained how she had lived a miserable existence in South Korea, subject to all manner of discrimination. She might then take it upon herself to decry the plight of the millions of other, less fortunate, South Korean girls who were forced into prostitution or had been the victims of assault and rape, probably by US soldiers.

Thus went our reasoning as 'experts'. But as usual we underestimated the ability of the North's propaganda machine to put one over on the South. What actually happened was that Rim Su Gyong remained at Panmunjom and went on hunger strike. Night after night she appeared on television, chanting slogans and denouncing the South Korean authorities who were keeping her apart from her dear family, so close at hand. Within days she was lying feebly on a mat on the floor, scarcely able to raise a defiant fist as the ravages of hunger did their worst. Meanwhile, her colleagues in South Korea spoke out in her support and in denunciation of the stance of the authorities. And the North metaphorically sat back and enjoyed this propaganda coup.

Complete victory was assured when the South Korean authorities finally relented and agreed to let the Flower of Reunification step across the 38th Parallel at Panmunjom. To add a finishing touch that North Korea's propagandists could not even have dreamed of, a Catholic priest, Father Moon Gyu Hyon, turned up to accompany the thin and woebegone Rim, a professed Christian, back across the demarcation line. Both were arrested and the next sight North Koreans got of the Flower of Reunification was of this pretty girl dressed in orange prison uniform, her wrists linked together by handcuffs.

In itself it was a powerful image. Just to underscore the point, in newspapers and magazines, the photograph would be accompanied by another: of the cheerful, ebullient girl who had charmed everyone who saw her in Pyongyang.

Chapter 6

It is common for North Koreans to express the hope that a foreigner, by visiting their country, will learn to understand their situation. Seeing is believing, they tell you, which seems to imply that understanding will naturally develop into support. From my own experience, I can say my reading and observation did tend to make me more sympathetic to the plight of the country and its people and more critical of its opponents. But still there were claims and statements contained in what I heard and read that left me feeling disturbed.

In his autobiography, Choe Dok Sin, a former general, senior diplomat and foreign minister of South Korea, who in his twilight years came to the North to see out his days in the great leader's embrace, is highly critical of the 'enormous number of illegitimate people of mixed bloods' in South Korea, a state of affairs that is principally a result of the presence of US troops. What he calls 'international marriages' are rampant and entered into 'with impunity'.[1]

Up to this point, the *The Nation and I* has been a fairly interesting and moving tale of a Korean patriot and anti-communist who experiences anguish as a leading citizen of South Korea, a country misruled and divided, before fleeing to the United States, from where he eventually travels to North Korea to settle. He bemoans the humiliation the Korean nation suffered under colonial rule and complains of the weakness that led to the Japanese being replaced as rulers in the South by the

[1] The references to international marriages and the purity of the Korean bloodline are found in *The Nation and I* by Choe Dok Sin. Foreign Languages Publishing House, Pyongyang, 1987.

Americans. He rails at the successive military dictators who ruled South Korea at the bidding of the Americans and weeps at the part he played in supporting them, all the time acting out of a misguided loathing of communism. Only after visiting the North and meeting Kim Il Sung does he realise that he has been deluded and that the Communists are the true Korean patriots who honour the country's traditions.

But then he starts talking about the community of bloodline, which in North Korea is regarded as 'the primary of the national communities that bind a nation together'. Naturally, Choe insists, this has nothing to do with the racist 'pure blood' theory of Nazi Germany. It is not simply a matter of preventing different races from mixing. Rather, it is 'a question of great affection for fellow countrymen and the national pride of the Korean people'.

The conclusion is that, 'After all, the most important idea of the theory of bloodline is that the Korean people of the same blood are all compatriots and brothers and sisters wherever they live'.

All of which tends to suggest that the foreigner, however much of a Korea expert he may be and however understanding, will always be kept at a distance.

CHAPTER SIX

Silent Witness

The bet was that Romania would stand firm. Hungary, already beyond the pale as far as North Korea was concerned after establishing diplomatic relations with the South, had been the first to show signs of weakness when the Communists entered into negotiations on setting up a multi-party system. Poland had soon followed, with Solidarity sweeping the Communist old guard aside as it stormed to power. It wasn't long before East Germans had taken to the streets in their hundreds of thousands to demonstrate, and to their cars in tens of thousands to flee westwards. In Prague the rulers stood firm for a while, but by the beginning of December they had stepped aside, too. Bulgaria was being pushed into change and before long succumbed with barely a whimper. Silly little isolated Albania, of course, didn't really count. All of which left only Romania.

The regime built by Nicolae Ceausescu was somewhat in North Korea's own image. State control was absolute, a powerful security force maintained a strong grip over the population and Ceausescu had succeeded in building up something of a personality cult; it was rumoured that he'd got the idea during several trips to Pyongyang. Anyway, he clearly had no intention of giving up power.

I'd spent part of the summer of 1989 in Britain and had watched in fascination as the early stages of the drama in Eastern Europe unfolded on television. Back in Pyongyang, the people were being kept very much in the dark. I had the advantage of a radio, and I kept those of my colleagues who asked up-to-date with what was going on.

I agreed with Song Do Nam, our new resident interpreter at the guest house, when he said Ceausescu would survive. There was no chance that he would step aside peacefully, we reckoned, and the country's security forces could be relied upon to use whatever brutality was necessary to put down any dissent. Taking the opposite view was my American colleague, Carol, who had recently arrived from Beijing.

Song Do Nam had spent a year in China studying French, which had also brought him a reasonable command of Chinese and, by coincidence, a friendship with Carol, who had been studying in Beijing at the same time. Like most of my Korean colleagues, Song Do Nam viewed the events in Eastern Europe not so much with the horror, trepidation and perhaps even anticipation one might have expected from North Koreans, but with the attitude of an intrigued onlooker. Carol, by contrast, was fervent in her delight. The latest collapse of a fortress in communism's evil empire was the cause of almost daily celebration. It was only a matter of time before North Korea, too, would succumb, so she thought.

My Soviet colleague Boris, though, tended to side with Song Do Nam and myself, and he was outraged on the day that Nicolae

Ceausescu and his wife were executed. No friend of communism himself, Boris feared that things were happening far too quickly. If the collapse that was overtaking Eastern Europe was to be sustained, it had to be brought under some control. The execution of the Romanian leader had been ill-considered and too hasty.

Everyone seemed to have their own view of what was happening. My Korean friends were apparently united in the conviction, even after Romania fell, that things would be back to normal before too long. Of the foreigners, there were those who were distressed that the work of decades was being undermined on a sudden impulse; there were others who believed that finally the oppressed masses were giving vent to their frustrations and winning the freedom they had craved.

Miles, the American professor, and I were in the habit of meeting up after work a couple of times a week at the Potonggang Hotel. He was an intelligent, well-read man who always struck me as looking the part. With his thinning sandy hair and moustache and his horn-rimmed spectacles, he had a professorial air about him. Unlike many of Pyongyang's foreigners, he could hold a conversation on a range of issues that extended well beyond the country we happened to be living in.

I'm not sure which side Miles came down on in the fall of communism debate because he never really told me. Of course, we discussed the daily unfolding developments at great length, but his approach was academic, that of someone who realised he had a unique perspective on historical developments that would fundamentally change the world. What would be the impact on North Korea he had no idea, and he didn't seem particularly interested in speculating. For once, I think our reluctance to discuss potential repercussions in North Korea stemmed more from pure uncertainty than it did from a fear of being overheard saying something too critical.

Within two days of the Ceausescus' deaths, half of an entire edition of *The Pyongyang Times* was given over to an article that went under the headline 'Let us advance vigorously along the road of socialism, repulsing the challenge of the imperialists'.[2] It was a translation of an editorial that had appeared in *Rodong Sinmun*, organ of the Workers' Party of Korea, and had been written before the events in Romania reached their climax. I knew this because I'd been working on the English translation at the time.

The tone of the lengthy article was set in the opening paragraph, which read:

> The imperialists have of late become more heated than ever before in slandering socialism, talking loudly about the 'decline of socialism' and the 'victory of the free world'. They are behaving impudently and arrogantly against history, and committing greater crimes against mankind, but they are running headlong to their destruction.

The somewhat optimistic argument, given the course events were taking in Eastern Europe, was that the overthrow of capitalism by the forces of socialism was a law of human development. While not referring directly to changes in the international situation, the article did make an oblique reference, thus:

> That which is outdated and reactionary does not recede from the arena of history of its own accord, but resorts to more vicious and crafty moves as it draws closer to its downfall.

[2] *The Pyongyang Times*, December 27 1989.

And so:

> The modern imperialists, who are internationally allied with the US imperialists as their chieftain, are trying more desperately to turn back the tide of history from capitalism to socialism. They are directing the sharp edge of their attack to the socialist countries, the bastion of peace and progress.

But never fear, the triumph of the just cause was assured! The article went on:

> No force on earth can check the historical process of the turn from capitalism to socialism, and the victory of socialism and the downfall of imperialism are likewise inevitable.

Essentially, all was and would continue to be well for North Korean socialism, thanks of course to its ideal guiding philosophy and the leader the rest of the world could only look up to and admire. Hence the article ended on a rousing note:

> If anyone asks wherein the source of the indestructible strength lies and what the key to our victory is, we will answer without hesitation. It is that our people have continued with the revolution without the slightest vacillation, holding high the banner of anti-imperialism and independence, the banner of socialism, advancing along the road indicated by the immortal Juche Idea, united in a single heart behind the Party Central Committee headed by the great leader Comrade Kim Il Sung.

The stepped-up rhetoric against capitalism made regular reference to 'reactionary bourgeois culture' as an instrument for 'debasing'[3] people morally. The allegations were lacking in specifics, but to judge by the strict controls over the content of North Korean film and song and the restrictions on the country's people listening to or seeing any foreign culture, there was the clear belief that nothing the outside world had to offer would suit North Korea's highly refined ideological and moral tastes. Certainly one would have thought a busty blonde singer dressed in a miniskirt, who sang raunchy songs about love and relationships as she strutted not only around the stage but also through her audience, would be the last thing North Koreans would be permitted to see.

I'd never heard of Alla Pugachova. She was a Russian singer and I watched in utter amazement as she pranced and preened in front of her Pyongyang audience, in an exhibition far removed from the very staid and static stage performances North Koreans were used to from their home-grown singers.

Understandably, the audience didn't know quite what it should do. Instead of throwing themselves wholeheartedly into the celebration of Western-style decadence and dancing on their seats, which I imagined was what the singer was used to from her fans back home, the Koreans sat stiffly erect and clapped politely and in unison at the end of each song. Professional that she was, Ms Pugachova carried on regardless, although I did sense she was thrown a little out of her stride by the mass giggling at her attempts to embrace and kiss a poor chap who had been designated to get up on stage and hand her a bunch of flowers during the performance.

The only people apart from us foreigners who seemed to be aware that this restrained response might have been taken amiss

---

[3] *The Pyongyang Times*, December 27 1989.

by the singer were some chaps in the side aisles, who were making frantic attempts to stir the spectators to cast off their inhibitions. Maybe it was a duty they had taken upon themselves, or maybe the theatre's management had shown remarkable foresight; either way, they were leaping up and down, pirouetting, clapping wildly with their hands in the air and generally making complete fools of themselves, in a desperate effort to stir the crowd out of its lethargy.

As long as they leapt and danced and waved their arms the audience showed some signs of stirring, even clapping along during one number. But as soon as these brave souls took a breather there was a general relapse into the state of passive indifference. Whatever the rest of the world might think, North Korea didn't seem to be ready for any decadence.

The clearest signal that Pyongyang had been shaken by international developments came at the end of 1989, when nearly 2000 students were recalled from Eastern Europe. Undoubtedly the authorities were worried that these young and impressionable people were being infected by the counter-revolutionary elements at work in the countries where they were studying. A sign that this was the case had been the defection to South Korea of a handful of North Korean students from Czechoslovakia, Poland and East Germany.

I felt quite sorry for one student thus recalled, although I never met him. His girlfriend worked at the Ansan Club and had been dutifully heartbroken when he landed a place for a couple of years at a university in Czechoslovakia. The poor girl had waited for months for a first letter home and had been mortified to find enclosed with it, when it finally arrived, a photograph of the object of her devotion surrounded by a giggling group of locals, including several girls. It was a display of male insensitivity that would, I assumed was his thinking, have been forgiven and forgotten by the time he made it home, which he had anticipated would be a couple of years hence.

So being recalled on the orders of his government must have come as quite a blow. A lengthy political debriefing from the authorities to ensure that he was ideologically still on track must have been a daunting enough prospect for the poor chap. But even that was likely to be nothing compared with the unsympathetic welcome he could expect from his betrothed, if that was what she still considered herself to be.

Miles briefly had a colleague, an American girl called Sam who was teaching English conversation. I met her quite often, mainly in the coffee shop at the Changgwangsan, the hotel where she was lodged, and before long she confessed to me that she was, in fact, in Pyongyang searching for lost love.

She, like Carol, had been recruited – in her case by Kim Il Sung University – in Beijing, where she had been studying. There she had formed a relationship with a young Korean. After his departure she had decided to follow him home. I never discovered whether the young man had been a party to this plan – asking her while she was pouring her heart out never seemed quite the right thing to do – and I wondered cynically if, in fact, he would have appreciated the gesture, given the rather difficult explanations that would be demanded by her arrival on his doorstep.

They had several mutual friends in Pyongyang, none of whom appeared to know about any romantic involvement between the two and none of whom would or could tell her about her boyfriend's fate upon his arrival back in Pyongyang from China. Of course, Sam was convinced that the authorities had found out about their affair and that her boyfriend was being punished in some way. Reports from friends she dispatched in search of him, that he seemed to have vanished, simply confirmed her fears.

Then a few snippets of information began to filter through. Yes, there had been a dark car and sinister men waiting for him at the airport. So the worst had happened, concluded Sam. But no, it later transpired, this was not necessarily so. Yes, they were agents of some description, but they were in fact waiting for him because he was a new recruit to their organisation, which conveniently explained why it was proving so difficult even for his friends to contact him.

She never found out what had really happened, but then she appeared to lose interest anyway. She left North Korea as soon as the university would let her, which was more or less as soon as she asked. Philippe, who knew her and her group of North Korean friends from Beijing, was convinced that she'd invented the whole story. Pity, then, the poor Korean who was the object of her search, was Philippe's attitude; he would have an awful lot of explaining to do for someone so innocent.

I wondered if perhaps the Korean might have assumed there was no chance of anything coming from the relationship and had decided that doing a disappearing act was the best way of dealing with a potentially very awkward situation. I liked to think that nothing untoward had happened to him; probably he had settled down with a nice Korean girl instead.

To my mind, the certainty that foreigners and Koreans could never wed seemed to be dissipating, although I had to admit this might be just wishful thinking on my part. One of Philippe's friends, the son of someone quite high up in the leadership, even introduced Philippe to his sister, something that would have been perfectly innocent in Western circles but for Philippe, who seemed to have no desire to settle down, was just a little too close to a formal Korean-style introduction for comfort.

A rather earthy approach to the issue of interracial marriage was adopted by Kim Ho Gwang, who had joined Director Li and Song Il as the third member of the publishing house's foreign affairs team. He told me jokingly over a beer on one of his visits to my flat that the real reason marriage with Koreans was forbidden was that foreign males were 'too big'.

Such were the thoughts that had preoccupied me one quiet Sunday afternoon.

She was sitting on her low stool behind the bar, reading. I'd asked her if she would like to hear a funny story. She'd said yes and I'd apologised that my Korean might make it difficult to understand.

My Korean friend, I'd told her, had been introduced to a girl and she was very pretty. He invited her to the cinema and he arranged for a car – it was my driver – to take him to meet her. Unfortunately my friend had been given a higher job that day. Why unfortunately? Because he visited my room and we celebrated. He stayed to drink several beers. And he had to go quickly to meet the girl.

At the cinema they sat in the middle. But because of all the beer he had to go to the toilet four times. It made a big disturbance. For the girl it was very embarrassing. She called him a drunkard and said she would never see him again.

She'd seemed pleased by the story. She'd said I understood her country well.

It was a compliment, something Koreans said when they sensed that a foreigner appreciated and respected them and their customs. It didn't matter that I'd ruined a possible romance; what was important, I guessed, was that I'd gained someone's trust sufficiently to celebrate his promotion and talk to him about his date, as a friend.

The problem was that I was still living in a separate world. True, there were things I knew and appreciated about the people and their culture. But there was one thing I didn't know, something I wanted to understand more than anything else, and that was how far into the Koreans' own world I would be permitted to venture.

Miles was careful about whom he confided in, out of a fear that saying the wrong thing to the wrong person might land him in difficulties, a possibility that he, as an American, was more sensitive to than were the rest of us foreigners. Anyway, it was much more interesting and informative just to listen to what other people had to say, he reasoned, as well as being much safer.

Naturally visitors were keen to find out what Pyongyang's long-term foreign residents knew and there was always the danger of letting your tongue run away with you. The trick, I'd worked out, was to nod a bit or shake my head during conversations with inquisitive outsiders. 'Yes, but from the work I do I can tell you the official line is ... ' was always a handy phrase that, while appearing to show a willingness to talk, led merely into a harmless repetition of the propaganda, while 'A lot of Western media reports aren't as accurate as they should be' allowed me to refer to critical comments made by someone else.

The point was to appear open to debate, but without compromising myself in the event that someone was eavesdropping.

On one occasion after the World Festival of Youth and Students, however, I'd let my tongue slip. Over a Sunday afternoon beer in the Changgwangsan Coffee Shop, I'd suggested to a British engineer that in the event of the great leader's death I couldn't see the dear leader lasting too long. In fact, I'd given him three months. For days afterwards I'd dreaded every knock on my door and had found myself far more than was usual in Song Il's room downstairs, fearful of finding him in conversation with a sinister-looking stranger. When his telephone had rung I would listen in trepidation to the conversation, anxious to pick up on any signs of what actions might be planned against me. For weeks afterwards, whenever Song Il or an interpreter or even a driver had spoken to me, I'd turned over in my mind every word, searching desperately for any hint or innuendo referring to the dreadful mistake I had made.

Even after a month had passed and nothing had happened, I wasn't completely reassured. Perhaps nobody had been listening. Or maybe I was well enough regarded to get away with minor indiscretions. Another possibility was that they might be waiting to tell me that, after three years, they wouldn't be interested in extending my contract.

I held my breath as the end of my third year approached.

Miles and I were sure we'd seen them somewhere before, the two strangers playing pool on our favourite table in the Potonggang Hotel. But we couldn't place them. They were Koreans, sure enough; they spoke the language. But there was something different about them, about the way they dressed. Their clothes were smart, just like those of their hosts, but they had a quality and casual style that North Korean clothing generally lacked. Also, it was most unusual for a Korean girl to be playing what was considered a man's game.

They were, we picked up from the barmaid's whisper, from South Korea. Of course they were! We'd seen their photographs in *The Pyongyang Times*.[4] Still, we were quite taken aback to find that the two of them had precedence on our favourite pool table.

There had been quite a rush of people escaping from the brutal regime south of the border, we had read in the local press. The official line in the news when South Koreans 'came over to the northern half of the Republic' was always that they were escaping a life of personal misery in a colony of the United States, where they were robbed of all national dignity. Society was corrupt and the only hope of salvation lay in the embrace of the Party in the North. However, the fact that the two defectors staying at the Potonggang Hotel were an elderly male director of a tourist agency and his much younger female assistant had tongues wagging, at least Pyongyang's foreign tongues.

It was interesting, I reflected, how we so readily dismissed the claims of those defecting from the South to the North, speculating instead that there was some lurid reason why they had escaped. On the other hand, the Northerners we read about in the foreign media who defected to the South – of course there was no mention of them in *The Pyongyang Times*, which led me to wonder if South Koreans were told about those who had headed in the opposite direction – could expect the stories they told – of poverty and starvation and the violation of human rights – to be lapped up and widely believed.

---

[4] The arrival of the two dissidents was reported in *The Pyongyang Times*, February 10 1990.

Such was the situation on the Korean peninsula that, whichever side you were coming from, you were guaranteed a hero's welcome on the other. No awkward questions would be asked about your past. The deal was that you had to make the right condemnatory noises about the half of the peninsula you had come from and express due delight at the wonders of the new society you found yourself in.

One might have expected North Koreans to be heading southwards in their droves to enjoy the riches and decadence of capitalism. But they didn't, and for three principal reasons. For one thing there was the lack of opportunity. Their movements were so restricted inside North Korea that they could hardly leave their home town or village without anyone knowing it, let alone make it to the coast or a border. Even if they got that far, there were still the hazards to face of getting out of the country. A second consideration was that any defectors could expect the family they left behind to face harsh reprisals, of such severity as to deter others from taking the same course. Finally, the idea of going to South Korea probably never entered the head of the average Northerner, who was told it was a land of misery and poverty where crime, disease and homelessness were rampant and where human rights were trampled underfoot. And they had no source of information to give them reason to doubt this.

The faltering search for reconciliation between North and South Korea was subjected to another setback when talks broke down in February 1990 on fielding a joint team to compete in September's Beijing Asian Games. Predictably, each side blamed the other.

For almost a year discussions and meetings had been held as the two sides attempted to make some practical headway in the wake of overtures made in the political arena by the two countries' leaders. The climate of goodwill was, however, inadequate to putting out a joint team. Not even deciding its name was as simple as might be imagined. 'Korea' was, not surprisingly, approved by both sides. But then, to believe North Korean accounts, the South side prevaricated even on this.[5]

North Korean officials insisted that they had done all they could to facilitate agreement: putting forward reasonable proposals, accepting many of the South's demands and even making unilateral concessions.

The talks finally collapsed after the South rejected what the North described as a 'reasonable proposal'. This included a demand that the South admit that it had been responsible for delaying the formation of the team by raising unrelated problems. In such a climate of petty name-calling, it was difficult to see how the breakthrough might be achieved that so many people on both sides of the 38th Parallel were so desperately hoping for.

Defectors reinforced the negative perceptions of South Korea. Kim Won Sok, the tourism executive using my pool table, was reported by *The Pyongyang Times*[6] as telling a press conference a month after his defection that South Korea was a land where injustice and irregularities prevailed. As a result he had been unable to realise his simple dream of making a contribution to

[5] See *Korea Today*, 1990, 7.

[6] *The Pyongyang Times*, March 24 1990.

the nation by running a decent travel business. The reputation of the industry in South Korea was of 'sex-package' tourism, he said.

His companion, Yu Sol Ja, said that in South Korea women were humiliated and discriminated against. President Roh Tae Woo himself, she said, was behind a trade in which 8000 babies a year were sold abroad. In short, South Korea was not a land fit for women to live in. So when Kim Won Sok had told her about North Korea, whose leaders President Kim Il Sung and Mr Kim Jong Il had been praised by people he had met in Singapore with expressions of boundless respect, she had agreed to accompany him, in expectation of being able to lead a worthwhile life.[7]

The two defectors also referred in their press conference to a bizarre argument between the North and South of Korea, about a concrete wall that Pyongyang accused Seoul of having built across the width of the country in the southern part of the demilitarised zone. This, the North insisted, was yet another example of the South Korean authorities flying in the face of the national desire for reunification. Phrases such as 'severed blood veins' and 'perpetuate the division' were bandied about in the North Korean media.[8] South Korea said that no such wall existed. Kim Won Sok said that yes, it did; he'd seen it with his own eyes.

By the middle of March, the North had brought in an international fact-finding mission for the verification of the wall's existence, and magazines featured photographs of the left-wing former European foreign ministers and leaders of various pro-Pyongyang international groupings peering through binoculars and telescopes, above ecstatic headlines such as 'The concrete

[7] *The Pyongyang Times*, March 24 1990.

[8] For example, *The Pyongyang Times*, March 24 1990.

wall exists!' Oh, said the South Koreans, you mean the anti-tank barrier.

To make matters worse and in a way even more ludicrous, it was around this time that the South Koreans accused the North of digging another tunnel under the demilitarised zone, designed for use in an invasion. The so-called '4th Tunnel Incident', the North countered, was yet another ploy by the South to discredit it. To my mind, squabbling over whether a wall, which would have had to be several hundred kilometres long, and a tunnel supposed to be wide enough and to extend far enough into South Korea to present a credible threat of facilitating an invasion, actually existed or not epitomised the futility of the attempts to bring North and South Korea together.

At the Ansan Guest House we had a brand new wall of our own that became the subject of discussion. One morning I arrived for breakfast and, while I waited for my milk, eggs, toast and coffee to arrive, glanced out of the dining room window, as was my habit, to watch the people turning up for work at the factory next door.

Normally I could see them, at just below the level of my eyes, trudging along a driveway not more than ten metres away. Martial music blasted in the background, interrupted from time to time by the voice of a political agitator, carried over loudspeakers, that rose in waves of hysteria until he or she sounded close to tears, entreating the workers to perform their day's labours for the greater glory of the Party and the leader.

On this morning, though, I couldn't see the workers because the wall separating the guest house's grounds from their drive had been raised. It had been done overnight and I wondered if the builders would be back later to finish the job, because rather than making the wall higher along its whole length they had only bothered with the section immediately outside our dining room window.

I asked the waitress what the strange construction was for when she came in with her tray. She didn't know.

I asked if the factory workers had complained about the foreigners staring at them when they were coming to work.

She laughed.

More likely, I concluded after several weeks had passed and the middle section of the wall remained the only part raised, someone had decided that, at a time of growing economic hardship, it was sensible that the workers should not be aware of the plentiful food supplies available for the privileged few.

There was a spate of defections by South Koreans at the end of the 1980s and the beginning of the 1990s. Those who had 'come over' were lodged in the hotels. No doubt this facilitated debriefing since if, as was widely believed to be the case, the hotels were bugged throughout, even their private conversations could be listened to. The drawback for the officials charged with looking after the new arrivals was that they came into contact with people like me. Even though they were celebrities, individual propaganda triumphs over the South, they were at the same time potentially spies. At the very least they might not necessarily have the most wholesome of reasons for defecting. So the least contact they had with anyone, especially foreigners who spoke a little of their language, the better.

The bugging was pretty hard for these South Koreans to accept. The couple at the Potonggang Hotel on several occasions told me, when their 'guide' wasn't present, that he had told them not to talk to me. It was pretty naïve of them, I thought, since no doubt he was listening anyway.

One of the 'guides' did, however, earn my sympathy, since he was looking after a young man, in his early 20s I guessed, who had 'come over' and was clearly suffering under the strain. He would get obnoxiously, and at times violently, drunk in the bars of the Potonggang Hotel. From what I could gather from his yelling, he had quickly become disillusioned with his new home, if he'd ever been enamoured of it in the first place. His 'guide', of course, was in an impossible position. His charge was extremely valuable propaganda-wise as a defector, but was hardly exhibiting the signs of delirious joy that might have been expected of him in his father's warm embrace. He was supposed to enjoy every comfort in his temporary hotel home, but at some point the supply of drink had to be turned off. Punching him to shut him up was hardly an option, however violent his protests became. To my knowledge, his was the briefest debriefing of any South Korean defector.

In the Changgwangsan Hotel from time to time I met a South Korean who spoke English. He it was who told me about the rigorous debriefing South Korean defectors were subjected to. The questioning was particularly intense in his case, since he was a former interpreter for the US forces in South Korea. Aside from extracting useful information for intelligence and propaganda purposes, the aim of the debriefing, he told me, was to decide what to do with the defectors in order to assimilate them into North Korean society. An appropriate job had to be found for them, and arrangements made for their social and family needs. The obvious course of action in his case, given his somewhat blatant approaches to the hotel's waitresses, was to find him a wife as soon as possible, which the authorities duly did.

Next stop Glory: Restoration Station on the Pyongyang Metro

Monument to liberty: Pyongyang's Arch of Triumph

Giant pretensions: Pyongyang's Ryugyong Hotel, 105 storeys tall and never completed

Taming a legend: The Chollima Statue

Testament to faithfulness: The Loyalty Monuments, Kaesong

Vision of grandeur: Kim Il Sung Square and the Juche Tower from the roof of the Grand People's Study House

Man in the street: Waiting at a trolleybus stop, with the Grand People's Study House in the background

Playing with fire: Clam bake, North Korean style

Night fever: Celebrating the founding of the Republic; evening dance in Kim Il Sung Square, September 9th, 1993

Poor relations: The old home at Mangyongdae, with the twisted rice jar that demonstrates the poverty endured by the future great leader's family

Break from the fields: Celebrating National Farmers' Day at the Tomb of King Kongmin, Kaesong

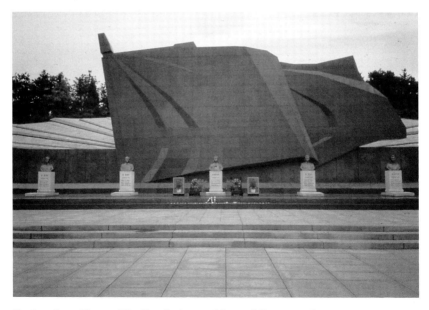

Resting place of heroes: The Revolutionary Martyrs' Cemetery, Pyongyang

Temple of dreams: The Pohyon Temple in the Myohyang Mountains

Ancient and modern: Nam (South) Gate, Kaesong

Life on the line: The 38th Parallel at Panmunjom

Photographs by Denis Harrold

Madame Beatrice had left us and, in accordance with what seemed now to be tried and tested recruitment practice, the publishing house found her replacement in Beijing. The argument was that anyone who had lived in China would find it easier to adapt to life in North Korea.

Christophe Leblanc single-handedly disproved this theory. That he was odd even by the standards of Pyongyang's foreigners became evident very soon after I first met him. He was polite enough in English, which he spoke with a clipped correctness. But it was in his native French that he voiced, apparently to himself, the poisonous thoughts that became a feature of meals at the guest house.

That Leblanc talked to himself was nothing particularly out of the ordinary. The pressure on the foreigners in Pyongyang brought out many unusual characteristics. Miles, for example, had an off-putting habit of looking over his shoulder from time to time while he talked to you, as if seeking out someone who might be following him. Until I got used to this, many a time I would follow his gaze, wondering who it was that he was looking out for. He in turn would clearly want to know who I'd seen and our conversation, already faltering, would grind to a halt while he turned around to see who or what I was looking at.

It was what Christophe Leblanc said to himself as he sat bolt upright at the dinner table, with his Chinese wife imploring him to stop, that I had a problem with. It was generally nasty vitriol against the Koreans, the Chinese, the English and any other nation except the French. That he could say the most spiteful and downright unpleasant things about individuals with no regard to the fact that they might be my friends, with a look of childish serenity on his face, could be quite disconcerting. This was bad enough. But what really unnerved me about Christophe Leblanc was his obsessive pursuit of binoculars.

He wanted binoculars, and for weeks on end at every meal he would go on about them. He'd had drivers and interpreters scouring the shops of Pyongyang in search of a pair. Letters to China asking friends to send him binoculars had failed to yield results. None of the foreigners in Pyongyang, it seemed, had any to lend him.

Quite why he wanted binoculars I could only imagine. He said he was a bird-watcher, but I rather suspected they represented a handy stick with which to beat the North Koreans. Ending each account of his latest expedition in search of binoculars, he would rant about a country where an honest 'bird-fancier' was prevented from pursuing his innocent hobby.

It was when he asked me if I could help import a pair from Hong Kong – Philippe and I were in contact with a mail order company, which had already supplied us with Walkmans and tapes – that I finally put my foot down. He hadn't taken the hint when I'd told him there wasn't much demand for them in Pyongyang, so now I demanded to know what he thought would be the reaction in a city that considered itself in imminent danger of attack, was inhabited by a highly militarised population that he himself mocked as obsessed with spies, and was surrounded by military installations, to a foreigner wandering around with a pair of high-powered binoculars.

Carol, when she left after a largely unhappy year spent revising propaganda condemning her own country, discovered that she hadn't been American at all, but Irish. She had an Irish passport as well as an American one and when she left she was told she would be put on a plane to Dublin. She argued that she lived in New York, had never been to Ireland and wanted to be flown home, but this carried no weight with the vast bureaucracy that had determined that she couldn't possibly be American. So she had to pay the rest of her way home, from Dublin to New York.

Miles didn't tell people he was American. Whenever he was asked he said he was Canadian. I never really appreciated the wisdom of this until I went out for dinner with an American journalist.

Vince was a veteran reporter on Asia and no supporter of his government's policy in the region. He viewed the authorities in South Korea with suspicion and didn't find it necessary to rubbish the Kim personality cult in the North. North Korea had its problems, he agreed, but which country didn't? There were plenty of places in the region where the people were starving; free medical care was the exception, not the norm; in many parts of Asia and beyond children could only dream of an education and in many cases were lucky if they weren't working in sweatshops by the time they were teenagers.

I proposed we should have dinner in the Koryo Restaurant, a Japanese *sushi* bar adjoining the Koryo Hotel, and he asked me what he should say when he was asked where he was from. The US of course, I said. If there was any hostility I would explain that he was sympathetic to the cause. I might even call him a friend of Korea.

It was no good. As usual the waitress wanted to know where my friend was from and her reaction when I said America was along the lines of yes, yes, I've heard that one before. She probably had, since it was a popular joke among the foreigners in Pyongyang to claim that either they themselves or a companion was from the US. The light-hearted banter would generally continue with the waitress saying, 'There are no American bastards in our country.'

So it took some effort on my part to convince the waitress that Vince was indeed American and when I finally succeeded she lost all interest in serving us. When I protested, the entire staff got involved. 'Why did you bring that American bastard here?' they demanded.

'But he's very sympathetic,' I replied vainly. Vince didn't understand the words, but the sentiments were all too clear, to my acute embarrassment. I was grateful to him for remaining so relaxed even as, under the hostile glares of the restaurant staff, we quickly ate the food we eventually managed to order. I then took him to the Koryo Hotel for a beer, where I introduced my friend as a Canadian.

The Victorious Fatherland Liberation War Museum in Pyongyang is a vast building that rather incongruously resembles Buckingham Palace. This is the place to visit for those who have any doubts about just how strong is the North Korean antipathy to the US.

Throughout its vast halls and expansive chambers are displayed photographs and inscriptions, armaments and weapons, uniforms and flags, testifying to the heroism and self-sacrificing spirit of the Korean People's Army and the North Korean population at large and to the savagery and treachery of the US imperialists and their puppet allies. To be fair, I suppose that in this sense it is not so different from war museums in other countries. What makes the Victorious Fatherland Liberation War Museum somewhat unusual is the inference that it commemorates a war that is still being fought.

North Korea keeps itself in a permanent state of readiness against the possibility of renewed US attack. Such vigilance is essential to protect not only the country and people, but also the gains of the revolution, in other words the infrastructure and factories, the towns and cities, the farms and waterways, built at the cost of the sweat and blood of the North Korean people. The fear is that the Americans, having reduced the country to rubble once already, may do so again at the drop of a hat.

There is little doubt that what North Korea achieved in terms of rehabilitation in the years after the Korean War was remarkable, even allowing for the usual tendency to exaggerate their successes. They managed largely to re-establish their heavy industry and, by the early 1960s, Kim Il Sung was able to concentrate on doing something about improving the lot of the country's farmers and knocking the management of factories into shape. A general upgrading of technology was also made a priority.

The tale was told how the Kum Song Tractor Plant made the first indigenous tractor, the Chollima No. 1. The only problem was that it only ran backwards. Still, the great leader was pleased and reassured the workers and technicians by telling them that if it ran backwards, it could also run forwards.[9] For years afterwards it was an example he would refer to in his speeches of how Koreans, if they only put their minds to it, could overcome any adversity and, using their ingenuity, design and produce anything that anyone else could.

In a personal demonstration of inspired leadership, in February 1960 the great leader visited the farming village of Chongsan-ri. In the course of a stay lasting several days he observed the way the farmers worked and listened to their

[9] See *Korea Today*, 1991, 11.

opinions, and he duly developed the Chongsan-ri Method. Essentially this involved officials getting into the habit of talking to, listening to and helping the masses, all the time ensuring that political work among them was given priority. Similarly, the Taean Work System, dreamed up during a trip to give on-the-spot guidance at the Taean Heavy Machine Works not far from Pyongyang, envisaged factories being managed under the collective leadership of their Party committees.

By the time of the Fourth Party Congress in September 1961, with the economic basics sorted out, raising technical standards could be placed on the agenda. In launching the new national economic plan, Kim Il Sung was able to say:

> The fundamental tasks of the Seven-year Plan are to carry out a comprehensive technological reconstruction and the cultural revolution, and to make radical improvements in the people's living conditions by relying on the triumphant socialist system. We must carry out socialist industrialization, equip all branches of the national economy with modern technology, and decisively raise the material and cultural standards of the whole population. Thus, we will attain the high peak of socialism.[10]

But every success was overshadowed by the menace lurking in the South that might at any time lash out once again and undo all that had been achieved. The menace itself provided ample proof of its intent. A whole section in the basement of the Victorious Fatherland Liberation War Museum is devoted to photographs and exhibits chronicling incursions committed by

---

[10] 'Report to the Fourth Congress of the Workers Party of Korea, September 9th 1961'. In *Kim Il Sung: Works*, vol. 16, January–December 1961. Foreign Languages Publishing House, Pyongyang, 1989.

the US imperialists in the decades after the signing of the Armistice. There are bits of planes and helicopters shot down over North Korean territory. But pride of place goes to memorabilia associated with the *Pueblo*.

In January 1968 an American spy ship, the USS *Pueblo*, was captured while operating illegally, so Pyongyang claimed, in North Korean waters. One crewman was killed and the other 80 or so were taken prisoner. The United States was outraged and demanded the immediate return of its innocent sailors. Insults were traded and attack was threatened. It wasn't until December of that year that the men were finally released, having signed a letter of confession in which they admitted to conducting espionage activities against the North.

The US authorities subsequently insisted that the confession had been extracted through coercion and that the ship, which remained in North Korean hands, had been engaged in wholly legitimate activities. Be that as it may, the capture of the *Pueblo* came as a huge propaganda coup for the North Koreans. Not only did the crew with their hands up provide some pretty sterling images of the mighty US being humbled again by the heroic Korean People's Army, but it also provided further proof of the need for vigilance at all times against an enemy preparing to attack at any moment.[11]

Leblanc was openly scathing about the propaganda he worked on, to the point that, so one of his colleagues confided in me, they had to be extra vigilant in checking his work, just in case he

---

[11] An account of the *Pueblo* incident from the crew's point of view is found on www.usspueblo.org.

had slipped in some subtle change that left the text giving a damaging impression of North Korea. As far as I was concerned he was entitled to his views, and to my knowledge he was never so unprofessional as deliberately to alter the meaning of texts he was given to edit. But I did think he was too outspoken. While the rest of us tiptoed around certain subjects, intent on not causing offence to our hosts, Leblanc made no effort to hide his contempt for the country and its leadership.

So he was disliked, but tolerated. He clearly went too far, though, on a visit to the foreigners' hospital. An interpreter from the publishing house's French Section had accompanied him and he told me how he had witnessed Leblanc, while they were in the waiting room, pick up a copy of the *Korea* pictorial magazine, open it to a page with the inevitable portrait of Kim Il Sung, and deliberately spit. He then said something horrible which the interpreter claimed he had not understood.

When I recounted the story to Miles that evening, I concluded with a shrug of my shoulders and a comment along the lines of, 'Well, he'll be on the first flight out of here.' As it was, Leblanc was allowed to see out the remaining few weeks of his contract. Probably it wasn't worth the hassle of making an example of him so soon before he was due to leave anyway; either that, or perhaps the thought had crossed the mind of someone in authority that there was the potential for enormous embarrassment in admitting that the great leader's image had been violated so horribly.

Within a day of Leblanc and his wife being put on a plane out of the country, Mr O, the guest house handyman, came to my flat with an assistant. Without explanation the two men removed the portraits of the great leader and the dear leader from the walls. They had, I discovered, done the same in the home of every foreigner in the guest house.

Frankly, I was a little insulted. It was safe to assume that the removal of the portraits was connected with Leblanc's offensive behaviour. But the suggestion that I might be considering some similar sacrilege ignored the fact that, whatever my other transgressions, I had never shown anything but respect for the country's leadership.

Pyongyang took advantage of the anniversary of national liberation in August 1990 to occupy the propaganda high ground. It organised a Pan-National Rally for the Reunification of the Fatherland. Koreans from all over the world – from the US and the UK, Canada and Australia, Japan, China and the Soviet Union, as well as a couple of brave souls from South Korea – converged on the North to take part in a highly symbolic march. The plan was for them to set out from Mount Paekdu, the sacred mountain of the Korean nation on the border with China in the North, and walk all the way to that other great mountain, Mount Halla on Cheju Island off the south coast of South Korea. For this to happen, the border at Panmunjom had to be opened, something that, predictably, the South Korean authorities declined to do.

Feeling a little miffed at for once having no part to play in a major event, I wondered spitefully what the North Koreans would do if the South did agree to open the border. The television showed the great crowd of disgruntled and incensed Koreans standing on the northern side of the 38th Parallel at Panmunjom, waving their fists at the puppet clique that was acting on the orders of its US masters to frustrate the people's desire for reunification. 'Let them in!' I cried at the television, gleefully anticipating the panic that would be induced in

Pyongyang at the sight of tens of thousands of its citizens strolling into South Korea.

Seoul never did open the border and the North was handed a whole new artillery battery to fire in the propaganda war. Here they were again, the puppets and their masters; they had caused the suffering of the millions of separated Koreans in the first place and they were still perpetuating their grief.

North Korea had a field day. But in embellishing the larger reunification picture they could, I felt, be guilty of callously ignoring the sensitivities of individuals.

My favourite such tale involved a husband and wife who had not seen each other since 1952, when during the war he had been taken south by the Americans. He had been sent to a prisoner of war camp on Cheju Island and by the time of his release the border between North and South had been closed. Up to this point it was a sad and all too familiar story.

Eventually the husband made his way to Canada, while his wife remained waiting tearfully for his return in her small village in the North. The years passed and he made no appearance. He must be dead, her fellow villagers told her. She had waited a decent length of time and should remarry. But she refused, in the vain hope that one day they might be brought together again. In the meantime their son married and the mother wept at the thought of the father who had missed this most important of family occasions.

Then out of the blue she received a letter from her long-lost husband in Canada, with news that he planned to come to the North to attend the Pan-National Rally. They met at the Koryo Hotel and wept as they embraced after nearly 40 years of separation. She took him back to their home village, where he expressed his admiration for a social system that had given his son, despite the absence of his father, an education and a job.

But there was a slight hitch to what in all other respects was the perfect tale of a tearful and happy family reunion. The father had to return to his wife in Canada. The original wife apparently took the news very well. All she required of her husband, if he could still be called that, was a promise that back in Canada he would bend all his efforts to achieving the reunification of the country.[12]

Autumn, I had been told, was the finest season in North Korea and I could not disagree. The winters are cold, often bitingly so. The spring is fine enough, but tends to be a little windy and is anyway far too brief. In the summer the rains come, sudden, heavy downpours that can leave the streets flooded for days; the temperatures aren't particularly high, something that unfortunately cannot be said of the stifling humidity levels.

By contrast the fine, warm, dry autumns are very pleasant, the ideal time for a visit to the mountains. So the prospect of a trip in September to Kumgangsan, the most beautiful mountains in the world so every North Korean told me, was an enticing prospect. I'd been twice before, both times in the summer, and enjoyable though the trips had been, I was looking forward to a visit in the cool of autumn, when the mountains were said to be ablaze with the reds, oranges and yellows of the leaves. To add to my anticipation, we were to enjoy the luxury of travelling by car.

I mulled this information over for a few days and resolved that, despite the evident honour being done me, I should be a good citizen and insist on travelling by train, as we usually did. Thus I would be doing my bit to preserve the country's desperately low fuel reserves. But Song Il would have none of it.

[12] See *Korea Today*, 1991, 1.

Our driver was to be Mr Paek, a large and lugubrious man who drove a pale green Mercedes. With my still limited Korean I found it impossible to hold a conversation with him, since he spoke entirely in grunted monosyllables. Still, I liked him well enough, as he struck me as the good, honest type who asked for nothing and was grateful just to be bought beer and cigarettes.

My interpreter for the trip was Hong Du, a young man from the English Section who had recently returned to Pyongyang after spending a year as a student in Africa. His travels gave him a cosmopolitan air, which I found rather endearing. He told me that while abroad he had occasionally read *The Times*. He was intrigued by 'Thatcher', although he appeared to have little interest in her politics; miners' strikes and demonstrations over taxation and health care he dismissed as run of the mill for a capitalist society. What he liked about her was the uncom-promising attitude she had brought to bear on summit meetings. It was funny, Hong Du thought, that a woman had been able to bring all those male heads of government, and hence their countries, to heel.

Song Il was coming, too, and discussions with the three of them as we loaded the boot of the car with food and beer revealed that the itinerary would be leisurely. It was fine with me, I told Song Il, as long as we didn't have to spend the night in Wonsan.

Being driven outside Pyongyang, along the wide and empty roads, was a rare experience and I was interested to observe the farmers. Seeing the slight, wiry figures working in the fields, their movements slow and deliberate, trousers rolled up above their knees, large conical hats protecting them against the elements, was a reminder that I was really way out East. It was a fact that was easily forgotten in the showcase city Pyongyang, where the magnificent buildings were designed on a lavish scale to give an impression of modern grandeur.

From time to time we would pass people, either singly or in small groups, trudging along the sides of the road, sometimes with huge bundles balanced impossibly on their heads. As we sped by I would wonder what business they were on, since rarely did the deserted landscape yield any sign of human habitation.

The occasional signs of civilisation I did see were small villages, perhaps no more than a cluster of half a dozen low, plaster-covered apartment buildings surrounded by a brick wall with a mud track leading through an opening. Inevitably a red banner would be strung high above this gateway or on the front of a main building, emblazoned with some exhortation to the farmers to work harder and produce more grain for the leader, the Party, the people and the army. Briefly I entertained notions of how romantic and healthy it would be to live in such a small community among the mountains, enjoying the camaraderie of working the fields by day and sitting round the campfire in the evening. But then my mind would turn to the rumours I had heard of desperate poverty, of freezing winter evenings with no fuel for warmth, of barely enough food to survive on, of nasty diseases caused by the insects lurking in the paddy fields, and of the rudimentary medical care and lack of proper medicines.

These farming communities were few and far between, since most of the country is mountainous.[13] On many of the gentler slopes I would see long lines of placards bearing large Korean characters eulogising the great leader and the Party. Our road took us straight through the more precipitous hills on our route and each time we came to a tunnel Driver Paek would slow the car, turn on his headlights and toot his horn – unnecessarily, I

---

[13] According to North Korean estimates, 75–80% of its territory is covered by mountains.

thought, since there was hardly likely to be any traffic coming the other way. I'd edited many descriptions of the heroism of the workers who had risked death to blast their way through the mountains and, as we crawled through the tunnels they had created, I wondered why they'd gone to all the trouble for the pitiful number of vehicles that used them.

At intervals along the way there were police checkpoints and I took uncomfortable pleasure in sweeping past them. Locals could expect to be flagged down regularly to show that they had obtained the necessary permission to travel outside Pyongyang. By contrast, in my specially marked car I wasn't supposed to be stopped. Driver Paek even ventured from time to time into the middle carriageway, clearly defined with two white or orange lines, that was supposedly reserved for the great leader's car.

We stopped once on the way to Wonsan, at a two-storey restaurant standing by a small lake at the side of the road. The staff there served the trickle of motorists travelling between Pyongyang and the East coast. We drank some tea and beer and I thought, here was one of the benefits of socialisms: a business continued to serve customers in such tiny number that it could not possibly be viable commercially to do so.

There was no avoiding Wonsan for those who wanted to go to Kumgangsan. The road out of the city that wound south along the coast in the direction of the demilitarised zone was the only route to the mountains. I had nothing against Wonsan; it was a very pleasant beach resort. I'd asked that we not spend the night there simply because I wanted to get up into the mountains as soon as possible.

We arrived in Wonsan in time for lunch and pulled up in front of the main hotel. I was surprised when the driver began to unload our belongings from the car. Song Il told me hastily that I should keep my things with me for safety. We even had our own rooms reserved where we could have a wash and leave our bags while we went downstairs to the restaurant.

Song Il was looking worried when he joined me at my table. Mr Paek, he told me, was very tired and didn't feel up to the tricky drive along the coast road to the mountains. But it was, of course, up to me when we left.

I should have known, really. There had to be some good reason why we'd come by car. Of course they'd always planned to stay in Wonsan. But what was the attraction? All I could think of was that someone had a girlfriend there. The interpreter was the only one who wasn't married.

Having worked out what the little secret was, I felt inclined to be magnanimous and agreed to spend the night there. Still, I was irritated that I'd been excluded from the plot and to show my displeasure I disappeared in the afternoon, thinking that Song Il might get into trouble for letting his foreigner out of his sight. I found a foreign currency restaurant not far from the hotel and drank a bottle of beer.

Having assumed that Hong Du had a girlfriend in Wonsan, I was surprised to find him hanging around the hotel after dinner. The driver, though, was nowhere to be seen. Song Il, Hong Du and I went to the tiny hotel bar, where we had a very enjoyable evening. The driver, though – the good, honest type who was grateful to be bought beer and cigarettes – never showed up. I asked where he was and was sufficiently relaxed by that stage of the evening that I laughed when Hong Du told me innocently, 'He's with his family. He brought some things for them. You don't know he's from Wonsan?'

The drivers enjoyed a unique place in the circles in which I moved. They, more than anyone else, had their fingers on

Pyongyang's pulse and in a sense they wielded considerable power. They knew everyone, the foreigners and the usual coterie of Korean guides and interpreters, and it was always as well to stay on their right side.

Our cars came from a pool based not far from the Koryo Hotel. Generally we had three drivers at a time, who stayed with us at the guest house for six months. This system of rotation brought them, when they were not with us, into contact with other foreigners, occasionally visiting dignitaries. Often in the hotel bars I would run into drivers I knew who were now working for another 'delegation'. I enjoyed chatting to them – obviously I was expected to provide the beer and cigarettes – because by the standards I had become accustomed to, they were quite open.

As long as you knew enough Korean to hold a basic conversation, they became a wonderful source of information about what was going on in Pyongyang, where the best places to go were and what new places were opening up. The drivers could also be relied on to have a detailed inventory of supplies at all Pyongyang's dollar shops. This was very useful, particularly at the not infrequent times when even such everyday items as batteries were in short supply. In a city where nothing was advertised and everything was passed on by word of mouth, the drivers provided at least a semblance of local knowledge.

The drivers tended also to be less inhibited than most of the Koreans I knew in talking about scandal. Thus it was from one driver that I learned about the German engineer who had drunk too much one night in the Koryo Hotel, had loudly and pointedly been very insulting about North Korea and its leaders and had, within a few days, found himself on a plane out of the country.

The story was a reminder that, however secure I felt, I should never get too complacent and neglect being very careful over what I said and did. I was well into my third year by now, so I'd got away with the comment about Kim Jong Il's chances of survival. But I still went cold at the thought of my stupidity in giving a Korean a tape of music from the South.

We arrived at our hotel in the mountains the next day in time for a late lunch; so late, in fact, that it was deemed unwise to head out for a climb. It was exactly as I had feared; spending the night in Wonsan had robbed us of an entire day of enjoying the fresh mountain air.

The following morning we set out early with our guide, Song Hui, an old friend from previous visits. A tiny girl, she was dressed in beige trousers and a floral shirt and carried a small handkerchief with which she would from time to time discreetly mop her brow. She was called a guide, but the routes were not many and the paths were clearly marked and she was in fact more a story-teller, a fund of tales associated with the mountains, of legends that had grown up about the curiously shaped rocks and ancient trees, and of stories about the visits there by the great leader and the dear leader.

At one point she stopped by a gully, at a spot from where we could look up and see a waterfall. She pointed to a very ordinary-looking boulder that was roped off by a low chain fence, rather in the manner that a particularly revered gravestone might be protected in a church. 'Here,' she intoned, 'the great leader Comrade Kim Il Sung rested while he climbed the mountains. He said that truly the Korean people are great because they have the greatest mountains in the world.' Further up the mountain there was another boulder, where the dear leader had sat and imparted thoughts of almost equal importance. Sadly, though, we didn't pass the memorial I was most hoping to see, the one I'd heard about – I think it had been featured in a Polish-made television documentary – that marked the spot where the beloved wife of the great leader, Comrade Kim Jong Suk, had halted when she realised she had forgotten to bring the great leader's lunch, and had turned back to prepare something to eat for when he returned from the mountains.

It was a fine day and there were many people out on the trails. Most were on what was clearly an organised trip. They had arrived in fleets of old buses and coaches and swarmed up the mountains, laughing and calling to one another. It was quite easy to tell who belonged to which group, since generally they wore matching tracksuits of navy blue, red or maroon. Adults and children, all wore sensible shoes and caps, very much as if someone had taken the trouble to ensure they were properly kitted out for the trip.

Among the crowds it was the old ladies who drew my attention. Bent and frail with age, long skirts hitched up trouser-like between their legs, they would astonish me by speeding past us, huge panniers on their heads which presumably contained a picnic lunch for the whole group. We, by contrast – me, Song Il, Hong Du and Paek the driver – were puffing and wheezing our way along under the weight of little more than a few sandwiches and several bottles of beer. Song Hui offered to help, but Song Il declined, declaring, 'We are English gentlemen!' Instead we decided the best thing to do would be to sit down and drink some of the beer, thus lightening our loads.

The sky was a clear blue, the weather was warm and the scenery was truly spectacular. There were stories to be told about every spot, it seemed, delightful tales about foxes and bears and the cinnamon trees on the moon. A sprinkling of pools in a vast flat rock turned out to be the place where eight fairies had descended from the sky to bathe. There they were espied by a young woodcutter who fell in love with one of their number. The woodcutter had recently saved a deer from a group of hunters and to repay his kindness the deer hid the winged robes of the fairy he loved. Unable to ascend back to the heavens, she became the woodcutter's wife. Years later, the woodcutter revealed to her what had happened and returned her winged robes to her. She flew up to her home in the sky with their children in her arms where, again with the help of the deer, the woodcutter was able to join them. But despite the wonders of the heavens they never forgot the beauty of the Kumgang Mountains and eventually they returned, to live happily ever after.

The climb was exhilarating and not too tough. The paths were well laid out, there were protective chain fences at the most precipitous spots and sturdy wooden plank bridges spanned the ravines. The most testing parts of the climb were the occasional steps cut into a rock face, where we had to haul ourselves up on handrails.

It was at the foot of one of these 'ladders' that we realised one person was no longer enjoying himself. For Song Il a visit to the mountains was no novelty; he had accompanied countless groups of the publishing house's foreign employees there before. Moreover, his liking for drink and cigarettes was taking its toll. He told us he would stop and rest on a rock while the rest of us continued to the top. I asked if he was expecting a little chain fence to be placed around the rock and if Song Hui would be telling future visitors that Song Il had rested there.

Hong Du, on the other hand, had never had the opportunity to visit the Kumgang Mountains before and so he was determined to get to the top. Driver Paek also wanted to go on and Song Hui said she would accompany them. I carried on, too.

We rounded a bend in the path and before us, across a wide, deep gully, a sheer rock face soared high up into the sky. Hanging perilously over the side was a rough wooden cradle, little more than a piece of wood suspended on two ropes. It was unoccupied, but its purpose was all too evident. There was no telling when the carving had been completed. Now they were working on the painting, in red, of two massive characters, one above the other and each ten times the height of a man, I judged. They read 'Ju-che'.

I continued to the top with the others, but the scenery had lost much of its fascination. The most beautiful mountains in the world, the place to where fairies came down from Heaven to bathe, were no place for disfigurement by political slogans that were, to judge by their scale, clearly designed to last for centuries.

That afternoon we visited a local beauty spot, Lake Samil. Song Il had been unusually keen to take out a couple of boats and, as we sweated at the oars, me with Song Hui in one boat and Song Il with Driver Paek and Hong Du in the other, I wondered why. It was hot and three small islands[14] offered inviting places to stop and rest and admire the clear dark turquoise of the deserted water, but as we rowed past it was clear these were not our destination.

Song Il took us across the lake to the far shore. We disembarked and followed him up a low hill. At the top my four companions shaded their eyes and gazed into the distance. Song Il pointed and told me, 'You can see South Korea over there.' We stood in contemplative silence for a few moments.

---

[14] *Samil* means 'three islands'.

Chapter 7

I came to believe, and up to a point still believe today, that despite their obsession with presenting themselves, their country and their system as the perfect embodiment of their leaders' designs, North Koreans can take a bit of criticism, as long as it does not involve any insult to the leaders themselves. Their problem is that so all-pervasive and overpowering is their propaganda that they have largely lost the ability to put their case simply and convincingly in a way that might win over sceptical foreigners; instead they end up preaching to the socialist faithful. Nobody else will listen. I think there are some North Koreans who understand this and realise they could do with a bit of outside help.

This is not to say, however, that a foreigner who fancies he or she has an insider's understanding of North Korea would not face a pretty thankless task in trying to bridge a cultural gulf with the West that has only been made wider by ideological divergence.

For example, Western reporters who think they might like to try would be well advised to take a look at a thin volume called *The Great Teacher of Journalists*,[1] which details the contribution of Kim Jong Il in the media field. The introduction gives an indication of North Korea's unique approach to reporting, saying of the dear leader:

> He is always among journalists and teaches them every detailed problem arising in their activities, and kindly leads them to write and compile excellent articles that arouse the sentiments of the masses in keeping with the Party's intentions.

By way of an example of this kind leadership, the book offers *Taking the place of a reporter*. It is an anecdote dating back to May Day 1966,

---

[1] *The Great Teacher of Journalists*. Foreign Languages Publishing House, Pyongyang, 1983.

when Kim Il Sung was visiting a military college. A journalist from the Central News Agency is spotted by Kim Jong Il, turning up late for the event. Rather than chastise him, the dear leader fills the reporter's heart with joy by revealing that he himself has already jotted down what he should write:

> The great leader reviewed the guard of honour and acknowledged the enthusiastic cheers of those who welcomed him.
>
> All the soldiers and their family members came out and, waving bouquets, fervently welcomed the leader.

The story goes on:

> As he was putting down in his memo what was dictated by the dear leader, the journalist could see before his eyes the stirring scene when, upon the great leader's arrival, the teaching staff, cadets and the family members of the soldiers began to stamp their feet with flower bundles in their hands, shouting at the top of their voice, 'Long live the great leader Comrade Kim Il Sung!' He also seemed to see the fatherly leader who was inspecting the formation of parading soldiers in front of the main entrance, the soldiers with intense loyalty in their hearts, and acknowledging the enthusiastic cheers of those who welcomed him with his hand upraised and with a bright smile on his face.

What few Western journalists realise, unless they have read *The Great Teacher of Journalists*, is that, as the dear leader says:

> It is advisable that the newspapers carry articles in which they unfailingly hold the president in high esteem, adore him and praise him as the great revolutionary leader.

Perhaps, I realised with time, it is better for foreigners to accept that in some respects North Korea is beyond their understanding and, if they wish to make use of their knowledge and experience, they should do so as an outsider pursuing familiar, capitalist goals.

Torn Between Two Worlds

I didn't feel it was the time to question my friend Boris's maths; not when he was single-handedly defending the Motherland. He was standing rigidly at the bar in the Potonggang Hotel, one hand planted on the counter, the other brandishing a pencil in the face of the barmaid, who was glaring with equal venom straight back at him.

'Not even a single pencil!' he was shouting at her through clenched teeth. 'It wouldn't buy even a single pencil for each Soviet citizen!'

If Boris's figures were to be believed, they have expensive pencils in the Soviet Union, was my thought. But Miss Kim's stance was founded on the argument that international solidarity and revolutionary principle had been betrayed. The Soviet Union had sold out an old friend and ally for a few miserable dollars.

'Absolutely!' was Boris's sarcastic rely. A few miserable dollars! A drop in the ocean compared to the tens of billions the Soviet

Union had poured into North Korea over the years, and with never any thanks.

It was a telling argument. So much so that Miss Kim ended the debate by closing the bar and saying I could settle my bill the next day.

The Soviet Union had been warned, and in no uncertain terms. Establishing diplomatic relations with South Korea would incur Pyongyang's most extreme displeasure and righteous anger. It would be the final blow – there could be no possibility of that most loyal ally China doing anything so treacherous – after the countries of Eastern Europe had, one by one, led by Hungary and followed by Poland, succumbed to the lure of money and stabbed an old ally in the back, by opening diplomatic relations with South Korea.

Ignoring Pyongyang's threats and cajoling, in September 1990 Moscow and Seoul went ahead and agreed to exchange ambassadors. For North Korea, the loss of one of its two great benefactors to the enemy camp represented much more than a diplomatic setback – the economic fallout would no doubt be severe. And the question now was, what would Pyongyang do about its growing isolation?

Predictably perhaps, it chose to sulk. *Rodong Sinmun*, the official daily of the Workers' Party of Korea, published an editorial accusing the Soviet Union of smearing its reputation at a time when it was 'going downhill to ruin, floundering in chaos and confusion in the vortex of "perestroika" '.[2]

_____

[2] Quoted in *Korea Today*, 1990, 11.

The article reported that an 'economic cooperation fund' worth $2.3 billion had been made available to the Soviet Union coincidentally with the announcement of diplomatic ties. Clearly, though, Seoul could not afford such a sum and it would be supplied out of a special reserve set up by the US imperialists for the express purpose of 'disorganising' socialism.

As *Rodong Sinmun* put it starkly: 'The Soviet Union sold off the dignity and honour of a socialist power and the interests and faith of an ally for 2.3 billion dollars.'[3]

Boris and my other Soviet friends, most of them at the embassy, were by and large delighted with the announcement that their country would be recognising South Korea, for the simple reason that they might yet find themselves in Seoul. I'd never failed to be impressed by the level of expertise the Soviet Union's diplomats and other experts such as Boris demonstrated in all things Korean, not only the language, but also the history, culture and politics of the country. Several of them, however, expressed regret at ever having taken up Korean studies because it invariably led them to dreary Pyongyang. Colleagues at university who had studied English, French, Spanish and so on could look forward to being sent to any number of exotic locations.

But now, unexpectedly, a posting to Seoul beckoned, with all its glamour and decadence. No longer did being a Korea expert limit them to a career of drudgery either at a desk in Moscow or in Pyongyang.

To me, Boris epitomised the attitude towards the country and their hosts of the Soviets who found themselves in North Korea.

[3] *Korea Today*, 1990, 11.

Not particularly enamoured of Pyongyang in the first place, he had grown increasingly irritated over the two years he'd been obliged to spend there as part of a government-sponsored academic exchange programme. He never stopped complaining about the two-tier pricing system and resented the fact that, even though his salary was in blue *won*, which meant he had to pay more than I did for most items in the shops, including food, he was paid less. The fact that he wasn't fed at the guest house merely rubbed salt into the wounds. He considered that his country and he personally were being taken for a ride by the North Koreans, who mopped up the generous assistance from his government and gave little in return, other than chatter about international solidarity. There was never any thanks for the Soviet help, financial or military; and there was no acknowledgement of the Soviet role in the liberation of the country, apart from a small monument tucked away on a small hill somewhere in Pyongyang that no-one was ever taken to unless they asked.

As changes on the international scene swept aside old allegiances, foreign diplomats and visitors from former socialist allies became more outspoken about their feelings for North Korea. Many expressed horror at the many obsessions: the cult of personality, the systematic indoctrination, the intrusive surveillance, the anti-American fixation, the parades and demonstrations. Even the many who professed themselves still to be communists invariably felt that North Korea needed to relax the rhetoric a bit, domestically and in the international arena. An elderly East German whispered to me one night that, in his experience, North Korea was more akin to his own country under Hitler than under Honecker.

><

Even as it surveyed with apparent dismay the ruins of the only world it had known since its birth, North Korea appeared to be rousing itself to join the new international order. While Pyongyang must have contemplated complete isolation in the wake of the collapse of socialism in Eastern Europe and the diplomatic recognition extended to South Korea by its allies, its enemies rallied round to offer an olive branch, and it seemed that it might just be accepted.

At the end of September 1990, North and South Korea got together to show the world that the dream of reunification was alive and kicking, when teams of supporters from the two sides united to cheer on all the Korean competitors at the Beijing Asian Games. Only a few months earlier the two Koreas had failed to agree on sending a joint team to the Games; but then the prime ministers of the two sides had met for talks in Seoul at the beginning of September. There was a new spirit of cooperation on the Korean peninsula and the joint cheering of the two teams was a powerful symbol of it.

Also at the end of September, a high-level delegation from Japan's ruling Liberal Democratic Party was in Pyongyang for a ground-breaking visit that held out the promise of talks on establishing diplomatic relations. There appeared even to be a softening in Pyongyang's attitude to the United States, although Washington appeared more cautious than Seoul and Tokyo in responding to the overtures. In May North Korea had handed over the remains of five GIs Missing in Action from the Korean War, a goodwill gesture that four months later had yet to yield any significant results in terms of improved relations with the great enemy.

><

During the opening ceremony of the World Festival of Youth and Students I'd formed some idea of how much noise 150,000 people packed inside a stadium could generate. But that boisterous acclamation of international solidarity was nothing compared to the deafening blast of sound as the two teams walked out onto the pitch for the reunification football match of October 1990. What a difference a few footballing months could make, I reflected. The local television had carried extensive coverage of the summer's World Cup in Italy, showing every game, some of them more than once; every game, that is, except those featuring South Korea. The average North Korean must have thought it strange that only 23 countries had qualified for the finals, and stranger still that one of the groups played fewer matches than the others. Or perhaps the more enlightened might have been wise to the fact that the authorities could not admit to such a powerful example of South Korea, by qualifying for the World Cup finals, outperforming the North on the sporting field.

But now we in the stadium and probably practically every North Korean, either at home or at their workplace, were watching live the South Korean football team. The two sides, North and South, were greeted by a massive, head-thumping, unrelenting barrage of noise generated by a full house of football-crazy, reunification-obsessed fans screaming with all their might and I thought how sensible other countries had been in not building such enormous stadiums. Someone had once told me that a considerable handicap with the May Day Stadium, even on normal sporting occasions – which the reunification football match clearly was not – was that the players on the pitch could often not hear one another or, indeed, the referee, because of the noise of the crowd.

I'd never experienced such a racket before and it was maintained throughout the match, reaching unbearable levels just as much when South Korea scored the first goal as when the North equalised in the opening minutes of the second half. There was no let-up in the cacophony and the conduct of the players on the pitch was impeccable. There were smiles, pats on the backs and hands extended to help each other to their feet. It quite warmed my heart to think that here there was, by the public at large and by the sportsmen on the pitch, a true show of national unity, a heartfelt demonstration to the whole world that Korea could, should and wanted to be one again.

And so it was with disbelief that, as the match entered second-half injury time, I watched a North Korean player dive under an innocuous challenge somewhere on the edge of the penalty area. Even as the referee pointed to the spot, I speculated that the North Korean player charged with taking this most dodgy and undiplomatic of penalties might tap the ball gently and thus give the South Korean goalkeeper a reasonable chance of keeping the match level.

But no. With the last kick of the game North Korea scored and won the match 2 : 1.[4]

Song Il had told me he would soon be leaving the guest house to go back and work at the publishing house. He wasn't sorry, he said; by this time he had a young daughter and he would enjoy spending more time with his family. He would visit me regularly, he promised, and if I needed his help, I could easily get in touch.

As a matter of fact, I told him, there was something I wanted to ask him. I wondered if there was any chance of a visit from the

[4] A report on the Reunification Football Match of October 1990 is found in *Korea Today*, 1990, 11.

publishing house's general director. There was a matter I hoped to discuss with him. I knew it was a bit awkward requesting someone so senior just to drop by, but if Song Il could help, I'd be grateful.

I told Song Il that I wanted to propose that I try and gain accreditation as a foreign correspondent. It was an idea I'd been toying with for some time. After years in the wings of the international arena, North Korea was finding itself increasingly at the heart of the action and I was right there on the spot. Moreover, I had a fair number of friends and acquaintances whom I could reasonably call contacts and who seemed to think I had a fair grasp on what was going on. 'You know my country very well,' was a comment I heard often after revealing some insight, such as reunification was the greatest desire of the Korean nation, which I could back up with an observation about the great leader's thoughts on the matter, principally his plan for founding the Democratic Confederal Republic of Koryo. And as I studiously poured my companion a glass of beer in the two-handed Korean fashion, I might also slip in the fact that the name Koryo had been chosen, since back in the tenth century AD it had been the name of the first unified state on the Korean peninsula; the Koryo Hotel, with its two towers linked near the top by a short passageway, was supposed to symbolise the reunified Korea. On top of all that I felt I had a pretty comprehensive knowledge of the thoughts and policies of the two leaders, built up in the course of my editing work, and I might yet summon up the courage to offer some intelligent commentary on developments. I'd also visited pretty well all of the sights in Pyongyang and most of the places outside the capital where foreigners were permitted to go.

The first step was to obtain the publishing house's support. I had to convince them of the benefits of having a resident

Western journalist in the country, someone with an understanding of the way things worked and who could be trusted not to spout the sensationalist and often erroneous nonsense that was usually served up by visiting Western reporters. I would tell the truth, would be my argument, but I would have to insist that my work couldn't be censored.

This was important, since even if I got the Koreans' approval I would still have to find someone prepared to fund a bureau. I reasoned that a Western news organisation would be tempted by the prospect of opening a Pyongyang office ahead of its rivals, but it would be an expensive investment and I would have to offer some guarantees about the quality and the impartiality of my reporting. Still, I could argue that the North Koreans were unlikely to give accreditation to anyone else; it was take me or leave me. There was the added advantage that the publishing house might allow me to work from my office at the guest house, which would save the cost of renting premises. It would mean that I was combining the job of foreign correspondent with that of language editor of the great leader's works. The Cubans managed it, but then I didn't suppose *Prensa Latina*, the official Cuban news agency, saw any significant risk of their impartiality being compromised.

It would be hard work, but it could be interesting. There would be difficulties, for sure, but it was time to lay the groundwork for a career after I left the country.

I'd already decided what my first story would be about. It would feature Marek, a good friend and a diamond merchant. He was a very amiable chap, always ready to help others out, and through his golf partners and his social contacts in the Koryo Hotel he kept up-to-date on local business developments.

Marek had taken me round the diamond cutting factory he'd helped to set up and I was sure he wouldn't mind being written about. The title of the piece would be something along the lines of 'Capitalism's gentle breeze stirs North Korea'.

It has to be the most unlikely factory in the world, the story would start. But you wouldn't know it from the outside. It's just another low grey building in a city full of low grey buildings and like any other factory or office in Pyongyang, a red banner bearing a slogan eulogising the great leader is hung above the entrance.

Even when you venture inside there is little to suggest that this factory is different from what you would suppose any other to be like in North Korea. It's a little gloomy, but it's clean enough and the offices are functional rather than comfortable. There are the inevitable images of the great and dear leaders on the walls, along with displays charting the fulfilment of production quotas. The workplace itself is nothing special to look at either; rows of workbenches at which sit young ladies, engrossed in the task at hand.

It is when you look closely at what they are doing that you realise this factory hardly fits the stereotype of the communist cooperative churning out basic products to serve the masses. For the girls – it is a job we are assured is best done by girls – are cutting diamonds.

Our guide, and the man in charge here, is Marek, a South African who has been in Pyongyang for a number of years. He originally came as part of a team to supervise the setting up of this factory, but a nifty bit of entrepreneurial footwork saw him take over the foreign interest in this most unusual of ventures. The basis of the business, however, remains the same. Marek imports raw diamonds, the girls cut them and they are exported again. It's a simple matter of making use of cheap labour.

But there might just be a little more to it than that. Because what Marek has managed to prove is something that is often talked about, but is not always evident to the foreign business-man: the North Korean is by nature a darned good worker. As long as the rewards are forthcoming, that is. Still, it doesn't take much. Marek's girls aren't bedecked in jewels; not one of the tiny stones is ever gifted out – not even to visitors! But still they work flat out, absenteeism is virtually unknown and no complaining voice is ever heard. Hardly what one expects from a communist sweatshop.

The secret, Marek explains, is to treat the workers fairly; a little more money for a little more effort or a job well done; promotion for those who excel. And the occasional gifts on the appropriate occasions. Perhaps some cheap cosmetics for the May Day holiday. Too much and they would get greedy. Buying a heater for the factory went down very well when temperatures plummeted. The girls are only slightly better off than their counterparts at other factories. It's enough.

So no-one's being corrupted. There's no essential violation of socialist principles here, at least not as far as the Koreans are concerned. Marek makes his profit, of course. So really it's a case of communism and capitalism coming together for the benefit of all.

In an effort to attract such businesses as Marek's, in 1984 North Korea adopted a Joint Venture Law. But the results have been disappointing, at least to those North Korean officials charged with boosting the flagging economy. On the other hand, the ideological purists, those who talked about 'pagan influences' in anticipation of the hordes of foreign businessmen arriving, are no doubt relieved.

Herein lies the essential difficulty for North Korea in doing business: the clash between ideology and the harsh reality of economics. The great leader himself, never one to encourage unnecessary contact with the outside world, has called for increasing the country's foreign trade, but he has consistently insisted that it should not be at the cost of compromising the country's Juche philosophy of self-reliance. To make matters economically worse, China and its billion plus consumers are just up the road. Compare the lure of this vast market and its more relaxed investment laws to little North Korea, where visiting businessmen frequently complain they are left to drag their heels while someone is found who can take even a simple decision and where attitudes to meeting payment deadlines are pretty cavalier.

To date, fewer than 50 businesses have been established under the 1984 Joint Venture Law. The vast majority involve investment from Japanese Koreans, or Korean Japanese – no-one ever seems too sure which is correct. These are ethnic Koreans whose families were taken, usually by force, across the Sea of Japan during the Japanese occupation of the Korean peninsula in the first half of the century, to do mining, forestry and other dangerous and backbreaking work. It is estimated that at its height their population numbered some two million. Today it is believed to be somewhere between 600,000 and 700,000.

The loyalty of this population of Korean residents in Japan is divided roughly 50 : 50 between North and South Korea. For the North in particular, the economic support it receives from its backers in Japan is vital. They have funded a number of high-profile projects, such as an international golf course and several restaurants, used mainly by the Japanese Koreans themselves and wealthier Western visitors. The rest are small factories, research institutes and the like. In 1986 Pyongyang signed an agreement on founding an 'International Joint Venture Company' with Chongryon, the pro-North organisation of Koreans in Japan, in an attempt to tap into the capital of the group's business members.

The Japanese Koreans are also involved in commodity trade with Pyongyang. Whether it is all entirely legal one wonders, when it is possible to buy in a Pyongyang department store a packet of John Player Specials clearly marked 'For Sale Only in Japan'. Tourism is another way these Koreans bring money in. Throughout most of the year, hotels that otherwise serve a trickle of foreign visitors are regularly taken over by groups of generally young and tracksuited 'home-visiting' compatriots.

Despite the importance of these tour groups as a source of valuable foreign currency there is another, and perhaps more important, consideration. As in every aspect of North Korean life there is nothing more vital than politics, and by choosing to visit the North they are tacitly, in North Korean eyes at least, recognising the Pyongyang government ahead of the puppets in Seoul.

Some of the Koreans who found themselves in Japan as a result of their homeland's occupation have, over the years, chosen to return home. The first boatload was permitted into North Korea back in 1959, when there would no doubt have been a great patriotic eagerness to return to family and friends back in a home town or village. Today, there is barely a trickle of returnees. One can only speculate what those who came back decades ago must be thinking now. No doubt their *yen* must have made life more tolerable, initially at least. They may well have brought their entire wealth with them when they made the move back home, or they may have left some money in a bank account for tapping into later. They may even still have family and friends in Japan who will send them goods and money. Whatever, they bring in valuable foreign currency for the North.

Some of the returnees, though, enjoy no such economic luxury or freedom and have become fully integrated into North Korean society. Others, with their experience of life in Japan and their contacts there, have found themselves at the forefront of Pyongyang's efforts to open up economically. With their common Korean heritage and exposure to Japan's liberal market they can bridge the gap between two very different cultures and business philosophies.

All the more reason, then, to admire Marek and his success in steering a middle course. But if Marek offers a glimpse into a future where a sprinkling of Western capitalism may brighten up the gloomy state-run economic landscape, one is left to wonder where are the other Mareks to make it happen. People like him, with experience of the North Korean system, who have seemingly limitless patience, are hard-working and determined, all combined with the most laid-back of approaches and a bluff good humour, are pretty thin on the ground.

I would need a few quotes from Marek. I might even talk to Philippe, who was turning his hand to doing business. Having left the publishing house, he had set up an office near the Koryo and equipped it quite impressively with a fax machine, a cordless telephone and all the paraphernalia of the professional business-man. He had even managed to generate a few interested foreign clients and I would run into him from time to time in the Koryo, holding discussions with business-suited foreigners.

According to Philippe, he was doing quite well, and I had no reason to doubt him. His contacts in Pyongyang were evidently very good, he spoke the language fluently and the world was anticipating a North Korea that would soon be open to business.

He told me on one occasion that he had even had an approach from a South Korean businessman who wanted to set up a cutlery factory in the North. I'd laughed at the very suggestion.

Mind you, my own flirtations with business scarcely qualified me to express any sort of opinion on the matter at all. From time to time Korean friends offered me the opportunity of making some money but to be honest, most of the offers struck me as being frankly bizarre, if not bordering on the illegal. Anyway, I was sure it would take someone with far more business drive than I could muster to make a success of bridging the cultural and ideological gulf between Western and Korean entrepreneurs.

For North Koreans, especially those who spoke English, doing business had become the most sought-after occupation. It offered an opportunity to travel and to earn a personal profit in hard currency. But it wasn't an easy career to break into; changing workplace in a country where jobs were for life was virtually impossible at the best of times – to establish yourself in this most desirable and lucrative of professions, you had to know the right person and you had to have the right sort of influence.

Anyway, as I got to know North Korea's international businessmen – naturally with their money they would hang out in the same Japanese restaurants and hotel bars that I did – and as some of my better-connected friends also made the move into business, so I would find myself immersed in bizarre conversations that promised to make my fortune. Simply being foreign meant I must be in touch with someone who wanted to invest a few million in a cartoon film-making enterprise. If I happened to know anyone in the UK interested in importing a few hundred thousand dollars worth of North Korean stamps, of course I would get my cut. And I really shouldn't laugh at some of the strange tonics and medical appliances advertised in the *Korea's*

Foreign Trade monthly. This stuff was in great demand in southeast Asia. It was once put to me that rather than going to the UK for my annual holiday, I might go instead to Singapore and drum up a few buyers for hair-restoring tonics.

But my favourite approach was from Rim, an English interpreter I'd first met when he was working with a Hong Kong businessman and some of whose entrepreneurial spirit had apparently rubbed off. I was walking through the Potonggang Hotel one evening when he came up to me, rather furtively I thought. 'I want to talk to you, Michael,' he said. 'It's very secret.'

I was intrigued, anticipating some scandal, so I said fine, I'd buy him a beer. 'No, not at the bar,' he said. 'This is really secret. Come to the billiard bar in five minutes.'

When I got to the billiard bar, rather than sit down and talk he led me back outside and as we walked, he talked. 'I'm in business now,' he said, looking around nervously, 'and I have a very interesting offer. You can make a lot of money. But you must keep it quiet. You understand. You've been here a long time. I can trust you. It's a big deal.' And then, standing very close to me, he whispered: 'Who do you know who'll buy a tonne of dried seals' penises?'

Unfortunately, I told him, I couldn't think of anyone off-hand. Someone later told me that, while a noted aphrodisiac in Asia, seals' penises were banned from international trade. If I'd ever entertained any ideas of doing business, I think that was the incident that put the lid on my ambition.

The general director, Song Il told me, wished to call on the publishing house's foreign employees. Song Il was excited; now I could put my proposal formally. I wondered if he had visions of himself as my assistant, earning a healthy hard currency salary. It was unfortunate for him, then, that by the time of the general director's visit my enthusiasm for becoming Pyongyang's first Western correspondent had abated.

First of all, there was the business side of things. I still felt uncomfortable when I thought of the casual acquaintances in the past who had expected me to buy them beer and cigarettes. I dreaded having to go through all that again – and perhaps worse – when people found out that I had an expense account. I could picture the self-righteous looks and hear the protests: 'No, no, Michael. You mustn't spend your own money on me. But it might be in the interests of your agency if we took a few people out to dinner and bought them a bottle of whisky, a carton of cigarettes. You know how things work here.'

Then there were certain other peculiarities of the way things worked – or didn't – in North Korea that would involve some tricky explanations to an office in the West. My staff – I would at least need an interpreter and driver – might be excused some of the common diversions, such as the *kimchi*-making, rice transplanting, voluntary construction and political meetings that dotted the weekly and annual calendars of the average North Korean worker. But how would I explain to my employer such oddities and admit that they might possibly disrupt my work?

Perhaps it would be better not to mention them. As long as the big news story didn't break on a Saturday during the weekly political meetings and study sessions, I reasoned, it would be all right. As for *kimchi* season, sexist though it might seem, I would be better off employing a male interpreter, since it was the women who would disappear for a week or two in the late autumn to transform the cabbages brought into the city on fleets of trucks into the pickled dish that was the staple of the winter diet; many a foreign visitor was bemused to discover that this was why a lot of the hotel bars were closed for a fortnight. The transplanting of rice seedlings, which took half of the guest house's staff as well as the publishing house's younger interpreters out of Pyongyang for several weeks at the beginning of summer, might be avoided. But not, I imagined, the military training which seemed to involve everyone, even the elderly Director Kim when he had been with us, for about a week once every year or so.

Say, for example, the South Korean authorities had opened the border at Panmunjom in August and let the pan-national marchers in. It was a story worth covering and my agency would doubtless have expected me to submit a first-hand account.

'I need a car,' I would have said to my assistant-cum-interpreter.

'No problem,' he would have responded. 'Where are you going?'

'Panmunjom,' I'd have said, disappointed that it hadn't already clicked with him that this was the big news story and we should be there.

'So, when would you like to go?' he would ask, already showing the first signs of worry.

'Right now,' I would say. 'This is the breaking news story.'

'Ah,' he would say. 'There may be a problem. I don't know if the driver has a permit to travel to Panmunjom.'

'So we'll take the train.'

'We? Why do you want to take the driver on the train?' he might ask.

'Not the driver. You!' I would say, exasperated.

'But I don't have permission to go to Panmunjom.'

'So I'll have to manage without the driver or you,' I would say, infuriated.

'I will see if we can get permission for me and the driver to come,' he might say, now clearly worried. He was caught on the horns of a dilemma. He and the driver couldn't go, but he couldn't allow me to go on my own.

He would make phone calls, his hand over the receiver just in case I might understand what he was saying.

'No problem,' he would declare in triumph, after keeping me in a state of suppressed fury for nearly an hour. 'We can go with the driver.'

He would sit down, clearly satisfied with a job well done.

'When will the driver be here?' I would ask.

'Tomorrow morning,' he might say.

'But that's no good,' I would tell him, trying to remain calm and polite. 'The story's happening now.'

'I'm sorry,' my assistant would say. 'That's not possible. The driver is absent. He's helping the farmers.'

'What about another driver?' I would ask in desperation.

'They're all absent.'

'So we'll go by train, then.'

'There are no trains today.'

Clearly somebody somewhere didn't want me travelling to Panmunjom that day to witness the opening of the border, an event that had caught the North off guard because it was never supposed to have happened.

'We'll just have to file our report from Pyongyang,' I would say with a sigh.

'That may be difficult,' my assistant might tell me. 'The fax machine doesn't work. Anyway, I think there's a problem with the international telephone connections today.'

I didn't care to think of my news editor's reaction when my story, a reworked version of a Korean Central News Agency report that somehow contrived to condemn the South Korean authorities for their treachery in bowing to the North's demand that the border be opened, arrived on his desk two days after the event. It was an entirely hypothetical situation, of course, and negative in the extreme in its depiction of North Korean attitudes. But there was a grain of truth there, and it was just big enough to give me second thoughts. So when the general director came for his visit I barely raised the matter of gaining press accreditation. Instead I asked Song Il to explain – a lukewarm approach that was guaranteed to bring failure. The possibility that I might become Pyongyang's first resident Western reporter was never mentioned again.

It was a pity, with so much happening, that I wasn't in a position to provide first-hand reports from Pyongyang. By and large, though, I decided it was just as well. One sweetener I might have been able to dangle in front of a Western news agency thinking of taking me on was the promise of being the first to know, as speech editor, when Kim Il Sung or Kim Jong Il made significant statements of policy. I'd anticipated, once North Korea had decided how it would react to developments in Eastern Europe and the Soviet Union, being able to saunter down to the Koryo and tell the assembled foreigners, 'Yes, it's official. There's going to be more opening.'

Instead, my work still consisted largely of editing speeches almost a decade out of date that were to be included in the latest volume of the *Works*. Frankly I struggled to see the point in a lot of what I was doing; North Korea's fishermen would no doubt have lapped up 'On Speeding up Preparations for Winter Fishing and Stepping up Fish Farming', while a must-see for their counterparts in the rural areas would have been 'On Accelerating the Reclamation of Tideland and Increasing the Fertility of Fields'. But what interest could there possibly be for English-speaking readers? 'On the Standardization of Machine Parts' would hardly have been compulsive reading, unless one happened to be a North Korean machine tool worker, although 'Let Us Firmly Guarantee the Fulfilment of the Revolutionary Cause of Juche by Force of Arms' might, even as it stirred the fighting spirit of the Korean People's Army, have stirred interest, if not alarm, in foreign parts.[5]

Only adding to the sense of futility were the senseless arguments over obscure vocabulary and minor points of grammar I was still having with the dreaded Mr Ma, although by this time I had developed a flawless stratagem for limiting the damage he was doing to the English language.

One day he had staggered into the room where I was waiting for a *confrontation*, carrying an enormous volume of the *Oxford English Dictionary*. It was a massive tome, one of I guessed 20 or so that made up a complete set, that completely hid the tiny Mr Ma, apart from his legs, the top of his head and his clutching arms. It turned out that he'd gone to all the trouble of fetching the *Oxford*, despite having previously condemned it for failing to incorporate 'workingclassization', in order to justify another obscure piece of vocabulary, one that on my previous visit I'd vetoed as unknown to the average native speaker of English.

The word he pointed to in triumph was so obscure that it merited just a single line in the dictionary, while others, those that inhabited the main galaxy of English, had whole pages devoted to them. This indicated to me that Mr Ma's word was probably best left in the dictionary.

In so many words, I pointed this out to him. 'So, you don't trust the *Oxford?*' he countered.

---

[5] These speeches are contained in *Kim Il Sung: Works*, vol. 37, January 1982– May 1983. Foreign Languages Publishing House, Pyongyang, 1991.

This, I decided, was the final straw! Faced with such hypocrisy and such determination to prove me wrong I decided to abandon my qualms about resorting to subterfuge. If they weren't prepared to accept my views as the native speaker, I was fully justified in using underhand means to impose my opinion on people who, after all, had probably never set foot outside their own country, let alone visited somewhere where English was the first language.

And so I shook my head sadly over the disputed word and said, 'Ah, yes, you're quite right. But I think that's American usage. Now if you accept my suggestion, at least we can be sure that we're using British English.'

When I'd first used this argument it had been true. But I didn't see any reason why honesty should restrict me in the pursuit of good English. It was such a jolly good ruse and guaranteed to succeed. I would use it sparingly, and even if on occasion Mr Ma suspected that I was being a little dishonest, he couldn't argue, because he knew that I knew that he could not contemplate even the possibility of American English coming from the great leader's mouth.

Having been backed against a diplomatic wall, North Korea was, by the end of 1990, apparently realising that it might yet make the best of a bad job and find itself enjoying improved relations – and the economic benefits that could be assumed to go with them – with its most implacable enemies.

In December the prime ministers of North and South Korea met in Seoul for a third round of talks. As in the first two rounds, held in Seoul and Pyongyang in September and October, little progress was made. North Korea was still insisting on a non-aggression pact that would lead eventually to the withdrawal of US forces from South Korea; the South wanted a basic accord that would facilitate confidence-building measures. The South side's delegation also brought up the issues of alleged North Korean terrorist attacks against the South; the North Koreans raised the matter of the three South Korean dissidents imprisoned after making illegal trips to the North. Pyongyang also expressed concern over Seoul's attempts to secure a seat independently at the UN. The bickering aside, the fact that the talks were held at all was significant, since it meant that North Korea had tacitly acknowledged the legitimacy of the Seoul government.

As for the United States, only time would tell how far it was prepared to go in its efforts to keep North Korea from sinking into a state of dangerous isolation. An obvious step would have been to cancel the annual Team Spirit 91 joint military exercise, viewed by North Korea as a dangerous war game.

Holding out more promise were the Japanese. In a groundbreaking visit to Pyongyang in October, Shin Kanemaru, the elder statesman of Japan's ruling Liberal Democratic Party, had committed himself to work for the improvement of bilateral relations. He also held out the possibility of Japan paying some hefty compensation, providing a desperately needed lifeline for North Korea's struggling economy. Formal talks on establishing diplomatic relations were due to begin in January.

Pyongyang was nothing if not optimistic in its compensation demands. Like South Korea when it opened diplomatic relations with Japan in the 1960s, the North was demanding compensation for the damage inflicted on the Korean peninsula during the Japanese occupation. Pyongyang, however, was taking things several steps further; it wanted reparations also for losses inflicted since 1945 as a result of Japan's responsibility in the division of Korea, its siding with the US during the Korean War and its hostility to North Korea ever since. A sum of $3 or $4 billion was being touted.[6]

I couldn't be sure whether the story about the great statue of Kim Il Sung on Mansu Hill in the heart of Pyongyang was true. Twenty metres tall, it depicts the great leader standing with his right arm raised, apparently indicating the road ahead for the Korean revolution. There are thousands of similar statues of the man dotted across the country, but none can compare with this one in terms of its colossal presence.

The statue was erected in 1972 to commemorate the great man's 60th birthday, and for a time it was covered from head to toe in gold. I was told this by a number of foreign diplomats; the Koreans whom I asked tended to be rather evasive in their answers. Eventually I became convinced that at some point in its existence the statue had been gilded, after I came across a photograph in which it appeared to be a little lighter in colour and to glisten a little more than it does in reality. If so, then I supposed the point of such conspicuous expenditure was that, by lavishing their wealth on a statue of the leader, the people were yet again demonstrating their unbounded reverence for him. To my mind they showed even greater reverence by not turning up after nightfall to strip it of its priceless covering.

The story, as told by the diplomats, goes that a prime minister or Party leader from a friendly socialist country in Eastern Europe, possibly Bulgaria or perhaps it was Deng Xiaoping from China, was on an official visit to Pyongyang and was, as was the North

---

[6] The *Joint Declaration on DPRK–Japan relations* is found in *The Pyongyang Times*, September 29 1990.

Koreans' habit, being asked to give generously to support the revolution in a country that was very much on the front line of the battle against the imperialists. Unfortunately for the North Koreans, someone chose to drive the friendly dignitary past Mansu Hill and its colossal statue. No, his interpreter apparently told the prime minister or Party leader or Deng Xiaoping, his eyes did not deceive him. The statue was indeed covered from head to toe in gold. In that case, was the reply, if they can afford such extravagance they hardly need any aid from us.

And that is why, the unofficial story has it, the statue on Mansu Hill no longer shimmers in the sunlight like it once did.

Pyongyang appears to have had a somewhat uneasy relationship with its socialist brethren. Of course, while the Cold War raged it was all international solidarity and Workers of the Whole World Unite. But Kim Il Sung preferred to steer a fairly independent diplomatic course.

The great split between Moscow and Beijing in the early 60s probably had a greater impact on North Korea than on any other of the socialist allies, most of which were, for geographical reasons, planted in the Soviet Union's sphere of influence. Albania, bizarrely, opted for Maoism and found itself poor and isolated.

North Korea, which had a border with both China and the Soviet Union, used the great schism to its advantage. Kim Il Sung was, by all accounts, quite clever in playing the Chinese and the Soviets off against each other. Initially, having been placed in power by the Soviets, he was very much pro-Moscow. But then the massive military assistance from China in the Korean War tilted the balance in favour of Beijing. The death of his mentor Stalin in 1953 also served to incline Kim Il Sung away from the Soviet Union. It was in the 1960s as the rift between Moscow and Beijing grew that, by dangling North Korea's support in front of both sides, he attempted to get as much aid as possible out of both. In the 1970s, with a border dispute concerning Mount Paekdu resolved, Kim Il Sung and Chinese premier Zhou Enlai exchanged visits and Beijing once again seemed to be in the ascendancy. But all the time Kim Il Sung was pursuing his Juche policy of self-reliance, and seemed keen not to be too closely linked with either side.

Despite the billions of dollars in aid that poured and dribbled its way in over the years, North Korea insisted with gathering conviction that it was building an independent economy. There is some truth in the claim, although it left the North open to accusations of ingratitude and possibly even to some serious charges of violating patent protection. The technology and expertise that came in would be leapt upon and examined. The emphasis was consistently on learning and adapting, and North Korea's own technicians became skilled at dismantling imported machines and rebuilding them as a way of learning how to make their own.

There had been difficulties in meeting the targets of the Seven-year Plan adopted in 1960, and the plan period was extended by a year. But by the 1970s, it is widely accepted, the North Korean economy wasn't doing too badly. Despite the lingering international tensions, principally with the United States and South Korea, military spending was cut substantially, freeing up money for investment. Under the Six-year Plan for 1971–1976, there was a commitment to strengthening the material and technical foundations of socialism, and to liberating the working people from the burden of heavy labour. This led to a shift away from the emphasis in the 1950s and 1960s on the role of heavy industry and to greater cooperation with the West, aimed at bringing in capital and technology. As a result, the people basically had enough to eat, heavy industry was still churning out the metals and machinery needed by the rest of industry, and the people's basic needs for commodities were being met. All in all, things weren't too bad for a Third World country.[7]

Diplomatically, too, Pyongyang was achieving some success. The West naturally chose to recognise the authorities in Seoul as the only legitimate government on the Korean peninsula. But as for the rest of the world, Pyongyang was neck and neck with Seoul in the diplomacy stakes. Apart from the socialist brothers in China, the Soviet Union and Eastern Europe, North Korea also claimed diplomatic legitimacy through the Non-Aligned Movement. Hence it had relations with countries in Latin America, Africa, Asia and the Middle East, where most of the Arab governments, espousing various degrees of radical anti-Americanism, found a ready ally in North Korea.

To celebrate its diplomatic successes, in 1978 North Korea built a magnificent palace among the mountains of Myohyangsan. Against a backdrop of misty green slopes, this vision of green hip-saddle roofs and white marble pillars nestles.

But this is no presidential retreat. Rather, the International Friendship Exhibition is a present from a generous leader to his people, for in it are housed the tens of thousands of gifts Kim Il Sung and Kim Jong Il have received from world leaders and other foreign friends over the decades. There are armour-plated cars and trains from the likes of Stalin, Bulganin and Molotov; there are vast silk tapestries of the Great Wall, porcelain vases and exquisite lacquer works from the Chinese leaders, Mao, Zhou and Deng. Suharto of Indonesia came bearing gifts; Ho Chi Minh sent something, too. Beneath a photograph of Kim Il Sung embracing Fidel Castro during their one and only meeting, there are gifts from Cuba. In the vast halls dedicated to Africa there

---

[7] An overview of the development of the North Korean economy is found in *Vantage Point*, May, 1987.

are elephant tusks and carved figures, traditional spears and shields, erotic carvings, painted ostrich eggs and crocodile skins presented by the likes of Kenneth Kaunda, Robert Mugabe and Haile Selassi.

And so on through dozens of halls. Tucked away in a corner of this vast 28,000 square metres emporium I came across a single glass case containing the gifts from my own country. Nothing, of course, from Her Majesty or one of her prime ministers; just a couple of engraved plates from grateful reinsurance companies.

Cooper, the 20-something Englishman who was Carol's replacement, had expressed a desire to learn Korean. Everyone was delighted, to the point that he was warmly congratulated by the staff of the foreign affairs department at the publishing house – which had now been renamed the Foreign Languages Press Group – the guest house staff and the drivers. Wouldn't it be marvellous to have someone else from Britain – Michael already spoke the language quite well – speaking Korean, was the popular view. It would really help him to understand the reality of Korea.

Perhaps I should have warned him there were pitfalls in being known to speak Korean. People were very flattering about a foreigner who had even the most rudimentary grasp of their language. In my case, bar-room chit-chat was still more or less the limit of my Korean and so on the occasions I was asked to act as an interpreter I would, however informal the circumstances and however much praise was lavished on my command of the language, decline. It happened from time to time that I came across a foreigner who was in dispute with a barmaid over the bill or there was some difficulty with arranging a taxi, but as far as I decently could I would refuse to get involved. Even if I knew all the necessary words – which I probably didn't anyway – interpreting was a thankless task, since no-one wanted to listen. Both sides simply wanted to make sure that their own view was being put across with sufficient force and clarity.

So how on earth, I wondered as I surveyed the crowd around me that was restless in its confusion, had I got involved between the Muslim delegation and the management of the Potonggang Hotel over the provision of *Halal* meat?

I'd been at my usual place in the lounge bar talking to an English interpreter I knew vaguely. He was in a bad way; that his delegation didn't provide him with a drink from time to time was the least of his worries, he said. His experience was with working for Western delegations, and he was finding it very difficult to understand the special demands and needs of his Muslim charges, on the one hand, and then convey them effectively to their Korean hosts. Anyway, he'd thanked me for the beer I'd bought him and declared that he needed to go home, which he did.

I felt sorry for him, so I decided I should cover his retreat when a member of his delegation pounced on me.

He'd just seen me with his interpreter. He needed to talk to him, as did several members of the hotel staff. I didn't want to tell them he'd simply upped and left, and so they hunted for a while in his room, the billiard bar and the gardens. By the time everyone was convinced the interpreter was not to be found, the man who had approached me had worked out that I spoke a bit of Korean. 'So you help us,' he said.

His English was not good, scarcely better than my Korean, and as his frustration grew with his inability to make me understand the technicalities of what he was saying, so his gestures became more violent, to the alarm of the members of the hotel staff who had gathered. As he drew his finger savagely across his throat for the umpteenth time, I wondered idly if the Koreans thought he was describing the fate that awaited his absent interpreter. By this time, though, I was beginning to see some light. He was demanding to know if the meat they were being served had been ritually slaughtered. Apparently they'd stuck to fish for their dinner and were still quite hungry.

Having grasped basically what he was tying to convey, my next problem was to explain it in Korean. I knew most of the words I would need, such as kill, sheep and food, and that these gentlemen were Muslim appeared to be understood. But what about the ritual bit? Blood was another word I knew, but how did I explain the process of ritual slaughter and did I know enough of what was involved to explain it, even in English?

Anyway I tried, and by using a similar hand gesture of slitting my own throat I appeared to get my message across. At least I hoped so, because as soon as the Koreans had nodded understandingly for a few moments I judged it time for me to beat a retreat.

I felt quite proud the next evening, when one of the British engineers staying in the hotel told me a funny story. 'We've had to complain,' he said. 'I mean, how are you supposed to eat your breakfast when there's a bloke outside on the lawn murdering a sheep? You wouldn't believe all the blood.'

Song Il had, as predicted, returned to work at the publishing house, as it was still popularly known, after a rather longer than was usual stint at the guest house as resident representative of the foreign affairs department. He had been replaced by Ho Gwang, who was a little older but just as partial to a beer or two as Song

Il was and could, with his entertaining stories of his nagging wife's efforts to make his life miserable by stamping out the two great loves of his life – alcohol and cigarettes – be very entertaining. He smoked heavily, though, and I had to admit, whenever he came coughing and spluttering into my room, that he lacked Song Il's sophistication.

He was a wry observer, though, as he showed at one of the clam bakes in our courtyard that were a feature for us of the national holidays that fell in the warmer months. It was a cooking process, Ho Gwang and I decided as we sat side by side on the guest house steps some way from the action, that was best appreciated from a distance.

We watched as a large, thick rush doormat was laid out and one of the drivers went to siphon petrol from his tank. After the mat was liberally doused, the shellfish were laid out on top.

Someone set fire to the petrol, and a couple of drivers stood over the flaming mass of shellfish and shook petrol over it from bottles that had dried grass stuffed in their necks, presumably to aid the sprinkling. Inevitably, the grass would from time to time catch fire, but the 'cook', rather than hurling his blazing Molotov cocktail as far away from him as he could, would simply stand there, blowing furiously on the grass until the fire had gone out. Then he would continue sprinkling the petrol over the clams.

'Madness,' Ho Gwang muttered. When most of the shells had opened, he stood up and the two of us sidled over to the main group, making sure we arrived just as the first clams were being handed out. There was a slight taste of petrol about them. But this was soon dealt with, Ho Gwang showed me, by filling the empty shells with *Pyongyang sul*[8] and drinking it, which killed the lingering taste in the mouth.

---

[8] *Sul* is a general term for alcohol.

It was Ho Gwang who was delegated to discuss with Cooper his plans for studying Korean. The Diplomats' Club offered lessons, Cooper had heard. He would like to learn there. Ho Gwang thought this was a splendid idea. Leave it to him, he said, to make all the arrangements.

But nothing happened. Cooper would tackle Ho Gwang about the matter on an almost daily basis. Sorry, would be the reply. He'd been so busy. Eventually it transpired that there was a problem. Although he personally was very disappointed, Ho Gwang reported, it would be impossible for Cooper to study Korean. Cooper asked why that was. Because lessons were held in the afternoons, at exactly the time when all the drivers were busy. The new Palestinian reviser, the replacement for Ali from Lebanon – a month or so before his departure Ali had started talking to me again, but without revealing the reason for the years of silence – had two children who needed fetching from school; there were texts to be collected from the publishing house; and so on.

Cooper wondered if there was a way around the problem. Ho Gwang really hoped there was and, after a further call to the Diplomats' Club, came to Cooper with the good news that, since the lessons were taught on an individual basis, it would in fact be possible to have them at any time of the day. He asked what time was convenient.

Ho Gwang was looking forlorn on his next visit. He had bad news; the publishing house could not agree to Cooper taking time off work, however worthy the reason. There was simply too much editing for him to do. But never fear! Ho Gwang had come up with the perfect solution. He himself would be Cooper's personal Korean tutor.

I think it was Philippe who advised Cooper on what to do. Go and talk to the teacher himself, arrange for lessons and book a car for whatever time he was scheduled to be at the Diplomats' Club. Of course the publishing house would know straight away what he was up to, but no-one would say anything.

Just as predicted, no-one did raise any objections. Twice a week Cooper took a car to the Diplomats' Club, without explaining what he was up to there. Soon Ho Gwang was expressing mock surprise at how quickly Cooper was learning Korean. And it wasn't long before he was informing Cooper that the car was waiting to take him for his Korean lesson.

The publishing house was the only regular employer of Westerners in the country and tended to be cautious in its handling of us. We were, after all, with our capitalist ideas and decadent ways, a potential source of trouble and embarrassment if we became too friendly with the locals. Hence the controls the publishing house tried to impose on our movements and the ambiguous attitude to our studying Korean.

On the other side of the coin there was always the possibility that we foreigners might bring credit to our employer. Madame Beatrice had been deemed worthy of a medal when she left, in recognition of the years she had spent editing the great leader's works. Ignacio, the Cuban reviser, also turned out to be a feather in the publishing house's cap. He even found himself in the strange position of editing articles about himself, his wife and their friendship baby.

Antonia was Ignacio's second wife and while he had children by a previous marriage, as a couple they were childless – this after several years of marriage and, so Ignacio insisted, a great deal of effort to do something about it.

Their plight was like a red rag to the North Korean propaganda bull and before long Antonia was stampeded off to the Pyongyang Maternity Hospital for tests and treatment. A jewel of the free health care system, the Pyongyang Maternity Hospital was built out of the love of the dear leader for the women of the country. It was equipped with the latest technology including, bizarrely to my mind, an internal television system linking the various rooms to a waiting area where the happy fathers could talk to their wives not in person, but via a video link.

Lo and behold, it wasn't long before Antonia was expecting, and in due time she gave birth. My Cuban friends were treated pretty well by the hospital and its staff, and were very grateful. As a foreigner Ignacio was even permitted, despite the hospital's hygiene concerns – which necessitated the video link – to sit in his wife's room and handle the baby. Once they had taken their baby home, though, propaganda etiquette took over and the dear leader was brought in on the act. Antonia and Ignacio found themselves writing to him personally, to ask him to give their new son a name. Whose idea this was, I don't know; what I do know is that the embassy and the highest levels of the publishing house were involved. Anyway, the argument was that it was the custom in Cuba to ask a respected elder to name a baby, and Kim Jong Il fitted the bill perfectly.

The dear leader duly obliged and the name Saebyol was bestowed on the infant, along with the more prosaic David added by his parents, presumably for use back home in Cuba. Saebyol, so the dear leader's reasoning was explained in an article in *Korea Today*, since it meant 'Morning Star', would reflect the wish that the child would shine forever over the solid road of Korea–Cuba friendship.

Such occasional success stories did nothing to diminish the suspicions of the publishing house about the foreigners they employed. It was an attitude they didn't feel the need to justify; but if ever they had, they would have had to look no further than their very own French Section, which was proving fertile ground for trouble-making foreigners.

I should have realised Song Il was up to something when he invited me to accompany him to the airport to meet the new French language reviser, who was flying in from Paris. After the experience with Leblanc, the publishing house had apparently abandoned its policy of recruiting old Asia hands in Beijing.

Sophie was a largish woman with her hair streaming behind her who marched through customs with her guitar in one hand and her daughter Annette grasped by the other. She looked formidable, as indeed Song Il already knew she was. He revealed to me back at the guest house, after thanking me for my moral support at the airport, that somehow she had persuaded North Korea's UNESCO mission in Paris, which had been instrumental in Sophie's recruitment, to extend permission for seven-year-old Annette to attend a regular North Korean school. She'd even got an official to sign a piece of paper to that effect.

The publishing house was not happy. There were arguments and Director Li intervened. But the lady was adamant; her daughter would, as had been promised, attend a regular North Korean school. The publishing house continued to protest. It would not be good for her. She would be much better off at the International School. 'You mean,' I said to Song Il when he brought me up-to-date with progress in the negotiations, 'it would not be good for the publishing house.' I was sure they were thinking of all the potential problems: little Annette upsetting her fellow pupils and her teachers when she spoke out of turn about the great leader; of fights in the playground when the other children ganged up against the outsider; of the added responsibility someone from the publishing house would have to assume as a surrogate parent who could speak to the teachers in a language they understood.

Finally, and with great reluctance, the publishing house said it agreed, but on her first morning at her new school little Annette was taken by our driver to the International School in the diplomatic quarter. Sophie protested and the arguments started again. It was the driver's mistake, the publishing house said. Anyway, Annette would be much better off at the International School. She wouldn't fit in as the only foreigner at a regular Korean school. Apart from anything else, she didn't speak the language. But her mother stood her ground and so Annette was duly dispatched every morning in one of our cars to Pyongyang Junior Middle School Number One.

I could quite see the publishing house's point of view. But it was nothing to do with me, which was what I told Song Il when he suggested I might like to talk to Sophie and make her see reason. I supposed his thinking was that I could be a little blunter about what she could expect from the school's Juche-oriented education. Quite what the use to Annette would be, once she was back in France, of a comprehensive knowledge of the revolutionary activities of the fatherly leader and an ability to sing the *Song of General Kim Il Sung* was beyond me. Of course, a proper education, stuff like maths and science and English, would be in there somewhere. But what sort of history would she be learning, what literature would she be reading?

North Koreans were put on the straight and narrow revolutionary path almost as soon as they were born. After a spell at nursery, by the age of four or five they would be attending kindergarten, where they would learn songs about the father leader. They would read stories about him and his kindness; how he cared for all the little children in the country and sent them presents on his birthday. All their school things, their pencils and their uniforms, were provided personally by the great leader. To express their thanks, they would start to recite poems about their beloved father and would learn how to stand to attention and declaim: 'Long live the great leader Comrade Kim Il Sung!'

The children were the kings and queens of the country, the great leader said, and it was the duty of society to ensure that they wanted for nothing. So they were provided with food and milk on a priority basis. Children's union camps were scattered across the country, in the most beautiful locations in the mountains and at the seaside. At home, the children enjoyed the love and support of the traditional extended Korean family, living not only with their parents, their brothers and sisters, but also in all likelihood with a grandparent or two. They had another family at their kindergarten or school. And always there was the benevolent father leader looking after them.

I had a pleasant surprise one day while in the car with Sophie. She was going to pick up Annette and when we arrived at the school gate there she was, surrounded by a group of little friends. They were chatting away quite cheerfully and the group waved her off very nicely as we drove away. Her mother seemed extremely happy.

But then Sophie asked me something that had the alarm bells ringing. Did I know if she would be free to meet the other parents?

This was important. Did I know anything about regular parents' meetings or perhaps social events? I pointed out that I had no reason to know anything about parental involvement in North Korean schools.

I heard her pestering the other foreigners at the guest house that evening, asking the same questions. I began to find her persistence strange. Stranger still were the stories that started to filter through about her activities. She had been spotted leaving the guest house alone at night. There was nothing wrong in that. But then it turned out that all she did was wander up and down the banks of the Potonggang.

Then there was a complaint, Song Il told me, from the chief of the group of women responsible for keeping the banks of the river clean and tidy. They were sick and tired of having to follow this crazy foreign woman every night, picking up the litter she left lying around. Song Il, whose French language skills meant he was spending more and more time at the guest house to deal with Sophie and her daughter, was naturally embarrassed about raising the matter and by the time he got round to it the affair had taken a more serious turn. Sophie had complained that she had been illegally detained by a group of furious and violent women in a small hut. The furious women – the cleaners – said they had been very polite and had merely asked mildly that she stop creating work for them by leaving litter lying around.

Song Il showed me a sheet of paper, one of the many Sophie had left lying on a bench by the river, and suddenly everything became clear.

I'd admired her perseverance in getting a car to come every Sunday morning to take her to one of Pyongyang's two churches. The official policy was religious tolerance, but the churches, located some way out of town, were not easy to get to and our drivers took some persuading to turn up for work at nine o'clock on a Sunday morning, even if they were, by doing so, proving the country's commitment to freedom of religion. But persuade them, Sophie did.

Going to church was one thing; distributing religious material along the banks of the River Potong was something else entirely. It was provocative, I decided, when I noticed on the sheet of paper Song Il had shown me, just below what appeared to be a bible quote in Korean, that it had been printed in South Korea. And I began to wonder: was her desire to spread her beliefs behind her determination to meet the parents of Annette's school friends?

The authorities took what I thought was a lenient attitude towards Sophie, given North Korean sensitivities – even at a time of improving relations – concerning anything that might be construed as South Korean propaganda. As far as I could ascertain she was given a strong talking to by the publishing house and told not to do it again. I supposed they were, as had been the case with Leblanc, keen to avoid any hint of scandal. But unlike Leblanc, Sophie was to go further with her indiscretions and oblige the police to intervene.

There had been high-level talks; there had been the reunification football match; finally there was the unified sports team.

And unified, Korea triumphed. It was May 1991 when, to the strains of the traditional melody *Arirang*,[9] the white flag with the blue outline of Korea was raised and tears of joy were shed, after

---

[9] *Arirang* is a popular traditional Korean tune and tale, various versions of which are told, but which share the common theme of the girl, Arirang, waiting faithfully for her departed lover.

the Korean girls took the title in the women's team event at the 41st World Table-Tennis Championships in Chiba, Japan.

The victory was greeted with delirium by the people of North Korea. Here was proof, not that they had ever needed it – but just in case the rest of the world had any doubts – of the greatness of a reunited Korean nation. Surely now, the inference was, those who by their meddling were perpetuating the division of Korea must see the error of their ways and stand aside, so that the powerful forces at work in the two halves of the peninsula could realise the desire of the people for reunification.

Putting out a joint sports team was a long way from uniting two mutually antagonistic political systems, but at least it offered some hope, especially to those millions of Koreans who were still living separated from family members. The real tragedy was that, with no communication links between North and South Korea, they had no way of knowing whether the loved ones they had been dreaming of were even alive. The longer the division of the peninsula lasted, the greater the number of people who would experience the crushing disappointment of having waited in vain.

But North Korea remained optimistic, so much so that its people were told to prepare for the great day of reunification, which would come in 1995, the 50th anniversary of national liberation.

A thought that entertained me was of Annette taking part in a mass game. What would the great leader think of the little girl with flowing blonde hair among the thousands of Korean children performing mass gymnastics on the pitch in the May Day Stadium?

To my mind, the mass games that North Korea was so proud of – lavish gymnastic displays performed by tens of thousands of children to mark all the major celebrations – focused the debate on the pluses and minuses of being a child in North Korea. A mass game was all about collectivism, organisation and discipline, the three key words in the doctrine of leading a worthwhile life. They were qualities that were fostered during the regular school life and honed during months of rehearsal to ensure that all the gambolling and cart-wheeling, trampolining and pyramid-making of the mass game went off without a hitch, and that all the individual gymnastic elements came together to create the perfect, grand spectacle against the orchestrated backdrop provided by thousands of anonymous children occupying the side of the stadium opposite the seats of honour. Holding aloft coloured cards, they created wonderful scenery of waving fields of golden corn that would give way in perfect coordination to ships fishing on a turquoise sea, to a glowing steel furnace, to a rocket flying to the moon. Workers, farmers and intellectuals, also created by the thousands of cards, would parade in vivid colours, proudly and happily across the background, above slogans written in bold Korean letters declaiming their loyalty to the leader and the Party and their determination to defeat their enemies and build a Paradise on Earth. The orchestration of the scenery was such that in a single movement a vast canvas of laughing schoolchildren could be replaced by images of tanks and artillery and soldiers defending their motherland. Even within single images there was sometimes movement; I could scarcely believe my eyes, the first time I saw a huge fish caught in a fisherman's net actually winking at me!

I wondered if schoolchildren in my own society could ever be persuaded to work together in their tens of thousands to put on such a display. Was it such a bad thing, if they couldn't? Wasn't the discipline that was routine to North Korean youngsters – the marching through the streets, for example – more appropriate for soldiers than for little children? Instead of the months of doubtless tedious and physically demanding rehearsal that went into a mass game, wouldn't they be better off at home or out in the street pursuing natural juvenile interests: listening to pop music, watching television, playing football, throwing sticks at dogs and cats, charging in mobs through shopping centres, standing in brooding menace on street corners?

Madame Beatrice had been a great fan of the mass games. Nagging concerns aside, I thought they were a wonderful spectacle, too, and I was prepared to acknowledge that they were on the whole a good thing, for the simple reason that every Korean I asked who had, as a child, taken part in a mass game was without exception proud of the fact.

There was another consideration that occurred to me: as adults they would lead a highly organised life as part of a collective, whether it be the army or part-time defence unit, an agricultural cooperative, an industrial enterprise or a work unit, a Party cell, a neighbourhood unit or a professional society, and the discipline instilled in them as children was no doubt essential preparation for this.

Marek claimed that he couldn't have survived life in Pyongyang were it not for his monthly sorties to Beijing. Philippe, too, felt the need to make regular trips to China. So accustomed had I become to the discipline of Pyongyang life that I never really understood why, until a group of us were taken by the publishing house on the six-hour train journey to Sinuiju on the Chinese border from where, after a night in the city's hotel, we foreigners set out early the next morning across the Friendship Bridge to Dandong on the Chinese side of the River Amnok.

Dandong was by Chinese standards a small town of just two million people. A ramshackle place of narrow streets and tiny shops, jerry-built restaurants and sprawling markets, street vendors, hawkers and spitters, nose-twitching smells and filth in the roads, battling taxis and shambling pedestrians, bicycles, tricycles and flat-bed cycles, calling, cursing and cackling, and cassette recorders screeching rock music; it was for us emigrants from the well-ordered Pyongyang a chaotic and confusing Shangri-La.

The markets sold all sorts of junk; cigarette lighters that boldly played *The East Is Red* as they struggled to produce a flame; plastic statues of a figure that could have been either Chairman Mao or the Buddha; genuine terracotta warriors packed in cardboard boxes; lethal toy daggers and little red books; music tapes and bananas. We could haggle, be ripped off, yet still buy shoes and clothes for a fraction of the price we would pay in Pyongyang. We could go to a restaurant, and by pointing at what other diners had on their tables, tuck into plates piled high with wonderful Chinese food – and it was all so cheap.

There was an innocuous-looking restaurant, so tiny it couldn't have seated more than eight people, where I went to eat with Cooper. We liked the place because the lady owner was Korean and this meant we could ask what meat went into the dishes we were ordering. Clearly the family was very poor, but she insisted on giving us a plate of fried bananas, free of charge. Her daughter was sent with us to the local market to help with bargaining. We went to her restaurant for our last meal before returning to Pyongyang and furtively she showed us a book, her Bible. Then she turned and gazed in the direction of the nearby river border, and as she did so, she shook her head in great sadness.

For a long time after that trip to Dandong I wondered what thoughts had so saddened the lady in the restaurant. A Christian, I supposed that compassion for her fellow people living in suffering just across the border might have filled her heart. But was she much better off, I wondered, eking out her own meagre existence from her tiny restaurant? Clearly she thought she was.

Obviously, the foreign sceptics would no doubt tell me, she had been despairing for her fellow Koreans who were living in desperate poverty, were robbed of their basic freedoms, including that of worshipping their God, were persecuted, and whose very thought processes were so controlled that they had been deprived of their natural human emotions, such as the ability to show the very sadness that the woman herself in Dandong had displayed.

I would have to admit that in the work I edited there were chilling references to remoulding people's thinking so as to eradicate from their minds improper ideas. But North Koreans were not the cold, unfeeling emotionless automatons that some foreigners saw all about them and declared to be the monstrous products of a monolithic system. Koreans revealed their feelings rarely, it was true, but when they did their emotions could be powerful. In the case of anger it could explode in an uncompromising, uncontrolled onslaught.

As I had discovered.

I hadn't been to see her for several weeks, although I'd been to other bars in the Koryo. My doubts had been growing stronger again, about encouraging a friendship that, if it developed, would sooner or later have demanded from me a commitment that I feared to make because it would be based neither on the close and tested companionship of my own culture nor on the structured role observance of hers. The only foundation of what was still no more than a friendship, I had feared, was the romantic notion of a lonely foreigner, and if I was to take a step towards a relationship that I still hadn't been told was not forbidden, I needed encouragement. But it hadn't come, and so for a while I'd kept away.

The girls working in the other bars had started asking why I didn't go to see her any more, and I would shrug and think that I'd been right not to go there because it was dangerous how people talked, and so I'd stayed away longer.

Then one night I'd gone back, anticipating her happiness at seeing me after so much time. Her fury had been frightening because she hadn't cared that others were watching and listening. And then, after the sudden heat of her anger had subsided, the cold set in. But I'd had to endure it. I'd had to come back night after night and feel the chill of her indifference that was, I imagined, punishment for what she had taken to be my own indifference.

People had noticed, and as once again I'd sat there waiting for the wordless, dismissive service, someone – a casual acquaintance – had told me Koreans only ever showed the true strength of their emotions to those they cared for.

I'd wondered if I'd found the encouragement I was seeking.

Even when the police were brought in to deal with Sophie, there was never, I suspected, any real possibility that the punishment would amount to much. For one thing, there was little Annette to consider.

Again, Song Il was my source. He came to me one morning looking tired, having apparently spent the night trying to persuade Sophie to turn her radio off. That explained the music I'd been hearing; that someone in North Korea should be having an all-night party had seemed quaintly naughty but a little unlikely. Anyway, what Sophie had done was barricade herself in her room, place her radio on her balcony and turn it on full volume. As if that wasn't provocation enough, she had tuned it to a South Korean station, and the neighbours had complained.

She had refused to open her door and the police were called. They had asked her and ordered her to let them in. Still she remained – with her daughter – locked inside the flat and the decision was taken to break the door down.

Song Il could hardly contain his excitement as he told me the story. The police had used small axes and at the first blow Sophie had flung open the door and squirted some sort of anti-rape spray on those outside. Yes, Song Il assured me, it was absolutely true. One of the policemen had been quite badly affected and had been sent to hospital.

For three days Sophie was kept under house arrest, which meant we had two plain-clothes policemen living in the guest house with us. I was quite happy with the arrangement because there was a marked improvement in the food we were served. Our Korean colleagues, though, were extremely nervous, and Li Jong Sun, the young Chinese interpreter resident at the guest house at the time, came near to panic on a visit to my room, when I told him I was thinking of popping downstairs to ask the policemen if they'd like to join us in watching a James Bond film.

'But what's wrong with that?' I asked him in mock surprise. 'You like James Bond.' North Koreans were not supposed to see 007 films, but among those who did so in secret, they were a big hit. I had a collection on tape and would occasionally show them to visitors, who all seemed to enjoy the action. All, that is, except a very serious young man whom Li Jong Sun had once brought with him. 'It's a lie,' he had shouted as James Bond's car had made some impossible leap, just missing a light aeroplane.

'What's a lie?' I had asked, surprised because he didn't speak English and so couldn't have understood the dialogue. 'He means the stunts,' Li Jong Sun had said.

The serious young man, sitting bolt upright in my armchair, bristling with self-righteous outrage, had then launched into a vehement condemnation of British propaganda. He demanded to know whether we seriously thought anyone would be taken in by it. Did we think our enemies feared us because we were all like this Bond spy?

'For goodness sake,' I'd said. 'It's only a bit of fun. A bit like your taekwondo movies.'

As for Li Jong Sun, I took pity on him and told him I was joking about inviting the police to see a film show. I settled his nerves with a beer.

Sophie was eventually escorted to the airport and put on the first available flight out of the country. And as so often happens in times of heightened tension, we – the foreigners and our Korean hosts – were brought together. We all felt sorry for the way things had turned out; we guessed she must have had some sort of nervous breakdown. But as for the way she carried out her missionary work, we were not sympathetic. Over a beer with my Palestinian, Cuban and North Korean colleagues we agreed that we all had our own beliefs and we all respected the right of others to have and, in the appropriate circumstances, disseminate theirs; but not to the extent that it was done so ineptly and thoughtlessly and involved a little girl being sent to a wholly unsuitable school.

Chapter 8

In the morning when the sky is aglow
We think of your kindly smile.
In the quiet night when the stars shine in the sky
We long for your warm love.[1]

So begins a song that, according to the two-volume biography *Great Leader Kim Jong Il*, became a popular ditty sung spontaneously by North Korean artists whenever they wanted to express their devotion.

Great Leader Kim Jong Il is made up of a series of anecdotes describing the noble personality and the outstanding leadership ability of the dear leader, in the vein of similar books about his father. For example, it tells of a school built on a remote island for just three children and of the Bridge of Love, likewise built on the orders of Kim Jong Il so that children in a remote part of the country could cross a dangerous stream safely on their way to school. There is the tale of the South Korean fishermen who inadvertently drift into the North's territorial waters, are brought ashore and leave singing the dear leader's praises after he personally ensures they receive medical treatment and good food.

There are stories also of officials receiving telephone calls in the early hours of the morning from Kim Jong Il, who is concerned about some aspect of the people's welfare. A popular image in North Korean song is that of a single light burning late at night in the building of the Party Central Committee. It is the dear

[1] *Great Leader Kim Jong Il*, vol. 1, by Tak Jin, Kim Gang Il and Pak Hong Je. Sorinsha, Tokyo, Japan, 1986.

leader's office window and he is again going without sleep as he works for the good of the people.

The underlying message of this and other books, reinforced by the well-documented tours of on-the-spot guidance that bring him, like his father, to every part of the country to meet ordinary people, is that there is always the chance that the dear leader might just hear of an individual's special efforts or needs and take a personal interest.

It's a romantic notion of a leader's love for his people that is, I think, a key element in creating believers out of people outside the country. As for North Koreans themselves, the point of the message is that however bad things may be, there is always hope.

CHAPTER EIGHT

Building Dreams

'*Je suis Kimilsungiste*,'[2] Madame Beatrice was in the habit of informing any foreign stranger she met, especially if they were impertinent enough to express any criticism of North Korea or its regime. Anyone foolish enough to take the great leader's name in vain would be roundly and loudly upbraided.

Madame Beatrice was to return in triumph in 1992, her commitment to the cause and her revolutionary credentials only strengthened by her absence, in the wake of the self-inflicted disasters the publishing house had suffered in attempting to replace her. She would be as staunch as ever in her belief in Kim Il Sung and she would wear her medal with pride. If anything, on her return she was a little more redoubtable; the finger would be pointed with a little more force and the tongue would be a little sharper. It was for the publishing house a relief, and for myself a

[2] I am a Kimilsungist.

pleasure, to have her back in a year that was such an important one for North Korea.

In 1992 three great events would be celebrated: the dear leader's 50th birthday, the great leader's 80th birthday, and the 60th anniversary of the founding of the Korean People's Army. Unlike 1989, when international developments had cast a shadow over North Korea's moment in the spotlight, the world situation as 1991 turned to 1992 promised that there might be cause for celebrating not only the domestic milestones but also diplomatic success.

But just a few months before the auspicious year dawned there had appeared to be little cause for optimism.

The international efforts to bring Pyongyang out of its isolation kept hitting the same wall; a nuclear one. Even after North Korea had bowed to the inevitable and joined the United Nations in September 1991, and in the face of overtures from Seoul, Tokyo and Washington, Pyongyang was playing hard to get with a world that was growing worried about its nuclear intentions.

In September 1991 Pyongyang stated that it would open its nuclear facilities to International Atomic Energy Agency inspection only if US nuclear weapons deployed in South Korea were subject to similar scrutiny. Thus Pyongyang appeared to be going back on a promise made in July to sign the nuclear safeguards agreement, which would clear the way for IAEA inspectors to visit the country.[3]

For years Pyongyang had been calling for north-east Asia to become a nuclear-free, peace zone and was feeling aggrieved

---

[3] See *Vantage Point*, December, 1991.

that it was being accused of nuclear misbehaviour even as the US had nuclear weapons on the other side of the 38th Parallel, aimed at it. But North Korea's bargaining was unlikely to win it much in the way of concessions from Washington, where there was concern in some quarters that it might be hiding a secret nuclear weapons programme.

Meanwhile, the nuclear issue was also cited by Japan for the lack of progress in talks on normalising relations, although Tokyo did point to other obstacles, principally the size of Pyongyang's compensation demands. There was also the matter of one of its citizens whom Japan said had been kidnapped and taken to North Korea in the 1970s.

The leadership in Pyongyang clearly felt vulnerable to what it saw as attempts to undermine its traditional policies. Even its UN membership had been forced on North Korea, which for years had argued that simultaneous entry by Pyongyang and Seoul would confirm the division of the peninsula and fly in the face of the national desire for reunification. The argument was maintained almost until the last moment, even after it became clear that the realignment of international forces would leave Pyongyang with no alternative other than to bow before Seoul's ultimatum to join simultaneously or leave South Korea to join alone.

In holding its ground on the issue of nuclear inspection, Pyongyang's apparent desire was to be treated as an equal dialogue partner. This being the case, some observers suggested that it was time to make concessions to North Korea rather than risk the consequences of a wounded regime being backed further into a corner.

><

Under the circumstances, it was hardly surprising that my offer of a piece of the Berlin Wall hadn't gone down at all well. I'd acquired a few bits during a visit home to England, and I thought this would be just the sort of historic souvenir Koreans might appreciate. They didn't. Interpreters and drivers, waitresses, cleaners and cooks; no-one was interested.

The reason was obvious when I thought about it. The destruction of the Berlin Wall had meant only one thing to the Korean people: that theirs was now the world's only country suffering the tragedy of division. The sadness of the lady in Dandong, it occurred to me, was like the sadness I saw on the faces of North Koreans when they discussed the plight of their country. I'd learned to parrot that the peninsula's partition was the greatest national tragedy and reunification was the most pressing demand of our times. But it had meant nothing to me; merely words. It was only when I discussed the matter with Korean colleagues and friends that I started to appreciate the strength of the feeling.

An elderly colleague talked of the aunt he had not seen since he was a little boy. There had been a time when he had dreamed that one day he would see her again. But the years had passed and he had to admit that she was probably dead. A friend I met regularly in the Koryo Hotel told me of the grandparents – his mother's parents I think – he had never seen or heard from. They didn't even know of his existence. The division of the country, I reflected, affected everyone. And the determination to achieve reunification united them.

Even those with no tale of personal tragedy to tell would speak with anger about the US imperialists who were, through their occupation of the South, preventing the Korean people from fulfilling their greatest desire. Increasingly, there was talk also of the economic hardship the Americans were inflicting on the

North by stationing an army in the South, obliging North Korea to spend one quarter of its GDP on defending itself.

The Cold War was over, my young friend who had never known his grandparents argued, and whatever excuse the Americans had used in the past to justify their occupation of South Korea was no longer valid. The US must withdraw at once and leave the Korean people free to settle their own fate independently and in accordance with the nation's will.

I sympathised. As well I should, he told me. Once the threat posed by the US army in South Korea had been removed, there would no longer be the need for such restrictions on the foreigners in Pyongyang.

And so the roller-coaster continued. North–South relations, despite peaking briefly in the spring when the unified table tennis team had taken part in the world championships, had spent most of 1991 struggling to raise themselves out of the morass into which they had been plunged after the US army had gone ahead early in the year with the annual Team Spirit military exercise in South Korea. But then they scaled a previously unknown height when the two prime ministers signed a non-aggression pact.

The high-level contacts between the two sides, which had begun at the end of 1990, had been interrupted when North Korea protested over the staging of Team Spirit. They had resumed again in October, and by December 1991 the two prime ministers were able to sign the *Basic Agreement on Reconciliation, Non-aggression, Exchange and Cooperation Between the North and the South*.

This landmark agreement was seen by both sides as providing momentum for bringing forward the reunification of the country. As *Korea Today* said, it:

> expresses the unshakable will of the north and the south to remove the political and military confrontation and achieve national reconciliation ... to achieve many-sided cooperation and exchange for the promotion of the common interests and prosperity of the nation, and to make concerted efforts to achieve peaceful reunification.[4]

By the time of his 50th birthday, Kim Jong Il was Supreme Commander of the million-strong Korean People's Army, an appointment that had been announced at the end of December amid much media trumpeting of his military genius. Only a few months earlier he had been raised to the position of deputy chairman of the National Defence Commission, making his rise through the ranks of the army even more spectacular than his ascendancy through the Party hierarchy.

Of course, the foreign cynics talked about the army being a spectacular birthday present, a massively dangerous toy. More sensible observers speculated that the appointment hinted at a subtle shift away from the leading role of the Party to that of the army. But to the ordinary Korean people it must have seemed that there was something in all the talk of military genius when the Americans announced, in keeping with the new climate of détente on the Korean peninsula, that they would cancel Team Spirit 92.

---

[4] *Korea Today*, 1992, 2. *Vantage Point*, December, 1991, also contains a report on the signing of the Basic Agreement.

Kim Il Sung University is the leading institution of higher education in North Korea, and it occupies a pleasantly leafy campus on the northern side of Moran Hill, not far from Rungna Island in the River Taedong. The university's most illustrious graduate is Kim Jong Il, who studied political science there in the early 1960s.

The dear leader's rise up the pecking order of the all-powerful Workers' Party of Korea, which by 1980 numbered more than two million members, began as soon as he left university. His first appointment, in 1964, was to an important position in the Party's propaganda department. He quickly demonstrated a flair for artistic creation and took upon himself the direction of films and operas. In 1970 he was named director of the party's culture and art department. He subsequently became the guiding light behind the Three Revolution Red Flag Movement, launched in the early 1970s, under which young people fresh from college were formed into small squads and packed off to factories and farms, to provide inspirational leadership and agitation to the toiling masses by encouraging them to devote themselves to carrying out the ideological, technical and cultural revolutions. In the meantime, he developed and enriched the Juche Idea, a process that conveniently involved laying down the revolutionary principles for a dynastic succession.[5]

The story goes that he became known as the 'dear leader' some time in the 1970s, not as a result of a decree sent down from on high, but by popular acclaim. The Party Central Committee had been inundated with letters calling for the president's son to

[5] *Vantage Point*, November, 1987, records Kim Jong Il's rise in the Workers' Party of Korea.

be given the affectionate title 'dear leader' and eventually the powers that be acquiesced to the will of the people.

Clearly, even under Kim Il Sung's monolithic leadership, a certain amount of preparatory work was necessary before he could take the bold step of putting forward his son as his successor. So a process of gradually raising Kim Jong Il to the right hand of his father was undertaken. He was appointed a Secretary of the Party Central Committee in September 1973. The following February, a plenary session of the Party Central Committee elected him a member of its Political Committee; this was in spite of the opposition of his father, who reluctantly agreed to the appointment only after bowing to the unanimous will of the meeting that a successor should be found to take some of the burden of leadership from his shoulders.

The dear leader's birthday became a national holiday and his portrait began appearing alongside that of the great leader in the mid-1970s. By 1980, it was time to take the fateful step.

In typical North Korean fashion, no declaration was made at the Sixth Party Congress, held in October 1980, that Kim Jong Il was to be his father's heir. He simply appeared on the platform and was elected to the powerful Presidium of the Political Bureau of the Party Central Committee and to the Secretariat of the Party Central Committee. There was a general reshuffling and expansion of the Central Committee, designed, many onlookers believed, to leave Kim Jong Il's supporters in the ascendancy; in Party hierarchies he was now listed at or just below number two. As the newspapers subsequently began pointing out with greater conviction and regularity, the succession to the revolutionary cause of Juche had been assured. The dear leader represented the next generation of the country's leadership.

I wondered if, back in 1980, it was the practice to sweeten a pill of uncertain reaction with a dose of reunification promise. But perhaps it was just coincidence or the force of circumstances that led the great leader to set out his vision of a reunified Korea at the Sixth Party Congress. This would be achieved, he had decided, through the founding of the Democratic Confederal Republic of Koryo.

In presenting the proposal, the great leader said:

> Our Party holds that the country should be unified by founding a Confederal Republic through the establishment of a unified national government on condition that the north and the south recognize and tolerate each other's ideas and social systems, a government in which the two sides are represented on an equal footing and under which they exercise regional autonomy respectively with equal rights and duties.[6]

All well and good, one might think, except that few in the South could have doubted that the hidden theme of the North's overture was the intention ultimately to reunify Korea under Communist rule. Even those in the South who either did not believe or did not fear this must have been worried by the prospect of closer economic cooperation, in which the North's lumbering practices and outdated industry would be a millstone likely to bring a sudden halt to their headlong charge to prosperity.

By this time South Korea was well ahead of the North economically and its trade was bringing it closer relations with the rest of the world, principally the West, which was turning a blind eye to Seoul's suspect claims to democracy. North Korea,

---

[6] 'Report to the Sixth Congress of the Workers Party of Korea on the Work of the Central Committee, October 10th 1980'. In *Kim Il Sung: Works*, vol. 35, January–December, 1980. Foreign Languages Publishing House, Pyongyang, 1989.

by contrast, was finding it difficult to achieve its economic growth targets and, since the mid-1970s, had been struggling to attract loans and investment from the Western industrial powers, which were put off by the country's inability to meet its international financial obligations.

So the Second Seven-year Plan adopted by Pyongyang in 1978 had marked a return to self-reliance. Development would be based on modernisation of the economy and the promotion of science. Priority would be given to the energy sector, to technical innovation, to the stepped-up exploitation of resources that could replace imports, to the modernisation of agriculture, and to a number of nature-harnessing projects.[7]

But the South Koreans were apparently unimpressed by such economic initiatives, just as Kim Il Sung's reunification proposal seemed to find little support. The North blamed the authorities in Seoul for deliberately fanning anti-Communist sentiment, claiming that they were hardly in a position to preach, given their own record of misrule and human rights abuses.

Five months before the Sixth Congress of the Workers' Party of Korea, an event took place in South Korea that the authorities in Pyongyang would exploit for years afterwards as evidence of the murderous nature of a regime that would stoop to committing the most barbarous atrocities at the behest of its US masters. In May 1980 the people of the southern city of Kwangju in South Korea had risen up in demand of an end to martial law. The puppet government, so the North Korean media reported, acting on the orders of their US masters, sent the troops in to deal with the uprising and a bloodbath ensued. Not surprisingly the statistics on how many civilians were killed in the subsequent massacre

---

[7] An overview of North Korea's economic development can be found in *Vantage Point*, May, 1987.

are widely divergent; the South said it was fewer than 200, the North came up with a figure of 5000.

Footage and photographs, documentaries and eye-witness accounts of the Kwangju Massacre were still the staple of North Korea's anti-South propaganda a dozen years after the event, a bloody and horrific reminder to the people of the North that salvation for their brothers and sisters in the South lay in reunification.

Pyongyang's vociferous criticisms of the South's human rights record left it open to accusations of hypocrisy. There was international condemnation of North Korea's labour camps and its treatment of prisoners, political prisoners in particular, which was scarcely dampened by lack of reliable information. North Korea defended itself by pointing out that under its socialist system the basic human rights to be clothed, fed and sheltered were guaranteed; its people enjoyed free education, free medical care and a pension if they were old or unable to work because of disability; and they could also walk freely and in perfect safety through the streets without being pestered by beggars, muggers or prostitutes. Those who attempted to undermine the system that made all this possible were harming the interests of the population at large and were thus deserving of punishment. That did not mean, however, that North Korea was prepared to let outsiders see its prison facilities. No-one pretended that the conditions in which it kept those of its citizens who had stepped out of line were not harsh, but North Korea preferred to keep the world, and those of its people who lived a blameless life in pursuit of lofty revolutionary goals, in the dark.

As foreigners, we were not supposed to know about the lengths North Korea went to in order to keep its citizens on the straight and narrow revolutionary path. Although the authorities made no bones about the ideological indoctrination the people were subjected to, a veil of secrecy was thrown over the activities of those responsible for policing the observance of that ideology. However, keeping us in the dark was difficult because the security around us had to be particularly tight, since we were the purveyors of evil and decadent influence, although it was those we associated with who felt the brunt of this vigilance.

On one occasion I was sitting in the small first-floor bar of the Koryo with a colleague from the publishing house. The telephone rang and the barmaid handed the receiver to my friend, who nodded a few times, handed the receiver back to the girl and got up and left. He returned a short while later, looking a little irritated, but it wasn't until we were in the safety of the street outside, on our way home, that he told me what had happened. 'The security told me to come up to their office,' he said. 'They said they wanted to check the identity of Michael's friend.'

I got the impression that he was embarrassed more than angry, rather like a little boy whose mother had called him indoors for a moment while he'd been playing in the street with his friends. Just like a little boy, he also seemed relieved that he hadn't been doing anything he shouldn't have; in his case, as a work colleague he had every right to be in the hotel with me. As for myself, long gone were the days when such an intrusion would have me fuming over the violation of a basic right to privacy; rather, I was annoyed by what seemed an irritating lack of courtesy for a foreign friend of the country and his companion.

As for those foreigners, such as Leblanc and Sophie, who came to what they clearly considered an alien country and, without making any apparent effort to adjust to circumstances they found strange or to compromise, or at least keep quiet, when their opinions clashed with what prevailed locally, ended up causing offence to their hosts, I had no sympathy when they fell foul of a system they held in contempt. Attitudes towards misbehaving foreigners had changed since the bad old days of the 1960s and 1970s, when speaking out of turn, as my Latin American predecessor at the publishing house, the one Madame Beatrice had told me about, had discovered, could land you in gaol. Sophie had experienced the worst that was likely to befall a foreigner who committed a misdemeanour that fell short of an actual crime. She had, sooner rather than later, been kicked out of the country. The punishment was clearly designed to humiliate, although she couldn't have been aware of the extent of her humiliation.

When the police had been breaking down Sophie's door, they had filmed the whole process. I imagined they wanted to be able to show, in the unlikely event that anyone asked, that they had behaved properly. Conscious of the country's image in some international circles, it was important, I reasoned, that they could demonstrate that their treatment of the troublesome foreigner had been justified and beyond reproach.

But such charitable thoughts were dashed by a casual comment from one of the barmaids at the Potonggang Hotel. She let slip that she'd seen my crazy French colleague with the spray at the guest house. There was only one explanation, I concluded: the hotel's staff had been shown the police video of Sophie's attack.

My reaction was to feel even angrier with Sophie, because it was the unthinking behaviour of such people that provided the more xenophobic elements in authority with the excuse and the means to reinforce the perception that all foreigners were dangerous.

It seemed only right that Madame Beatrice should have returned to North Korea for the celebrations of Kim Il Sung's 80th birthday, and it seemed particularly fitting that she should be asked to work on the memoirs of a man she admired so much.

With the Century, the first two volumes of which were published in April 1992, is a remarkable work for the enormous detail it contains.[8] The first two volumes recount the author's early childhood, the years he spent at school in Manchuria, where he had gone to be with his parents, and the early period of his struggle against the Japanese. It's hard not to be impressed by the remarkable maturity of the young boy described in its opening chapters and by the genuine affection he expresses, as he looks back, for the compatriots and friends who stood by him, taught him and helped him during those early days on the path of revolution.

The writer tells of how, as a small boy yet to celebrate his 7th birthday, he took part in the famous March 1st Uprising against the Japanese in 1919.[9] He describes his memories of that day, when he followed the marchers to the Potong Gate in Pyongyang, and comments:

> The March First Popular Uprising was the time that I stood in the ranks of the people and that the true image of our nation was implanted in my mind's eye.[10]

[8] *Kim Il Sung Reminiscences*: *With the Century*, vols. 1 & 2. Foreign Languages Publishing House, Pyongyang, 1992. Publication of the great leader's memoirs continued even after his death, and by 2000 eight volumes had appeared, covering the period from his birth up to 1945.

[9] A celebrated mass demonstration of Korean resistance to Japanese rule that followed the death of the former king, Kojong.

[10] *Kim Il Sung Reminiscences*: *With the Century*, vol. 1. Foreign Languages Publishing House, Pyongyang, 1992.

His power of recollection is phenomenal. He talks of people he met casually; the kindness of an innkeeper who helped the 11-year-old making his way alone from China to his grandparents in Pyongyang through the winter snows of Korea; the people he knew briefly in Jilin, what they looked like, what they ate; his fellow guerrillas and casual comments they made.

Fascinating though the accounts were in themselves, they merely put some flesh on the bones of the official story we already knew. I wondered how much had been written by the great leader himself and then thought it really didn't matter. Clearly his personal input had been enormous and I must confess the first two volumes had whetted my appetite for those that would come later, dealing with the late 1930s and early 1940s, the years when North Korea's official version of its history diverged most dramatically from the accounts of outsiders. Judging by his *Works*, Kim Il Sung made hardly a speech or wrote anything from the late 1930s until liberation in 1945, supporting his detractors' view that he'd been in the Soviet Union during most, if not all, of that period. But if he could describe his activities along the Chinese–Korean border at the time in the same detail and with equal authority as he had done his early years in the first two volumes, he would go a long way to tilting the judgement of history in his favour.

A week or so before Kim Il Sung's 80th birthday on April 15th 1992, I received a telephone call from the English Section at the publishing house, which was unusual since the translators generally seized on the slightest excuse to drag me there to share my cigarettes over a cup of tea. The reason for the call was that the matter to be discussed was of the greatest importance and urgency, Ho Gwang told me as he led me downstairs to the telephone. Having been appointed Supreme Commander of the Korean People's Army, the dear leader had now been given the military rank of Marshal. The problem was that this had necessitated promoting the existing Marshal, the ever-victorious, iron-willed brilliant commander Marshal Kim Il Sung. Some military rank had to be found that reflected the fact that he was the superior of the supreme commander.

'What do you think of 'Grand Marshal'?' asked Mr Han, the senior translator, a man whose attitude was a refreshing contrast to that of Mr Ma. Mr Han had an instinctive feel for English and, as such, could produce a translation that needed very little correction. The fluency of his work meant that, at a pinch, I could leave it more or less untouched. Even better, when I did make a change he generally accepted my point of view, rather than launching into a pointless argument.

Mr Han had gained my enormous respect early on in our collaboration by listening patiently to my suggestion, put with all the diplomacy I could muster, that the honorific 'great leader' was overused in English translations. My argument was that constant repetition in my culture tended to diminish the sense of respect, rather than reinforce it.

For a brief while the use of 'great leader' had been reduced in English language publications, to the consternation of some Western journalists I ran into one evening in the Koryo. They wanted to know what it signified. Was the great leader reducing his profile so that his son could take his place in the spotlight? Were there elements at work that were trying to water down the personality cult? Was it a sign that Kim Il Sung was losing his grip on power?

None of these, I could tell them. Just me and one of the more enlightened translators trying to give the propaganda a little more appeal.

I doubted whether they believed me. Anyway, before long 'great leader' was appearing just as often as before. Perhaps some foreign journalist had reported that the great leader's influence was diminishing and this had caused alarm in North Korea's propaganda circles.

I was always happy when Mr Han called, asking if I could come to the publishing house to discuss a translation. I enjoyed our meetings, in part for professional reasons and in part because over time he started telling me a little about his past.

He remembered the Japanese occupation. I'd read time and time again of how, among all their other crimes, the Japanese had tried to obliterate the Korean language and force all Koreans to adopt Japanese names. This, Mr Han told me, had happened to him as a schoolboy. Somehow, hearing his personal account of sitting in a classroom, being addressed by a teacher who called him by an alien name, brought home to me how brutal the reality was of being stripped of your national identity.

The whole Korean nation had suffered at the hands of the Japanese, none more so than the Comfort Women, girls who had been kidnapped during the war and packed off to work in Japanese army brothels. The women had come from across Asia, not only Korea, and their stories, once they told them after decades of silence, were quite horrific. In case anyone harboured thoughts that here was yet another example of North Korean vitriol against an enemy regime, their accounts were echoed by women in South Korea, China and other parts of Asia.

They told of being taken against their will in trucks from their villages or lured with promises of work in factories. By train or ship, they were then transported in their hundreds and thousands to Japan, China or parts of south-east Asia where the Imperial Army was stationed. At so-called service clubs they were thrown into tiny rooms with a mud floor and a curtain instead of a door and left to the devices of the Japanese soldiers who queued outside; officers first, followed by NCOs and finally the ordinary soldiers.

Their tales were gut-wrenching, desperate accounts of friends and acquaintances who'd been hung and drawn as an example to the others after trying to escape, of branding with searing hot irons, of pain, humiliation and degradation. Succumbing to infection or pregnancy meant they were useless for work and a drain on the meagre rations set aside for the girls. So they were afforded the most rudimentary medical treatment and, if it failed, they would be left to die.[11]

As to the great leader's new title, I told Mr Han I was against 'Grand Marshal', as it sounded rather contrived and anyway gave the impression of someone leading a parade. 'Great Marshal' also sounded unnatural and would leave us having to refer to the great leader, great marshal, Kim Il Sung. That was a little repetitive.

[11] For one of many accounts of the suffering of the Comfort Women, see *Korea Today*, 1992, 9.

Mr Han asked, rather uncertainly I thought, my opinion of 'Generalissimo'. He explained that his chief concern was the association with certain other, far from savoury characters who had given themselves the title. He mentioned Franco, Mussolini and Chiang Kaishek; but not, I noted, Stalin.

It wasn't really my place, I said, to comment on the political side of the debate. From the point of view of English, 'Generalissimo' was the only title he'd suggested that wasn't an invention.

'Who came up with 'Generalissimo'?' demanded my friends Choe and Kang, the two interpreters I was at that time hanging out with quite a lot in the Koryo.

'You don't think it's good?' I asked them.

'Look at all the other Generalissimos – Mussolini, Franco and Stalin. It's not right to include our president in the same group.'

'Well,' I said. 'I did what I could, but the final decision wasn't mine.'

For the great leader's 80th birthday the gifts from the people to the leader and, in that quaint Korean way of doing things, from the birthday boy to the people, were a little more generous than previously. The tram line was extended and all the children received a smart, newly designed school uniform, rather like a sailor suit. Even the publishing house got something: a gift of foreign currency, which it used to buy two computers. Much to the envy of the other language groups, they were given to the English Section. I suggested that I should have one of them, because of all the paper that would be saved. But no, the typists got both and I supposed it made sense. After all, they were the ones who were having to type out the original handwritten translation, then type the whole thing out again after I'd made my corrections, and then type it for a third time after the senior translators had checked it through. And it all had to be perfect. There could be no excuse for letting a spelling mistake make its way into the *Works* of Kim Il Sung.

The great leader even had a little something for the Americans to mark his birthday. At the beginning of April, just over a week before the big day, he gave an interview to the *Washington Times*. In his comments Kim Il Sung was reported to have revealed that US evangelist Billy Graham, on a visit to Pyongyang, had conveyed an oral message to him from President George Bush, and that in return he had expressed the feeling that 'spring has come to the two countries' and that it was his wish to see a US embassy in Pyongyang 'as quickly as possible'.[12]

It was Choe and Kang who explained to me the mystery of how Kim Il Sung had come to use such an unlikely envoy as Billy Graham. There was a family connection, they said. One or both of the evangelist's wife's parents – they weren't too sure of the details – had been missionaries in Korea in the early part of the century, and had worked at a school where the great leader's father was teaching.

It was in comments about another unlikely visitor that one of my two friends had earlier and in private done the unthinkable and criticised the great leader. That's how I'd thought of it, although I had to admit that what had actually happened was that he had questioned why Sun-myung Moon was being permitted to visit North Korea for a trip during which he was

<hr/>

[12] See *Vantage Point*, July, 1992.

scheduled to meet Kim Il Sung. This was as near to criticism of the great leader as I was ever likely to hear, I'd concluded.

As the head of the Unification Church, North Korea-born Moon had for years been an object of vilification on his home territory. Apart from anything else, he had done time in a North Korean prison on adultery charges, before the war had given him the chance to flee southwards.

In the past the North Korean media had been pretty uncompromising about Moon. He had been involved in numerous sex scandals in South Korea, it was reported, but thanks to the protection he enjoyed from the United States government he had always avoided punishment. In fact, my companion had told me, Moon was an outspoken anti-communist and as such was believed to be in the employ of the CIA. Don't be taken in by the name of the organisation, my young acquaintance had said; he was no advocate of true reunification.

Still, Kim Il Sung had met Moon. The message being put across was that a prominent overseas Korean was paying his respects to the great leader of the nation. The press revealed that the two men had held fruitful talks. That was true, my friend who had criticised the visit had reported to me, clearly unabashed to be changing his tune so dramatically; so fruitful in fact that the great leader had agreed to give an exclusive interview to Moon's newspaper, the *Washington Times*.

Because it was the great leader's 80th, special efforts went into another traditional aspect of the birthday celebrations, the April Spring Friendship Art Festival when, every year, performing artistes from around the world would put on shows in various theatres across the capital for a week, culminating in a grand performance by the best of them in the presence of Kim Il Sung himself on or near his birthday.

North Koreans were told that the Thai dancers and French magicians, German ballroom dancers and Chinese circus troupes, Russian opera singers and Mongolian warblers, Congolese dancers and Peruvian jugglers who turned up every year and whose performances they saw repeated for weeks afterwards on their televisions, were the cream of the world's performing artistes. If they weren't particularly good, I supposed the reasoning went, it only showed that the home-grown talent really was up there among and even exceeding the best in the world. But this wasn't really the point; what mattered was that the world had flocked to perform their party pieces in a demonstration of international respect and affection for the great leader of the Korean people.

I happened to fall into conversation with a member of the festival's organising committee a few months before the 1992 event, who told me they'd been a little disappointed with the previous year's British representative – after all, Russians were the best at playing Tchaikovsky's piano pieces, not the British, just as no-one could sing Korean songs like a Korean, was his argument – and said he was wondering who was the most famous of all British performing artistes.

The Beatles sprang to mind. The festival organiser asked whether they were any good. Would any of the other foreign artistes have heard of them? In that case, would I mind contacting The – what were they called? – yes, The Beatles, and ask them to come? He wondered if it was a problem if one of them was dead. How many were left? Three? Surely that would be enough.

I'd see what I could do, I said, and did nothing. If I remember rightly, a British pianist was once again invited that year, who played, as far as I recall, Tchaikovsky.

Of all the celebrations of 1992, it was the 60th anniversary of the founding of the glorious Korean People's Army that made the biggest impression on me. I'd attended march-pasts on previous army days, but never had there been such a display of tanks and armoured vehicles, missiles and rockets, planes and artillery pieces.

But it was Marshal Kim Jong Il who stole the show. There had been speculation among my Korean friends that he might use the occasion to deck himself out, for the first time in public, in some sort of uniform. I could only imagine what gorgeous outfit might be deemed suitable for such an august occasion. In the event, he turned up in his usual high-necked tunic, this one grey, and chose to mark the occasion with what was believed to have been his first utterance at such a public event. 'Glory to the officers and men of the heroic Korean People's Army,' he said in a clear enough voice, although not, I would say, with the deep resonance with which the propaganda habitually had him speaking. Even so, there was absolute hush while he said the words and for a few poignant moments afterwards.

I was delighted to discover in editing the English version of *With the Century* that I had something in common with the great leader: a love of the Myohyang Mountains. The preface to the first volume concluded with the words: 'Praying for the souls of the departed revolutionaries. The Myohyang Mountains.' Presumably he did his writing in the palace he had tucked away there.

I had to disagree with my friends and colleagues who claimed – and in this they were, as ever, toeing the official line – that the Kumgang Mountains were the most beautiful mountains in the world, because I preferred the Myohyang Mountains. I found the beauty of Myohyangsan just as unspoilt as that of its sister mountains on the east coast; its peaks were just as glorious, its waterfalls just as spectacular, and its pools just as crystal clear. But all this was only part of the attraction that made me a visitor very year.

In the Myohyang Mountains I felt completely at ease, a part of the casual camaraderie among my interpreters and drivers, the staff at the idyllic guest house where I always stayed and at the pyramid hotel where we went for a drink in the evenings, and the guides at the various places of interest, such as the International Friendship Exhibition and the Pohyon Temple. There was much less evidence of the restrictions and the pressures of life in Pyongyang. People seemed more relaxed and more open, with me and among themselves.

It was a pity, I thought, given the great leader's fondness for the Myohyang Mountains, that no-one ever bothered to tell him about how I'd saved one of its most famous landmarks from burning down. The Hyangsan Hotel, a pyramid-shaped building set amid lawns with the darker green of a mountain behind it, is one of the most popular images on North Korean calendars. Were it not for me, I like to claim, it might not have been the subject of calendars much past the beginning of the 1990s.

The irony was that, although I contrived to save the famous Hyangsan Hotel, I never stayed there. Instead I was lucky enough to stay at the Chongbyong Guest House, a two-storey traditional building with whitewashed walls and a green hip-saddle roof set in gardens and lawns that I fell in love with at first sight. It was small by hotel standards, with some 20 rooms only. Whenever I stayed there I was always given the same room, the 'presidential suite', as it was first described to me. Its finest feature was the wide marble balcony that took up an entire corner of the hotel's first floor. From the one side I overlooked the long driveway and lawns that led up to the main entrance and from the other I could gaze up at the rich greenness of a sheer mountainside that rose on the other side of the nearby road. The mountainside also dominated my line of vision from the guest house's dining room, whose vast picture window offered what I considered one of the finest views in all of Korea. In the background was the mountain and in the foreground was the hotel's small garden, a vision of streams and lakes, of pebbled pathways and of small, hunchback bridges. I especially looked forward to my dinners because in the evenings the whole garden would be turned into a fairytale scene, illuminated by coloured floodlights.

Our evenings in the Myohyang Mountains always took us after dinner to the top of the Hyangsan Hotel. Normally we – that is myself and a driver and two publishing house interpreters, one of whom would usually be Song Il – would take up a table in the revolving restaurant, overlooking the green valleys and small communities nearby.

It was during one of these Saturday nights that Song Il, Kim Sok Nam from the publishing house, a driver called Han and myself inadvertently became the archetypal unassuming heroes, whom the propaganda was at that time urging the population at large to emulate.

The circumstances were hardly what the propagandists had in mind, though. For a start, rather than being fired up with revolutionary enthusiasm we were a little sluggish, since it was after midnight and we'd drunk rather a lot of beer. So when the time for action was proclaimed by Kim returning from a visit to the toilet to report that he could smell burning, we told him it was our cigarettes and to sit down.

But before long we heard a commotion from the direction of the short corridor that gave access to the toilets and lifts and we hauled ourselves to our feet to see what was happening. Our barmaid, Mi Ran, was shouting 'Fire! Fire!' as she looked up at the ceiling, a section of which was in flames.

Unfortunately, though, she didn't swoon and so I had no excuse to throw her over my shoulder and struggle with her to safety down the staircase, wherever that was. Instead I stood in front of her and staged a pantomime of squirting an imaginary fire extinguisher upwards at the ceiling. 'I don't know the Korean word,' I explained as she shook her head.

The driver emerged as the man of action who didn't lose his head in times of crisis. He thought that the priority was to ensure the safety of the foreigner. Although I heartily agreed, I didn't fancy using the lifts, since they were perilously close to the fire. Apart from that, I was a little irritated that he thought I was surplus to requirements for saving the hotel, so I pointed out that I'd left a half-full bottle of beer on the table and intended to finish it, if we ever got round to putting out the fire.

This was just the sort of incisive observation the situation demanded, and it spurred us off in search of fire-fighting equipment. All we could find, though, were two small plastic washing-up bowls and these we filled with water in the kitchen and carried, racing, back to the fire. What surprised me, considering the amount we spilt *en route*, was how wet we got as we stood beneath the flames throwing the water upwards.

The mechanism that made the restaurant revolve was located above the ceiling, someone – probably the driver – suggested, and it occurred to me that water was probably not the best solution, if it was an electrical fire. By this time there was smoke, a lot of it; thick, grey, chemical smoke that was making me and evidently the others feel sick. We called a halt and stood, choking and dripping, to discuss what to do.

I think the driver was the clever dick who suggested that the fire should be tackled at source by someone who would climb up into the roof. I looked up at the tiny hatch in the ceiling and volunteered immediately, only to shake my head in apparent frustration when the others pointed out what I'd seen straight away; I was too big.

Instead, with the smoke getting thicker and more pungent, I rushed around the restaurant gathering table cloths and soaking them in water for people to cover their faces to aid breathing. Having done so with the other half-dozen tables I found myself contemplating our own, wondering how to remove the cloth without disturbing the half-filled beer bottles and glasses. 'No need,' said a nonchalant Song Il who had sauntered in from the scene of the fire. 'It's out.'

Incredulous, I went to check and the maintenance team that had finally turned up confirmed that yes, somehow we had contrived to put the fire out.

'You are a hero,' Kim the interpreter told me, as we sat choking and coughing, our eyes smarting, determined to finish our beers and work out how we'd managed to put the fire out. No-one had gone up into the ceiling; somehow the water we'd been throwing up at the flames had been enough to extinguish them.

Modestly, I hummed and hawed about how I'd done my bit. Really it had been a team effort, I told Kim. Even the driver had helped. It wasn't long, though, before I was brought right back down to earth. As we entered the lift to leave Song Il told me, 'Mi Ran says you can come back tomorrow and pay for the beer.'

The following morning, a Sunday, I took a stroll down to the Pohyon Buddhist Temple, ten minutes from our hotel. The temple was said to be almost 1000 years old. It had suffered during the war from American bombs and bullets and the bright painting of the door gods that guarded its gates and the splendour of the gilt statues in the main hall testified to recent renovation.

I was intrigued because a foreign friend had told me that, believe it or not, there was a bar at the temple. The claim, I'd decided, wasn't as unlikely as it had at first sounded; after all, there was a coffee shop in the basement of the Juche Tower and even a karaoke machine tucked away in the tiny café that served visitors to Kaesong's ancient Confucian college. Economic necessity, it seemed, was giving rise to commercial enterprise in some unlikely places.

The girl working in the bar at the Pohyon Temple asked me whether I knew the *kayagum*. I told her I did and she said if I waited a moment I could hear its music. She disappeared behind the large set of shelving on which the various alcohols were displayed, a mixture of well-known Western brands of whisky and cognac, clear and coloured Korean concoctions and cans of Japanese and Korean beers arranged in pyramids. I thought she'd gone to find a tape recorder, but when she reappeared not only was she carrying her *kayagum*, a large, oblong wooden stringed instrument, one end of which she rested on the ground, the other on her lap, after she'd sat down beside me; but also she'd changed into a beautiful blue and purple traditional costume of long and full *chima* skirt and tiny *chogori* jacket.

For an hour that warm summer morning, in a simple, open room with a stone floor on which red pillars supported a carved wooden ceiling, I gazed out over the temple's traditional curved roofs to the towering green mountains behind and, mesmerised by the sound of ancient melodies played in the most tranquil and timeless of settings, I dreamed.

I was with Song Il, Kim Sok Nam and Driver Han in a large, marble-floored room. We were walking, the four of us side by side, along a red carpet. Ahead of us stood a group of men, three of them, two of whom were highly deferential to the third. In the background were four women, tall and graceful, dressed in long traditional skirts.

The four of us reached the group and we bowed. The women stepped forward and the man whom the others deferred to took medals from cushions the women held and pinned them to our breasts. Then he invited us to sit with him and the other men.

He had been asked, the man told us, to convey the thanks of the Party and the people for our efforts. We had saved one of the finest structures of the Workers' Party era, a hotel built by the sweat and blood of the Korean workers and a building the whole country was proud of.

He spoke in a hushed voice for a little while to my three companions and then turned to me. He understood that I was a friend of his country, he said, that I was working hard to edit the speeches of the great leader Comrade Kim Il Sung and the dear leader Comrade Kim Jong Il. He had heard that I was well liked by my friends and colleagues. But he was concerned that I might in some way be unhappy with my life in Korea, that there might be something he could do to make my situation a little more comfortable.

I said I wanted for nothing. I was happy in Pyongyang; I loved my visits to the mountains; I was proud to be doing my work. In my dream I truly was living in Paradise; all the people were happy, helping one another and leading one another forward, and I said I hoped to stay for a long time among them, perhaps making a small contribution to removing the one cloud that sullied an otherwise perfectly blue sky. I wanted to help in whatever way I could to attain the goal of reunification.

It was true, then, the man said after a pause, that I understood the reality of Korea, how the greatest sadness of the Korean people was that the country was divided. The nation appreciated friends who understood the reality. But if I wanted to stay longer, I would find it difficult to do so alone. Did I have a fiancée in England, he wanted to know. I said I did not and he commented that I was indeed sacrificing a lot by staying in his country to help attain the noble cause of reunification. He suggested I should consider choosing a Korean girl to make my wife, so that I could stay for longer, amid the blessing of all the Korean people.

The only problem was, I thought, as Song Il roused me from my dream, how would I go about getting back to the man on the question of one day taking my bride home with me? The prospect of becoming the master of a traditional Korean-style home was very appealing and doing so 'amid the blessing of all the Korean people' dealt with my concerns about a foreign marriage not being accepted by the general population. But the premise appeared to be that I would be staying put, and to raise the matter, even before we were married, of taking my bride out of the country would give the impression that my intention all along was to steal away one of the nation's daughters.

Song Il had come to fetch me because we had to go back to the Hyangsan Hotel as promised, to pay.

When we arrived there was no hotel manager or brass band or staff on parade to acclaim us. Clearly it had been decided our heroics were to be of the unassuming type after all. There wasn't even any sign of Mi Ran, and it took us a good half an hour to track her down.

'You did a big work,' she said, with what I took to be typical Korean understatement, as she took the money I gave her to cover the previous night's bill.

It was thanks to Madame Beatrice that I finally met the three Americans. She had been invited to play a leading role in a film, as a UN human rights observer visiting South Korea, and Cooper and I had been asked to go along as extras, members of her delegation. There, on the film set in the Koryo Hotel, we saw a tanned, grey-haired, fit-looking Westerner. 'There's Lewis,' someone whispered to me. His was the one name I had heard mentioned during my long investigation into mysterious Americans living in North Korea.

It had taken some years after Philippe first mentioned them before I'd believed that any of the rumoured American defectors even existed. There had been several reported sightings of unidentified foreigners and the occasional claim by a student or diplomat to have talked to a group of Americans. Initially I had dismissed these stories as too unlikely, and even after the weight of evidence had mounted sufficiently to convince me, there was still much that wasn't clear: how many of them were there, and how and why had they come to North Korea?

I had asked my Korean friends and they only knew about Lewis. He was famous, although 'Lewis' wasn't his real name. It was the name of the character he had played in the 20-part film epic *Unknown Heroes*. But none of them knew anything more about him.

Cooper and I were left to snatch a few words with Lewis on the sidelines of the shooting, while Madame Beatrice, in her starring role, took centre stage. Our whispered conversation revealed very little about our illustrious companion. Even after the banquet at the end of the day's shooting to thank us foreigners for our help, I was left thinking that I'd learned nothing about the mysterious American, even though I'd been sitting next to him. I had, however, picked up quite a bit of information about film-making, North Korean style. The dear leader would be overseeing our production, taking a look at the uncut version and making recommendations, Lewis had told me. No, he was unlikely to give instructions that we come back and start all over again. He was mainly concerned with the editing.

We ran into Lewis again at the shooting of another scene for the same film. This time he was with two companions. They were friendly enough, chatty even. But I never learned their proper names. I'm sure I must have asked. They were only occasional film actors, they told me. They were, in fact, English teachers and their students were trainees at the country's top spy school.

I said I'd heard there were four of them. There had been, they said. One of their number had passed away only recently. They lived together in a compound somewhere on the outskirts of Pyongyang. As far as they knew they were the only Americans in the country. Reports that hidden away somewhere there might still be a few US prisoners from the war were, to their knowledge, unfounded. They themselves had individually deserted

– although I don't think this was the word they used – from the US army in South Korea during the early 1960s.

Of the three, Lewis was the most likeable. He came across as being quite thoughtful. He was married to a Lebanese woman he'd met in North Korea, although how she'd come to be in the country, he didn't explain. Of his two companions, the large, blond man was a little loud, somewhat too forceful in his jolly bonhomie. The third was a shorter man, older and more withdrawn and uncomfortable, who reminisced about a time in the past when he'd served in the US army in Europe.

A small attempt at market liberalisation was to be attempted, promising happier economic times ahead for the long-suffering Korean people. A 'free shop', the Hyangmanru Department Store on Kwangbok Street, was to be opened, where people could indulge in the little-known activity of buying goods across the counter. Three things preceded this: the entire population was awarded a pay increase of between 20% and 40%; all my money was taken off me and replaced with new notes; and bicycles were permitted on the streets. While this latter fact had only an indirect personal connection with the opening of the 'free shop' and we foreigners were not covered by the hefty pay rise, the withdrawal of all the paper money in circulation and its replacement with new notes – still not bearing the great leader's image – heralded, I believe, a tentative economic opening which, like much that North Korea attempted, was thwarted by external events.

The new notes I was given were predominantly blue and those exchanged for soft currency were red. Someone, I was later told, had been upset that under the old monetary system banknotes issued for use by the socialist brethren had borne a blue stamp, while it was we capitalists who had the privilege of red money. So under the new system the colour scheme had been reversed.

The Hyangmanru Department Store opened under its new identity as a free shop with very little fanfare and was immediately mobbed. That people had money stashed away, there was no doubt; possibly replacing the currency in circulation had been a way of finding out how much they had. There had simply been nothing worth spending it on. So when the first opportunity presented itself to go to a shop and buy goods freely, there was an overwhelming response.

Korean friends told me that what was on sale was exclusively Korean-made and the prices were astronomical. None of the fancy Japanese goods that I was used to in the dollar shops and hotel boutiques; here it was simple items like sweets costing a month's salary, plastic basins for the kitchen, and bicycles manufactured by a joint venture with China.

I had a friend, a regular at the Koryo whom I often invited for a beer for no better reason than he never asked, and he had decided to buy me a gift, now that he could do so freely. Ever since the advent of bicycles on Pyongyang's streets – no longer, it seemed, were they considered a danger to the traffic – I'd been talking about buying one. But I'd been put off by the hundreds of dollars price tag for the imported Japanese models on sale at the dollar shops. So my friend decided he was going to buy me a good, solid, Korean–Chinese model. Having heard how much even sweets were at the new free shop, I tried to persuade him not to, but to no avail. He insisted, and so one evening I met him in the Youth Hotel and there I waited while he headed off across the road to make the purchase, not, he assured me, by battling through the crowds, but at a back door, where a friend who worked in the shop would be waiting with the bicycle.

It was a splendid bike, big and solid, and I rather enjoyed sweeping through Pyongyang on it, grinning cheerily in response to the looks of astonishment. But after a while all the attention I attracted became a little wearing. It was bad enough foreigners walking through the streets and taking the public transport, I imagined people saying to themselves, but fancy letting them out on bicycles! Aren't they all supposed to have cars to be driven around in?

The real problem, though, was the mutterings – wasn't that one of our bikes that foreigner was riding? One or two people I knew asked me directly how I'd come by a Korean bicycle. My friend had beseeched me not to tell anyone that he'd bought it for me – I supposed there was a danger people might think he'd been involved in something dodgy, perhaps currency trading – so I would reply, enigmatically I hoped, that a friend had bought it for me; a very rich friend.

He had revealed to me rather proudly, when he presented me with my bike, that it had cost him the equivalent of a year's salary.

The experiment with Pyongyang's first free shop was soon ended. I thought it likely that the country's worsening economic plight had made it necessary to revert to the safe and familiar ground of socialist distribution.

Cooper and I ran into Lewis and his wife by chance in a hotel bar when we were on a late summer break in Wonsan. But even Cooper, without my reticence in tackling personal questions born of five years in North Korea, failed to elicit much more information from them, despite coming directly to the point on the matter of what had prompted Lewis to make his fateful move to the North back in 1963. The answer was the stock condemnation of South Korean society and disgust at the depravity surrounding the US troops there.

Cooper had left by the time, several months later, I ran into the three Americans again, on another film set. I was due to leave for a trip to Beijing within a few days of filming a scene in which I found myself playing a British colonel plotting with MacArthur – played by the large American – and his senior officers – the other two – the attack on North Korea in 1950. I made a point, in quiet conversations, of telling them I would be out of the country. Maybe they didn't get the hint, or maybe they weren't interested, or maybe they were fearful. Anyway, they didn't respond. I'd been prepared to take a message out for them, despite the inevitable furore news of their existence would cause in the outside world. There was also the matter of the danger I faced of incurring the displeasure of the North Korean authorities.

Despite their reticence, I was struck by the Americans' normality. But perhaps that was more a reflection of what I myself was becoming. They were outwardly relaxed; quite jolly, in fact. They enjoyed an easy familiarity with the Korean people around them. They never had a word of criticism of their lot. Then again, they never gave a hint of what was really going on inside their heads.

What made them different from me was that coming to North Korea had for them been a permanent move. It occurred to me that they might have been kidnapped, but they never gave any sign that their decision to cross the 38th Parallel had been anything but voluntary. So I had to assume that as young men they had, whether for ideological or for personal reasons, turned their backs on families and friends in the US and their army colleagues, and come to a strange country they could have no certainty of ever leaving.

They had missed out on being a part of the explosion of cultural excitement and political activism that had been the 1960s. Had they heard when their countryman had set foot on the moon? The 1970s and the Vietnam War had passed them by; if they had been relieved at missing out on the Vietnam draft, how must they have felt when that war had ended? The Watergate Scandal must have been presented to them as proof of the inherent corruption within the political system they had turned their backs on. Then there had been the thaw in the Cold War of the 1980s, the cause of relief for most of the world, but the first sign of the breaking up of an ideological camp that they had, for whatever reason, made their own.

What had been their reaction when the *Pueblo* was captured, or when the American soldiers were axed to death at Panmunjom? Had they rejoiced at the periodic signs of improvement in Pyongyang's relations with the rest of the world, the North–South talks of 1972, for example, when the famous joint declaration had been adopted?[13] Or had they dreaded the personal ramifications: being returned to the justice of a military they had deserted?

What exactly was their status in North Korea, and how did they cope with their situation? I had to assume that they weren't free to leave, if for no other reason than they were wanted for desertion by the US military. They seemed to get on well enough together, but what strains must their friendship have gone through during more than a quarter of a century? It was difficult enough for the rest of us to cope in such an alien environment,

---

[13] A Joint Communiqué announced by North and South Korea on July 4th 1972, following the first contacts between the two for more than a quarter of a century to discuss the question of reunification, called for establishing a 'North–South Coordinating Committee' and the exchange of Red Cross delegations.

but we at least had the option of leaving if the pressures became intolerable.

All these questions I would have loved to have asked. But for three men who had been starved of contact with the outside world for so long, they had a strange knack of not opening up in conversation.

For a time it seemed that fate had been leading me, like it had the Americans, to throw in my lot with North Korea, although the circumstances were wholly different.

I'd always known the dream I'd had in the Myohyang Mountains was desperately naïve; never more so than when the other girls in the Koryo had told me she was getting married. I had to go downstairs and confront her, they'd said. I should be encouraged, not put off by her anger. I'd gone to talk to her and she'd smiled. No, it wasn't true, she'd said.

Still, I'd decided it was time to act, but I hadn't known what was expected of me. I knew that a friend should be involved and so I'd told Song Il the story, and for him the matter was simple. He'd asked if I loved her. Yes, I'd said.

Song Il had returned with the vice-director of the publishing house. He had heard that I wanted to get married. He knew the whole story because Song Il had told him. I should look on him as my father, he'd said. He would talk to the girl himself, find out what her feelings were; make sure there was no misunderstanding.

But the vice-director hadn't gone to see her, Song Il had told me the following evening, and the next day Song Il had telephoned and got permission from him for us to go and talk to her ourselves.

It was Saturday afternoon and unusually the place was quite busy. She'd sat with us on one of the sofas. She was very sorry, she'd said, but there had been some misunderstanding. Yes, she was marrying – next week, in fact.

I appreciated the gesture; of a weekend away to think things over. The choice of destination, however, left much to be desired. Compared to the beauty of the mountains and the fascination of Kaesong and Panmunjom, industrial Hamhung had little to recommend itself, even at the best of times.

One of my two companions was Mr Li, the head of the English *Works* Section. I'd built up a genuine liking for him. He was very proud of the fact that he'd once visited England, as a young interpreter for the famous 1966 North Korean World Cup team, no less. Naturally this revelation sparked my interest, but I never managed to elicit any more information about the trip and his first-hand experience of the heroics of the national football team than that he remembered how good the fish was in Middlesbrough.

It was an overnight train journey from Pyongyang to Hamhung on the East coast, and as usual we had the foreigners' carriage to ourselves; I had my own compartment and Mr Li and my other companion, a young translator called Dong Il, were next door. A couple of guards were on hand to serve beer and snacks.

Hamhung was famous for its heavy machinery works and for its fertiliser factory, and when I discovered that these were the two main agenda items I realised why neither Ho Gwang nor Song Il had been anxious to come with me. The city also had a reputable dental hospital and I agreed, readily enough, that we should pay it a visit instead of the fertiliser factory, which, Mr Li told me without even a flicker of a smile, might be best avoided since he imagined it was rather smelly.

I was in the foyer of my hotel in the afternoon, waiting for my driver to take me to the Ryongsong Heavy Machinery Plant, when I ran into some African friends who were studying at the Hamhung University of Medicine. I knew them from Pyongyang, where they visited as often as time and their highly strained finances would permit. They were delighted to see me; a fresh face was always welcome, they said, in a city with only a handful of foreigners, one foreign currency restaurant, a noodle place and just one hotel bar, which opened 'when Ma Hui feels like it'. That tended only to be on the highly infrequent occasions when the hotel had any guests. With our fingers crossed, we agreed to meet there later that evening.

The factory tour consisted of depictions of heroic workers and heroic machines which, like the people, had earned distinction by working without interruption for long periods and vastly exceeding their production quotas. There were the usual photographs of the great leader and the dear leader visiting the factory and inscriptions of the wisdom they had imparted to improve heavy machinery production.

I tried to make the right noises and to ask some vaguely apposite questions, but within half an hour of the visit ending I could remember no more about the machinery and its production than I'd known before I'd set foot inside the factory.

Because I liked both Mr Li and Dong Il, I did the decent thing and informed them that I was going out with some friends for a beer or two that evening. In retrospect, that might have been a mistake.

I vetoed a proposal by the students to go to the noodle place. Hamhung was famous for its noodles, which were whiter and 'more elastic' than those in Pyongyang. Frankly, I'd never got used to eating cold noodles, and although I could well believe that the Hamhung variety was more appetising than the greying mush that was the great Pyongyang delicacy, the very sight of which made my stomach turn, I voted for the foreign currency restaurant, which turned out to be a small, dingy place cluttered with large wooden tables and benches that had pretensions of being Japanese.

There were four students, two each from Lesotho and Zambia, and myself. There were no other guests in the restaurant. As the students told me, hardly anyone in Hamhung had any hard currency. Life, they explained, was intensely dull, brightened only by the more ready availability of the local girls. While not prepared to be seen in public with any foreigner and especially not an African, they might be persuaded to join them in a secret assignation. The point was that the girls had nothing to lose; the trouble with Pyongyang girls was that they feared being deported from the capital in disgrace if they were discovered being involved in any sort of relationship with a foreigner.

I'd just ordered the latest of several rounds of beer and we were contemplating whether to order something to eat when the girl who was serving us announced that the restaurant was closed. She held the telephone receiver in her hand.

The students were astounded. There were still several hours to go before the regular closing time. At first they laughed it off, but they became quite irritated when the waitress insisted we had to finish our drinks quickly and leave. They remonstrated, but she was adamant.

We drank up and headed for the door. We intended to try the famous noodle restaurant, which one of the students, in high dudgeon, told the waitress was our plan.

'That's closed, too,' she said and looked straight at me.

I began to smell a rat. She'd received a phone call, had immediately closed her restaurant and had assumed – or had been told – that the only other place in town where beer was served, apart from my hotel, was also closed.

Two of the students went with me back to the hotel bar. A genial Mr Li was waiting for us. 'I was wondering where you had got to,' he said.

I shrugged and ordered him a beer. Dong Il joined us. I thought about asking them why they'd dragged me out of the restaurant. But I was tired, and what was the point? They'd deny it and anyway they were only doing their duty.

I don't know if it was his way of making up for spoiling my evening, but as we sat in the bar after the students had left, Mr Li told me a small secret. 'You are very important to the publishing house,' he said confidentially. 'That is why we take special care of you.'

He thought for moment. 'You know,' he said, 'there was a time in the past when I had to fight very hard to keep you in my country.'

'When was that?' I asked.

'Some time ago.' It was all he would say on the subject. I could only think that the matter of the South Korean music tape had been taken just as seriously as I'd feared at the time.

But my mistake had been forgiven. It was reassuring to know that there were forces at work looking after me.

Chapter 9

*D*espite its efforts to win friends internationally, North Korea is generally hostile to the outside world. It's an attitude that rests on two complaints, the first of which is that it is misunderstood, often deliberately so. North Koreans, especially after the fall of communism elsewhere, have been quite prepared to admit they are different. But that does not mean they are wrong, even if the unique ideology they are pursuing challenges certain principles taken for granted in other, capitalist societies. For example, the unquestioned leadership of the Party and the leader, they argue, is essential for providing the consistent guidance needed in the long-term pursuit of the noble cause of building a paradise on earth.

The second complaint is that the major powers have never really atoned for the harm they did to Korea throughout the twentieth century. For most of the first half of the century the peninsula was under Japanese rule; the end of the occupation, far from heralding a new dawn of freedom for the oppressed Korean people, brought further tragedy when the division of the peninsula was imposed on them by the United States and the Soviet Union.

And then came the Korean War, which the Americans had to be shown to have started if North Korea was to present itself again as the victim and the US forces left in South Korea afterwards were to be labelled an army of occupation. The trouble is that the rest of the world has consistently believed that North Korea started the war and that the US stayed in South Korea as protectors.

So, as the 40th anniversary of the end of the Korean War approached, a slim book written by a one-time adviser to the

American military government in Seoul, and subsequently South Korean ambassador to the United Nations, attracted considerable attention among North Korea's friends.

In *The Korean War – An Unanswered Question*, Channing Liem[1] relates an episode that took place in Japan on the morning of June 25th 1950, the day war broke out:

> That morning John Guntner, a prominent author, and his wife were on a sight-seeing trip in Nikko, accompanied by two of [Supreme Commander of the Allied Occupying Forces in Japan Douglas] MacArthur's aides. When they returned to their hotel for mid-morning tea, one of MacArthur's aides was called to the telephone. When he came back to rejoin the others, he whispered to them in suppressed excitement, 'A big story has just broken. The south Koreans have attacked the north.' But the Guntner party was told on its return to Tokyo by MacArthur's staff that the initial report was inaccurate; the fact was that the 'north Koreans had attacked the south'. Considering that the original version of MacArthur's aide's report continued to circulate in Tokyo during that afternoon, Guntner's retraction of it as a 'misunderstanding' seems unconvincing.

The evidence is hardly conclusive, but is nevertheless intriguing as it calls into question the version of events generally accepted outside North Korea. And if one reads the whole book, the conclusion is also interesting that the Korean War did not start with an unprovoked attack out of the blue, as both sides have claimed, but was preceded by years of incursion and counter-incursion, attack and counter-attack, across the 38th Parallel. The war, it seems, was inevitable.

[1] Found in *Korea Today*, 1993, 6.

War Games

*T*he man standing at the top of the flight of marble steps was surprised to see us. He was holding a clipboard, which he looked at before asking, 'Which delegation is your foreigner from?'

'He is from the Foreign Languages Press Group, from the English Section editing the great leader's *Works*,' said one of my interpreters, giving the stock response.

The man was suitably impressed. 'I'm sorry,' he said, making a note on his clipboard. 'There must have been some misunderstanding. I didn't know any foreign guests would be attending today. The other dignitaries will not be arriving for another hour.'

It was clear to me, though apparently not to the man with the clipboard, that my two companions were discomfited. 'It's our mistake,' one of them said. 'We will come back at the proper time.'

We had taken time off work to visit the Revolutionary Martyrs' Cemetery. It had been the idea of one of my two companions, Ho Gwang. Bored one afternoon, he had fancied a trip out. But in order to qualify for a car and the time off work he needed a foreign volunteer. So he'd asked me if I would like a trip to the cemetery and I'd said yes. The prospect of some time off work appealed to me, too, even though I'd been there at least half a dozen times before.

Developments on the international scene were promising improved relations for North Korea with the outside world, even after a diplomatic blow fell that was so devastating that even a month later the regime had not been able to bring itself to tell the population.

In August 1992 China had established diplomatic relations with South Korea. Unlike the furore when the Soviet Union had followed the lead of the Eastern European socialist countries and established ties with Seoul, China's betrayal went unreported in North Korea. Presumably the leadership could not own up to this final humiliation; perhaps also it was reluctant to let its people know that the economic situation, which declined rapidly in the wake of Moscow–Seoul ties being established, could be expected to get even worse.

The blow came at a time when Pyongyang appeared to be emerging, albeit slowly, from its diplomatic isolation. International Atomic Energy Agency inspections of its nuclear facilities had gone ahead during the summer and were continuing in the autumn, one of the preconditions set by Washington for the normalisation of diplomatic relations. Pyongyang had also met other conditions; in May it had returned the remains of some 30 GIs Missing in Action from the Korean War and had toned down the anti-US hysteria at the time of the June anniversary of the start of the Korean War. Then in July, President Bush made an announcement on the withdrawal of US tactical nuclear weapons from Asia and Europe and the Defence Department confirmed that there were no nuclear weapons on South Korean soil.

There had been further meetings between the prime ministers of the two Koreas, which had even brought agreement on family exchange visits. Japan and North Korea were continuing to talk. But still the concrete successes Pyongyang had been hoping for – formal ties with the United States, diplomatic recognition and compensation from Japan and acceptance by South Korea of its reunification proposals – had failed to materialise.

Our companion at the cemetery was Ho Gwang's friend, a translator from the publishing house's Spanish department who, according to Ho Gwang, had heard from a friend just back from a trip abroad that the Chinese had opened diplomatic relations with South Korea. They wanted to know whether it was true.

I told them it was. The timing, I thought, was unfortunate; only a month previously plans had been announced to build a vast monument to celebrate victory in the Fatherland Liberation War, a triumph achieved only after North Korea, in its hour of greatest need, had found support from its truest of friends and allies, China.

Even by Pyongyang standards the array of bronze statues would be extraordinary in their grandeur. Reached through a spectacular, high archway, a dozen bronze sculptures standing on marble plinths would depict various events from the war involving the three services of the Korean People's Army: the capture of Taejon, the sea battle off Jumunjin, the defence of Wolmi Island and of Height 1211. These would line a broad, stone-clad pathway that would lead up to one vast marble and bronze creation called simply 'Victory'.

The grand construction of the North Korean capital was proceeding apace, despite the country's economic situation, which had declined rapidly as trade with Eastern Europe and the Soviet Union had dried up. Fifty thousand flats had been completed in a brand new residential development, Tongil – or Reunification – Street, to mark Kim Il Sung's 80th birthday, and a further 30,000 were planned for completion across the capital in time for the celebrations of the 40th anniversary of victory in the Fatherland Liberation War.

The economic problems were so severe that for once the authorities admitted as much; people were being urged to tighten their belts and eat only two meals a day. But old habits died hard and even the suffering of the local population apparently did little to diminish the determination to pretend to us foreigners that all was well. So we were shielded from the worst of the economic crisis. Our food was not noticeably poorer in terms of quantity or quality; I supposed that Mrs Kim the guest house manager was obliged to cut down on the dinner invitations to her bosses. For a time there were two rather than three cars at the disposal of the foreigners at the Ansan Guest House. When our interpreters admitted that the reason was the need to conserve the country's desperately low fuel stocks, we rallied round and took to the streets on foot and by public transport. The gesture was appreciated, we were told, but we were asked to make more use of the cars after the drivers pointed out that, by returning to their parking place every night with tanks half full, they risked having their rations cut even further. Before long we had three cars again. The drivers had reported to their bosses that the foreigners were forced to take to the streets on foot and by public transport, and the third car had been reinstated.

Despite the reluctance to admit to the economic difficulties, there was some talk of reducing our salaries. When the idea was put to me directly, I said that I would accept as long as the cut applied equally to all those paid in dollars. I was prepared to cooperate because I was conscious more acutely than at any other time of the wealth and privilege I continued to enjoy, even as the people around me were suffering more. I hadn't needed reminding of this by the irate English-speaking Korean I met in the Koryo Hotel, who had found fault with a translation of a Kim Il Sung speech I had edited – a misplaced comma or something equally trivial – and had demanded to know what I thought I was doing, taking so much money for such shoddy work.

I asked him what he did to earn the foreign currency that allowed him to drink in the Koryo, and he told me angrily it was none of my business. But I had to admit to myself that he had a point about my salary. My feeling was that, if savings had to be made anywhere by the government, they could do away with the foreign language revisers. Surely they could accept a few odd-sounding English phrases and some dodgy punctuation in the interests of spending the thousands of dollars I earned every year to the benefit of the population at large, not to mention diverting the food I was given to a more needy cause.

So it was with mixed feelings that I was told our salaries would not be reduced. Other foreigners had said they would not stay on and work for less money. Thus they brought home to me the dilemma I was facing; I was anxious to be seen showing solidarity, but the privileges of the comparatively high foreign currency salary, the food, and the car and driver were the compensation that made bearable the restrictions, the lack of privacy and the monotony of life. Take away the privileges without doing something about the negatives and I, too, could see myself leaving. Keep them in place, however, and sooner or later it would be my sense of guilt that would probably be what eventually made me leave anyway.

But I would be contributing to the cause, I was told. I would be doing more work, editing *The Pyongyang Times* and the magazines. Cooper was not being replaced. The publishing house could no longer afford two English language revisers.

'So what's going on?' I joked as we walked back down the steps at the Revolutionary Martyrs' Cemetery. My two companions were looking anxious, rather like schoolboys fearful of being caught out after not doing their homework. What was the significance of the day, they wondered, that was bringing some high-ranking officials here?

The driver, it seemed, was the best person to ask.

September 22nd, he mused after we'd stirred him from his nap in his car seat, which he'd set in the reclining position. Of course, it was the anniversary of the death of the Mother of Korea, Kim Jong Suk. I kicked myself. I knew that. Kim Jong Suk had died in 1949, officially as a result of the hardships she had endured during the years as a guerrilla fighter. Unofficially she was said to have died in childbirth.

With part of the problem thus solved, we had to decide what to do. The man with the clipboard had my details and it would look very strange, if not downright rude, if I weren't to come back later as promised. Etiquette dictated that I should lay a wreath or some flowers before the tomb. Fortunately, the botanical garden was nearby. It was a safe bet they would have some flowers, the driver pointed out. Whether or not they would be for sale, well, we supposed, we could at least ask.

We managed to persuade a girl to sell us a handful of flowers. Clutching these and having made sure that people were starting to gather, I led the way back to the Revolutionary Martyrs' Cemetery, where it seemed I was expected. The original man had been joined at the top of the steps by another, evidently more senior, official who made a little speech about friends around the world who admired the indomitable woman revolutionary and thanking me for taking the trouble to turn up and show my respects.

The more important man led me to the front of the crowd standing at a short distance from the bronze bust of Kim Jong Suk, and asked me to wait a moment. He glanced to the left and, following his gaze, I saw a line of black cars with tinted windows pull silently up at the foot of a slight rise. One by one the drivers stepped out and opened a rear door for their passengers, one to each car, all of them dark-suited men with the exception of an immaculately turned-out woman dressed in what looked like a woollen suit, cream coloured. A hush fell on the crowd behind me and in silence the group, numbering about ten people, climbed up to the bust and laid flowers before it, formed a line, took a step back and bowed. Then they filed away to the left, back to their cars and as they did so the more important man was urging me forward. Alone, I stepped up, reverently laid my flowers, and bowed. I didn't, however, file away to the left. Instead I shuffled off to the back of the crowd to find my interpreters and driver who, sadly, had not been able to see and therefore identify my fellow VIP guests. They would look in the papers the next day, they told me.

I read the following day's Korean Central News Agency report on the ceremony to honour Kim Jong Suk and, while the senior

Party and Government officials who had attended were listed in full, there was no mention of me, the lone foreigner. It was just as I had expected. The propagandists had failed to take up my cause when I'd saved the famous Hyangsan Hotel from burning down, so it was hardly surprising that my demonstration of loyalty, albeit inadvertent, had gone unreported.

The Hyangsan Hotel is symbolic of a more pragmatic approach by North Korea to its dealings with the West. When it was built in 1986 the country was realising that it needed the rest of the world for its trade and that tourism might be a pretty good foreign currency earner. Tourists from the Eastern bloc, who had been the mainstay of the industry, were all very well, but it was those from the West who had the hard currency the economy needed.

Western visitors would no doubt be interested in the revolutionary sights of Pyongyang and in Panmunjom and the US aggressor army just across the frontier, was the traditional line of thinking. They would enjoy seeing a revolutionary opera and visiting the schoolchildren's palace, where young geniuses demonstrated the benefits of a Juche education by the perfection of their accordion playing, their remarkable dexterity in embroidering tablecloths and rebuilding a car's engine, and the speed with which they could dismantle and reassemble a Kalashnikov.

Special tours would be available, too. Visitors could spend a small fortune on mud baths designed to cure any number of ailments, from arthritis to impotency, at clinics located near some mud with special curative powers. The more romantically inclined tourists could come for a Korean-style wedding, although the itinerary of dinners for two and sailing in a flower-bedecked boat bore little resemblance to what I'd seen of Korean weddings, which appeared to consist of little more than being driven around Pyongyang to be photographed at numerous scenic or revolutionary spots, prior to lunch.

The tourist was also offered the possibility of coming for a study tour, which combined the regular itinerary of visits to the president's birthplace, the Juche Tower and the Arch of Triumph with the pursuit of some special interest, such as studying the Juche Idea.

The tourist people were nothing if not adaptable, as a group of British train enthusiasts I once met had discovered. They had rendered their hosts nonplussed by spending much of their two-week stay asking to take a trip by steam locomotive. This, I told them, was an incomprehensible request in a country that boasted loud and long about its success in electrifying the railways. Still, a steam train was rustled up for a short trip, and in the meantime the happy tourists indulged another of their interests, collecting beer bottle labels.

Eventually a certain amount of pragmatism found its way into the tourism promotion effort. Visitors, someone decided, might simply enjoy roaming across North Korea's mountains, enjoying the fresh air in spectacular scenery. With this in mind, a new hotel, the Hyangsan, was built in the Myohyang Mountains.

By the early 1980s construction had become the watchword, and grandiose projects were undertaken nationwide, as the country became obsessed with the idea that the rest of the world would be so impressed by its buildings as to be convinced that all was well with the North Korean economy and that the political system, which demonstrated such concern for the ordinary people, truly was exemplary. Pyongyang was being transformed; new residential districts, principally Changgwang-*gori*, were rising, as was the Koryo Hotel. More monuments, including the Juche Tower and the Arch of Triumph, were being built, along with facilities such as the Maternity Hospital.

All this was happening at a time when the economy was, in fact, struggling. There was still talk of meeting the people's basic needs for food, clothing and housing, suggesting that more than 30 years of economic planning had failed to achieve even this fundamental objective. It was said to have been around the beginning of the 1980s that the strict system of rationing food and other everyday items was introduced. But the building went on, as if to prove to the people themselves and to the outside world that essentially they were doing pretty well.

The grandest undertaking of them all was the West Sea Barrage at Nampo. It was one of four major construction projects for harnessing nature outlined by Kim Il Sung in October 1981, the other three being the Taechon Power Station, the reclamation of 300,000 hectares of tideland and the development of 200,000 hectares of new farmland. Clearly the great leader was worried about the food situation.

The eight kilometre-long West Sea Barrage represents a truly massive engineering feat. Construction was undertaken by the Korean People's Army and the word 'heroism' is lavished on descriptions of how the soldiers managed to complete the job. Sadly some deaths were reported, particularly when work was being done under water, although the numbers vary from the few who perished performing self-sacrificing exploits, as described in the North Korean media, to the pointless waste of hundreds of young lives, as was rumoured among Pyongyang's community of disgruntled foreign diplomats.

The dam's purposes are many: to regulate the water level in the port of Nampo, thus allowing large ships to dock; to prevent the flooding of the River Taedong that has devastated Pyongyang in the past; to stop ice floes from disrupting navigation on the river in winter; and to make irrigation water available for the newly reclaimed tidelands in its vicinity. To believe North Korean accounts, there have been further benefits. Wildlife has flourished as the temperature of the Taedonggang has risen slightly and its salt content has fallen.

But the foreign detractors and environmentalists have other ideas. The dam's construction in a matter of just five years – a reason for triumphant boasting by North Koreans – was a rush job and it was already crumbling within weeks of its completion, the detractors insist. The environmentalists say it was ill-conceived and has been an unmitigated environmental disaster. Whole species of river life, insects and plants, have been killed off, with disastrous consequences for the delicate ecological balance. The cause is the higher salt levels in the water, a consequence of the dam's construction that should have been foreseen.

Nampo and its great barrage were a 40-minute drive from Pyongyang and so a favourite place to spend a Sunday. We would visit the Seamen's Club, have a drink in the restaurant beneath the lighthouse and perhaps take some beers onto the beach. In between times we might take a stroll through the city's streets and visit a couple of shops. The place was neat and tidy but lacked the grandeur of Pyongyang. All in all it was possible to spend a very ordinary and – probably because of that – highly enjoyable day there.

One Sunday, Song Il and I were taking a car to Nampo when our driver dropped casually into the conversation that he was getting very low on petrol. Song Il, who I'd have thought would be anxious, if only about the prospect of being criticised for causing a foreigner in his charge to be abandoned in the middle of nowhere, merely smiled at the news and asked me for cigarettes. No, he didn't want a Dunhill, he said. He wanted a packet of Korean cigarettes.

We were pulling out to overtake an army lorry. At first I thought the manoeuvre had finished off the car's petrol, because we immediately started slowing. But then I saw that Song Il, who was in the front passenger seat, was leaning out of the window and waving the lorry down. It stopped and he and the two drivers got out for a chat. He passed cigarettes around and then handed a whole packet over to the man with the lorry. Then I saw our driver, who had gone round to the boot, reappear with a length of hosepipe and a bucket, which he used to siphon petrol from the lorry's tank. Overseeing the process was the lorry driver, who was making me very nervous by leaning over the bucket to oversee the operation with one of my cigarettes lighted and dangling from his mouth.

The army, Song Il explained as we watched our driver siphon the petrol into the car's tank, had plenty to spare.

A Korean businessman friend who, despite the country's economic difficulties, was clearly doing well for himself – so well, in fact, that the opinion of those who knew him was that he was an arms dealer, although he himself made vague references to commodity trade – once complained to me that his house was freezing cold in the winter. Buy yourself a heater, I told him. If he could afford to run his rather sporty car and to eat out apparently whenever he felt like it in the most expensive restaurants, an electric heater would represent only an incidental expense.

Had I seen any in the shops, he asked. Come to think of it, I hadn't. It was just one of those items, he explained, that, like electric ovens, were banned from sale, even in the dollar shops. The reason was that they used too much power. I suggested he should bring one back into the country with him, the next time he went on one of his business trips. No, he said. In this the authorities were serious and the customs people would confiscate it.

They were serious also, he said, about the ban on Koreans driving private vehicles on Sundays. The oil situation was becoming desperate after the Soviet Union had begun demanding hard currency payment for supplies. Under the strict new rationing system, Koreans were not even permitted to take a taxi on Sundays. Since the ban did not apply to foreigners, my friend said after buying a couple of rounds of drinks, would I mind calling a taxi and dropping him off at home?

Our drivers knocked off work at around six in the evening, which made it rather tricky to have dinner at the rather good Chinese restaurant that had opened above the Hyangmanru Department Store on Kwangbok Street. It was a long way home, so whenever I went there I tended to make an evening of it, walking to the Youth Hotel just across the street after I'd eaten. I liked the games room there, with Pyongyang's first *pachinko* parlour and the only fully equipped, full-size snooker table I ever came across in the capital. I was also rather taken by the neon sign above the bar where customers hired the cues and balls. It read: 'Pleasuring Equipment'.

The nearest taxi station to Kwangbok Street and the Youth Hotel was at the Potonggang Hotel and the drivers were reluctant to come such a long way – about six kilometres – to pick up passengers. As it was, I came to quite enjoy the walk home, even though it was a long one and I always had the thought at the back of my mind that I was crossing a military area.

One night I was going home very late; it must have been close to midnight when I found myself on the most open stretch of road, around the midway point between the Youth Hotel and our guest house. It was dark and I was almost up to the huge black shape before I noticed it.

It was a tank, the end one in a column that I could just make out stretching up the road ahead of me. There was another column of tanks on the other side of the road, which like those on my side had their huge guns pointing outwards. Down the centre of the road was what appeared to be a line of lorries.

I must confess I was frightened. I was on my own. Just ahead were hostile men and machines. Among the rolling hills to both sides were military installations and each shadowy undulation could hide a sniper, his sights trained on me. As for behind me, there was no heading back the way I'd come, as that would surely invite the suspicion of the unseen men up ahead who must be watching me. What would happen if some officer decided I had seen something I shouldn't have? Undoubtedly he was a spy, the officer's report would read. If not, what was a foreigner doing after dark in a restricted area? We did what was right to protect our unit.

The authorities would no doubt agree, but they would be concerned about having to explain a dead foreigner with a bullet hole in him. To avoid a fuss it might be wise simply to lose the body. It was a terrible accident, they might say. He so loved Kumgangsan and what a tragedy it was that he should slip on a cliff there and plunge to his death in the sea. And no-one would contradict the official story.

The whole convoy had come to a halt and so, on heavy, unsteady legs I passed beneath the guns of the line of tanks on my side of the road. As I walked I kept my eyes fixed straight ahead rather than inviting suspicion by looking to the sides and appearing to show any interest. I was entertaining the utterly bizarre notion that I could give the impression I hadn't even noticed this demonstration of North Korea's military might. And nothing happened, for which I was grateful. I dreaded hearing a shouted order to me to stop or the column starting to move again as I was passing. All I wanted to do was get through it as quickly as possible.

In the light of the following day it seemed reasonable to assume that someone had realised my encounter with the military had been entirely casual. So I decided I should make the same journey by foot a few days later, my somewhat illogical reasoning being that, by not changing my routine as a result of the incident, I would prove that I had nothing to hide. As things turned out, my confidence that I was presumed innocent was left a little dented.

I'd left the Youth Hotel and had just turned the corner onto the long road where I'd run across the military convoy and that led ultimately to the guest house, when someone greeted me. 'Where are you from?' said a voice in Korean. 'England,' I said, staring into the darkness in search of whoever was speaking. I heard some chatter. 'You speak our language very well,' said the same voice. 'Oh, just a little,' I replied. 'Where are you going?' I was asked, and four soldiers emerged from the shadows. 'To the Ansan Guest House,' I told them. 'It's near the Potonggang Hotel,' I added, since very few people had any idea where the Ansan Guest House was. 'Let's go together,' the soldiers said.

So we did and we had a good time. One of them leant me his rifle and I showed them how the British Army marched, which they thought was very funny. We discussed my life in Korea, what I thought about the country, and beer. I said I was very happy to be there and I was very fond of Korean people. They said they would be delighted to share a drink with me some time. 'When?' I asked, jokingly. 'Tomorrow evening,' they said.

I was fairly certain they wouldn't show up. Even so, at more or less the appointed time I passed the spot where we'd arranged to meet, just to make sure. I'd even bought some beer, just in case, which I drank when I got home.

My adventures walking back from the Youth Hotel, although making me conscious that I was probably still being watched, nevertheless left me feeling that I was on pretty good terms with the Korean People's Army. So I felt almost personally aggrieved at the behaviour one Saturday afternoon of the Japanese Koreans who were the regular customers at the golf driving range by the Sosan Hotel, not far from Kwangbok Street.

I found it a pleasant diversion, not only at weekends but also in the evenings when the light permitted, to spend an hour or so hitting some golf balls. I reasoned that if I ever got any good at it, I might occasionally pay the exorbitant price and join Marek for a round at the international golf course. If the weather was fine I might enjoy a barbecue on the driving range's terrace. It was a good place to meet Korean friends, since it was outdoors and they could relax and talk quite freely. It was also very pleasant to sit there alone, in reflective solitude, and gaze on the rolling scenery.

That was what I was doing when a troop of soldiers appeared on a rise just beyond the 300 metre mark. 'Fore!' one of the Japanese Koreans cried, unleashing a massive drive. 'Fore!' came several more cries as a whole volley of golf balls was fired off at the soldiers. 'Fore!' cried virtually the entire clientele, including several people who'd rushed outside from their dinners to grab any available club and ball.

The situation might be looking up in the international arena, I thought to myself, but it wasn't so safe as to treat the heroic defenders of the Motherland with such ingratitude.

An additional benefit brought by the West Sea Barrage, we were led to believe, was that the water of the River Taedong, when it flowed through Pyongyang, was clearer after the dam's construction, and that was good for the fish and hence the many fishermen who during the summer months lined the banks of the capital's two rivers. Fishing was a pastime the great leader encouraged his people – principally the men – to take up, and he gave orders that the Taedonggang and its tributary the Potonggang should be stocked with fish so that people could enjoy this most peaceful and harmless of diversions.

I didn't see the rivers before the dam was constructed, but afterwards their waters looked anything but 'crystal clear', as the propaganda described them. Rather, they looked quite murky, although this didn't seem to deter the fishermen, who spent contemplative afternoons and evenings sitting or squatting on their banks.

Song Il preferred to go out of town on fishing trips. He seemed to know where all the best places were and on one occasion he assured me that he had it on good authority that the Mirim Reservoir had just been restocked with fish from the local fish farm. To hear him speak, you'd have thought that we – that is himself, me, the driver and a cook – would hardly need bother attaching our hooks and bait. So teeming was the reservoir with fish that if they didn't simply leap into our buckets we could always merely lean over the water and grab a couple. It was just the place, Song Il assured me, for a novice such as myself to learn the ropes.

The cook was coming along because we'd decided that a good, spicy fish soup would do splendidly for lunch. Catching the necessary fish would be the work of but a moment and then it would be a matter of what to do in the afternoon.

We set off soon after breakfast and by three o'clock, after four or five hours of fishing, we were hungry and irritable. We'd caught nothing and apart from demanding to know from Song Il who was the joker who had told him the reservoir was teeming with fish, I was wondering who it was that had insisted on not bringing any food other than the spices for the fish soup. Song Il told me testily it had been my idea.

I took the line that I was new to fishing, yet Song Il and the driver passed themselves off as experts. Even the cook, in discussions about bait and floats and the length of the line, had revealed knowledge far greater than mine. So, I asked, if they were all such experts, how come we'd caught nothing while the chap at the end of the promenade had filled two buckets, using what appeared to be a stick with a bit of string tied to it?

Song Il thought for a moment and said, 'I'll go and ask him.' Incidentally, he wanted to know, did I have a couple of packets of my *Paek Ma*?

Two packets of cigarettes for five fish seemed a fair enough trade. At least we didn't starve and more importantly we would be able to tell people back at the guest house that yes, the fish soup had been delicious.

'Did you catch anything?' the elderly lady asked.

'Just a couple of little ones,' I replied. I was trudging along a narrow path that led to the main road back to our hotel in the Myohyang Mountains, having spent another unsuccessful day fishing with Song Il. My rod was over my shoulder and I had a bucket in my other hand. I looked the part, I supposed, and as fishermen's tales went mine was quite modest.

There was, in fact, nothing in my bucket, and I couldn't decide whether I would tell the lady we had eaten the 'couple of little ones' or thrown them back, if she were to take a look. It was as I was sidling past her, shielding the bucket from her gaze, that I was struck by the thought that it didn't seem to have occurred to her that I was a foreigner. She'd spoken in Korean and hadn't batted an eyelid when I'd replied in the same language.

As I waited on the road for Song Il to catch me up, I found my mind running away with illusions of achieving some ground-breaking acceptance into North Korean society. But then I was brought back to reality when I remembered the girl in the Pyongyang Department Store from whom I hadn't bought washing powder a month or so previously.

I'd asked her very politely in Korean what was the price of the washing powder and she'd clearly understood, since she called to her friend at the opposite counter, 'How do I say four *won* in Russian?' 'Four *won*,' was what I assumed her friend said in what sounded near enough Russian to me. 'Four *won*,' my girl said to me, or that's what I assumed she said, in what seemed reasonable Russian.

'I'm terribly sorry,' I said to the girl in Korean. 'But I don't speak Russian.'

'He doesn't speak Russian,' the girl called to her friend, sounding a little irritated. 'What's four *won* in English?' 'Four *won*, I think,' said her friend after a little hesitation. She was clearly more of a Russian expert. 'Four *won*,' my girl told me, in English.

'Excuse me,' I said, 'but what language are we speaking?'

Evidently it was a tricky question. 'I'm speaking Korean,' the girl said, after a little thought.

'And what about me?'

'You're a foreigner,' she said, with a look that told me I was clearly one of the least bright foreigners she had ever met.

I'd been baffled by her attitude. Not so my friend Chris, when I told him the story. A Canadian business consultant, he was an occasional visitor to Pyongyang who spoke Korean fluently after spending several years in the South. 'Imagine you're walking through a forest,' he said, 'and one of the trees leans over and asks you for a light. You'd understand the words; you might even give the tree a light. But you wouldn't believe that a tree had just addressed you. That's the attitude of some Koreans to foreigners who speak their language.'

Perhaps the old lady at the reservoir had only seen the props: the fishing rod and the bucket. My thinking was that if she could be taken in by my pretence of being a fisherman, then it was but a tiny step to passing myself off to her as a Korean.

Fishing, I reflected, was the epitome of what made life in North Korea appealing. Despite the propaganda bluster about battling to raise production output and resisting the enemy to the last drop of one's blood, life was peaceful, if not idyllic, and far less frenetic than what I was used to back home. There weren't the pressures associated with finding and keeping a job. There were none of the financial concerns of paying mortgages, taxes and bills. Housing was guaranteed, the children's education would be taken care of;

medical treatment was provided free of charge. And then there was retirement; it was the Korean tradition for the children to take care of their elderly parents and all I would be expected to do would be to wile away the hours with my fishing rod.

I might even, I thought, be able after so many years to laugh at the young man who'd made such a fool of himself when he'd loved and been rejected. But, where a foreigner in North Korea was concerned, nothing was ever that simple, and I wondered if, with a wiser and older head on my shoulders, I might one day be able to make sense of the bizarre events that had subsequently occurred.

Two weeks or so after the fateful Saturday afternoon at the Koryo Hotel, Song Il had insisted on taking me out for dinner. It was strange; I'd known him for most of the time I'd been in Pyongyang and he'd only ever invited me out to dinner once before, and that had been the previous week. After that first dinner he'd sent me to the Koryo, where a man I'd never seen before but who had everybody, including the hotel manager, jumping to his orders, had called me over to his table and spent the evening ordering us beer, served by a very attractive young lady he seemed to have brought with him for the purpose.

The following night a driver had been waiting for me after work, and had told me I was going to the Koryo. In the coffee shop I had met a young English-speaking Korean who never had any money. He had bought me beer, brandishing ten won I'd seen the barmaid hand him from the till, which he had given back to her when we'd got up and left for a restaurant, where I'd paid.

Back in the Koryo, at the door of which my companion had left me after our meal, I'd gone up to the small first-floor bar, where a group of the hotel's senior managers had soon gathered for a pointed conversation I couldn't follow about Kim Jong Il.

Strange that they used his name and not dear leader, I'd thought to myself.

So I'd gone for Song Il's mysterious second dinner and had been intrigued by the sight of one of our cars parked outside the restaurant and two of the girls from the guest house getting out with cloth-covered pots. They were, it seemed, delivering our food.

In the Koryo Hotel, where Song Il had again sent me after the meal, the girl in the billiard bar had told me I would soon be going to the Potonggang Hotel every night and not her hotel. The next night I'd gone to the Potonggang and the girl in the lounge bar had disappeared into her back room to finish a telephone conversation, having reported that someone had just turned up. There was no-one there, apart from me.

I'd ordered a car for after work the following day and asked the driver where he thought I should go, the Potonggang Hotel or the Koryo. He'd plumped very definitely for the Koryo and so I'd gone there. A group of the girls, the barmaid in the coffee shop had told me, were going out for dinner. Maybe I should do the same. No, of course I couldn't go with them. Nor should I go on my own. It wouldn't be right to drink alcohol alone. But, she'd told me, she had instructed one of the interpreters she saw me with quite often to meet me there. I'd waited, but no-one had turned up.

I'd been back in the Potonggang again a few days later, and the girl in the lounge bar had picked up the telephone when she saw me approaching and reported that someone was coming. She'd lowered her voice, but I think I caught her asking something about a meeting.

And so for weeks and then months I'd waited, spending my evenings alternately in the Koryo and the Potonggang, depending on the latest hint or suggestion. On occasion the mention of another hotel would send me scurrying off there.

The time had passed and I'd started wondering if I wasn't the butt of the cruellest of practical jokes or simply the victim of my own imagination. Or was there something I should have done and hadn't? I wanted to do the right thing, but not knowing what that was, it had seemed better to wait.

Eventually I'd asked the girls in the Koryo what had happened to her. At first the response had been knowing smiles; she hadn't married, they'd said; she just wasn't working there any more. But as time had passed they had started shaking their heads, sadly, but not disapproving of me. They had still called me a 'good person'.

Then one girl I'd spoken to in the roundabout, indirect fashion that is the way with Koreans discussing personal matters had told me I shouldn't call myself a bad person who didn't understand how to treat Korean girls. The publishing house, she had told me pointedly, was very bad.

It seemed that everyone knew what was happening, except me. In my frustration, I'd resorted to subterfuge.

What were the chances, I'd asked, of a foreigner becoming a member of the Workers' Party of Korea?

No-one had seemed to know. The general consensus was that a Party member had to be a citizen of the country.

Was there any such thing as honorary membership, I'd wondered.

It was a question – an academic one, I'd insisted – that I debated over games of cards in the interpreters' rooms at the guest house with our drivers, cooks and interpreters. Incidentally, I would insert ingenuously into the conversation, if a foreigner were to become a Party member, would this make it more or less difficult for him to take his bride, on the off chance that he were to marry a Korean girl, out of the country?

This was getting far too complicated. The best response anyone could come up with – I think it was one of the Spanish interpreters from the publishing house – was to write and ask Kim Jong Il.

I'd suggested that he might be rather busy to be bothered with such a relatively unimportant matter. Not at all, had been the reply from my companions. The dear leader was always concerned about the well-being of the people. I was doing very important work for the country and so there was every chance that he might choose to help me.

But I was already feeling I'd somehow handed over control of my own destiny. An appeal to the dear leader would surely take matters out of my hands entirely. So I'd waited.

As if North Korea's economic tribulations weren't bad enough, Team Spirit raised its head again at the end of 1992. The announcement that the annual military exercise conducted by the US in South Korea would be resumed early the following year provoked predictable outrage in Pyongyang.

The fury was all the greater because of the cancellation in 1992, seen as a goodwill gesture to North Korea at a time of improving relations with the US and South Korea.

The root cause of all the fuss remained North Korea's nuclear programme. International Atomic Energy Agency inspections had failed to remove all doubts about Pyongyang's intentions. The United States and South Korea wanted mutual nuclear verification on the Korean peninsula. Pyongyang, in an apparent and clearly futile attempt to drive a wedge between the two allies, insisted that it would deal only with the US.

My friend Hong Nam Il had got into trouble because he'd been seen too much in the company of foreigners and behaving drunkenly in the Koryo. His parents had been visited by a senior security official from the hotel, who had suggested that he should be devoting more time to studying.

This was the story told me by the forlorn Hong I ran into by chance in the relative security of the Taedonggang Restaurant. For a number of weeks he had barely said hello to me, and I'd been perplexed by the sight of his woebegone and nervous figure hanging sheepishly around the Koryo. He was so unlike the confident and carefree young man who'd asked me to teach him to drink beer and had even persuaded me to get my driver to drop him off at home.

It was as he drank the second bottle of *Kirin* beer I bought him that he became more bitter and started to lose my sympathy. His misfortune was all the result of the corruption that was rampant at the Koryo, he declared. For him to get into the hotel, he'd had to slip the doormen a packet of cigarettes or two. But recently, after having spent all the allowance his parents had given him, he'd become rather short of money and hadn't been able to give them anything. That was why there had been the visit to his parents.

No, of course they hadn't complained about not getting cigarettes. But by suggesting that he ought to be spending more time studying, the security people had been very clever, because his parents were important and it didn't look good if their son was seen to be lazy and abusing his position. So they'd cut his allowance.

Hong's family was in such an elevated position – his father was in the level of leadership only one step down from the great and dear leaders – that I'd never had any fear that he might land himself in trouble by meeting me in the Koryo. He hadn't even stopped going to the hotel after the visit from the security official, which showed how secure he felt.

Still, it was a relief to know that nothing serious had caused him to be so miserable. It was a relief also to know that there were forces at work, however obscure, that might limit the privilege enjoyed by the people with money and influence. There were rumours that those at the very top of the North Korean pile were leading lives of unimaginable luxury. It was all a disturbing contrast with the frugality imposed on the ordinary people, particularly the poor souls living outside Pyongyang in conditions of growing poverty and neglect.

But if our neighbour the vice-minister was anything to go by, either the stories of the lavish lifestyle of the elite were exaggerated or only the very top levels of the leadership were involved. The vice-minister and his family must, like us, have been enjoying only an intermittent hot water supply; they must have been subject to the same frequent power cuts; and they must have been left shivering during the coldest spells of winter by an unreliable heating system.

I'd seen a group of ladies from the vice-minister's block including, I have no reason to doubt, his wife, preparing *kimchi* outside in the October cold. The same ladies, aided by the children, regularly tended small vegetable plots outside their building, just like our guest house staff.

I did wonder, though, if the vice-minister's elevated position meant he could do something about the huge, revolting cockroaches that I was sure must infest his home, just as they did mine. My complaints after finding the disgusting black bodies littering my bathroom floor every morning had elicited a half-hearted effort to spread some powder on the floor, which the cockroaches apparently thrived on, since even more had made the trek out of the drain and up through the cracks in the floor and wall, to lie in bloated contentment on the tiles. Eventually, regardless of the waste of electricity, I simply left the bathroom light on all night, which kept them at bay.

Still, there was no denying that I was living very comfortably by local standards. I once asked Song Il if the life of comparative luxury I was leading didn't excite jealousy among ordinary Koreans. It was a concern that nagged with increasing persistence at the back of my mind as my resentment grew of the young Koreans with hard currency who chose to spend it on beer and cigarettes in the hotels, a thought that, had I ever voiced it, would have left me open to accusations of hypocrisy. Ah, yes, I would have countered, but they must have a better idea than I did of the misery that the vast majority of their fellow countrymen were forced to endure. And still, they opted for this openly wasteful way of life.

Song Il was adamant. I was doing important work and what I was earning was, in the government's opinion, appropriate, which was how the population at large would see it. It was just as well, because much as I would have liked to say otherwise, there was no getting away from the fact that money was important. I couldn't contemplate not being able to pop into a shop or bar for a beer when I felt like it; the prospect of not being free to go to a restaurant for a bite to eat whenever the food at the guest house wasn't up to scratch filled me with horror. What if I were ever obliged to survive on the diet of an ordinary North Korean: rice and *kimchi* and rarely any meat?

Ho Gwang got into trouble when the simmering dispute over North Korea's nuclear programme culminated in a state of semi-war being declared. Matters were finally brought to the boil when the United States, despite vigorous protestations from Pyongyang, went ahead and launched Team Spirit 93.

In response, Marshal Kim Jong Il, Supreme Commander of the Korean People's Army, issued an order declaring that, as of March 9th 1993, a state of semi-war existed on the Korean peninsula. It was more than being on a war footing, the translators told me when we discussed what should be the English equivalent of 'a state of semi-war'. *The Pyongyang Times* had described it as a war footing,[2] but other translators at the publishing house had been critical. This had been appropriate in previous years. And no; since the country was permanently in a state of war readiness, we couldn't describe it thus. Eventually I had to agree that, however unnatural it sounded in English, there was no alternative to the Korean phrase that meant, quite literally, that we were in a state of semi-war.

Ho Gwang had assumed that we were only on a war footing, and so he had thought there was no need for the guest house to observe the blackout enforced across the rest of Pyongyang, since in previous years we hadn't. But our building had been the only one in the whole of Pyongyang that had shown lights on that first night, and he had been criticised. Now, we were told, not only would we have to seal the black plastic sheeting over the windows; we would also not be permitted to turn on any light. I asked if I should move my television to the bathroom, since it had no windows. No-one found this funny. We could watch television, but only if the volume was turned down.

There were even whispers that we would have to take part in one of the daily air raid drills. It was chilling to watch every

---

[2] Order No. 0034 of the KPA Supreme Commander can be seen in *The Pyongyang Times*, March 13 1993.

evening as the workers at the factory next door assembled in the courtyard overlooked by my balcony as dusk gathered and the sirens sounded, and filed off noiselessly through the gloom in the direction of the nearby metro station. More than anything else, the sight of these ghostly figures, whose giggles, laughter and chatter were a feature of their regular outings to farms and other mass activities, now silent and bundled up in overcoats and shawls, brought home to me the seriousness of the situation.

Three days into the semi-war, on March 12th 1993, North Korea announced its withdrawal from the Nuclear Non-proliferation Treaty.[3]

Clearly, this wasn't just another of the exercises in mass hysteria that were the usual response to US actions that were perceived as hostile. There were the usual rallies and meetings, but the exhortations for solidarity and resolute determination to meet force with force were delivered with greater vehemence than ever. This was no time for the usual jokes about the US bastards. Perhaps the Supreme Commander was just flexing his muscles, but in hushed discussions in darkened rooms and bars there was never any suggestion other than that he meant business, and there was never any hint other than that the Americans deserved what they would get. The nightly news was filled with images of defiant soldiers. North Korean forces were prepared; attack was imminent and they were ready for battle. So convinced were people that war was about to break out that there was talk even of the date when the first shot would be fired: July 24th.

---

[3] *The Pyongyang Times*, March 20 1993, carried a front-page report: 'DPRK Government declares its withdrawal from NPT to defend its supreme interests'.

Ten days into the state of semi-war, North Korea was able to celebrate yet another propaganda triumph handed to it on a plate – or 'in a wheelbarrow', as one text I was given to edit originally put it – by the South. Li In Mo, the Incarnation of Faith and Will, returned in what was, in fact, a wheelchair, across the 38th Parallel and into the bosom of the fatherly leader whose name he had held dear throughout the 34 years he had spent in prison and several more years he had spent in abject misery in South Korea.

Li In Mo was an unconverted long-term prisoner. In other words, having been captured during the Korean War – in which he had served as a journalist – he had been kept in prison while the authorities tried to persuade him, using some pretty brutal means, to recant his communist beliefs. By refusing he had become a hero to people in the North and an embarrassment to the authorities in the South who, I'm sure, could well have done without this frail old man spilling the beans about torture and murder in its prisons, inmates forced to eat rats and the routine violation of human rights.[4]

What would I do, I mused, if it came to war? I had no objections to joining my Korean friends and colleagues in verbal expressions against US policy. But what if there really was an attack?

Team Spirit was, as North Korea insisted, a provocation. It was bad enough at the best of times for tens of thousands of US troops, along with large elements of the South Korean military, to conduct landing exercises within a stone's throw of northern territory; in circumstances where North Korea was more isolated

[4] See *Korea Today*, 1993, 6.

and vulnerable and less of a threat than ever, the exercise smacked of arrogance and insensitivity bordering on the 'reckless adventurism' that North Korean propaganda described it as.

Frankly, I didn't believe that Pyongyang had any intention of developing nuclear weapons, a possibility that the US gave as its excuse for resuming Team Spirit. Whatever diplomatic game North Korea was playing was served by making the opposition believe that acquiring a nuclear arsenal was a possibility; actually doing so served no useful purpose.

Say, for example, the Ansan Guest House was surrounded by a US unit and our waitresses and drivers, the interpreters and cooks, were defending it. I had absolutely no doubt that even the smiling, pretty waitresses would consider it their duty to fight. I knew they were all given regular military training and I supposed they would have been issued with weapons; come to think of it, I'd seen Myong Hui, our cleaner, arriving home after dark a couple of nights before with a rifle in her arms. Inevitably, she'd giggled when she'd seen me.

So, what would I do? I could hardly join them, even if they let me. Whatever my feelings about Americans, they hardly extended to killing them. Our waitresses and drivers, the interpreters and cooks, were all friends. Or were they? I speculated whether they might really have the same feelings for me. What would be their reaction, I wondered, if they were told to shoot me as a potential enemy spy? It was a line of thinking best not explored.

Still, I could hardly contemplate helping the American unit besieging the Ansan Guest House. The best scenario, from my point of view, would be for the guest house to fall without any bloodshed. I might do my Korean colleagues and friends a favour by talking them out of fighting, perhaps bopping them on their heads if they couldn't be persuaded. But then, when it was all over, they wouldn't thank me. Much better to die heroically than suffer defeat at the hands of the hated Americans, was very much the North Korean line of reasoning.

All in all, I decided, I had two choices. One was to stay in my room and embrace the triumphant American unit as liberators if they prevailed or heartily congratulate the Koreans if they saw off the assault. The other was to try and mediate, pointing out to the Americans that these were ordinary people they were attacking, girls who blushed when asked about their boyfriends, a cook whose wife had just given birth to their first son, a driver with his secret memories of the chocolate, not the bombs, dropped by the American planes during the last Korean War.

So I would stride out into the courtyard, carrying high a white flag and calling on everyone to stop firing. It was all a question, I thought, of which side would shoot me first.[5]

---

[5] On March 27th 1993, *The Pyongyang Times* reported that the army and people had been ordered by the Supreme Commander to stand down; the state of semi-war was thus ended.

PART 3

Right after the liberation of Korea from the Japanese colonial rule in 1945, Dear Leader Kim Jong-il visited a primary school at Chongjin in North Hamgyong Province. When he saw the Japanese map on the world globe which had been used by Japanese people, Dear Leader Kim Jong-il smeared black paint on the Japanese map in order to express his hatred of the Japanese people. Soon after, black clouds covered the whole of Japanese territory and heavy rain poured down.[1]

Considering the dear leader was three years old at the time of liberation and was, at such a tender age, able to wreak such vengeance on his enemies, it was no wonder that almost half a century later he could humble the United States in the semi-war of 1993.

Seven years later in the summer of Juche 89, therefore, even the loss of their great leader, a year after the semi-war, must no longer have seemed so devastating to the people of North Korea. With a man of such astonishing power leading them, they must have had real hope that, despite the ravages inflicted by nature on their Workers' Paradise, their other dream, that of reunification, was within reach ...

[1] Quoted *in Vantage Point*, October, 1991.

CHAPTER TEN

Inside Out

*M*ine was the only flight out of Pyongyang that day. I could see the plane through the airport's picture window, standing alone on the tarmac. The three of us were in the first-floor departure lounge. I'd saved ten *won* to offer them a drink. I'd never known Song Il to decline a beer before. 'Maybe you should buy Mr Li some cigarettes instead,' he said. So in the small restaurant I bought three packets of Mild Seven and handed them to Song Il, who passed them on to the director.

There was an hour and a half to go before the plane's departure. 'You should leave now,' Director Li said. He shook my hand and said goodbye. Song Il walked with me a little way towards the wooden cubicle that housed the immigration officer. 'Goodbye,' he said, 'and thank-you for everything.'

It took but a moment to have my passport stamped. I turned back to wave goodbye. Director Li and Song Il were already walking away.

In a whisper over dinner one night, with no-one else in the room, Madame Beatrice told me she was disappointed with Kim Il Sung. Almost a month had passed since the return of Li In Mo to the Republic and the great leader was yet to meet him. He was not ill or indisposed, she had ascertained. He was appearing as usual on the evening news. She couldn't understand why he had been unable to find the time to call on a man who had proved himself, by enduring so many years of hardship and even torture in the great leader's name, to be one of his most devoted supporters.

She needn't have worried, because Kim Il Sung paid the old man the greatest compliment of all by visiting him on his very own birthday; his 81st.

The photographs and the television pictures showed Kim Il Sung at the hospital bedside of the Incarnation of Faith and Will. He was smiling, clearly charming his listener. He was relaxed, sitting on an ordinary hospital chair. Around him stood note-taking officials and the family of Li, looking a little awestruck.[1]

This was Kim Il Sung in his element; the genial, charismatic leader at ease among his people. While the front pages of the newspapers seemed always to carry pictures of the great leader as international statesman in the company of a visiting foreign dignitary or delegation, the pictures on the inside pages would be of the leader among his people. With arm outstretched, he might be indicating where a dyke should be built for reclaiming tideland; hands behind his back, he might be making comments on the design of a garment as officials took notes; with a vase in his hands he might be inclining his head in approval of an artist's work; with arms spread wide and palms upturned he might be

---

[1] See *Democratic People's Republic of KOREA*, 1993, 7.

beaming with kindness and magnanimity on the group of farmers who gazed with rapt attention as they sat, just as he did, cross-legged on a rough floor.

The message was that the leader was always among the people, guiding and advising them. Together he shared weal and woe with them. He believed in the people as in Heaven and they placed their faith in him. He cared for each and every one of his millions of children. He was the source of all their happiness, their glory and their pride; he was the guiding light for every one of their triumphs. With kindness and understanding he helped them when they made mistakes.

It was all well and good for the great leader to be given the credit when everything was fine, I thought; it would, after all, be foolish to raise a dissenting voice when one's personal lot was a pleasant one. If any inconveniences were only minor, it might be expedient to look for their cause in one's own shortcomings. But when one felt let down by a system that one had believed in, it was only natural to blame the man at the top of the monolith.

Not since the Korean War of the early 1950s had North Korea been as self-righteous in its defiance of the rest of the world as it was in the summer of 1993.

The decision of the supreme commander to declare a state of semi-war and the massive show of unity by the entire population, who were as one with the army, had been vindicated; the US imperialists had not invaded. North Korea's withdrawal from the Nuclear Non-proliferation Treaty had been a diplomatic coup, forcing the unwilling Americans to the negotiating table.

In their talks in New York in June, North Korea and the United States reached agreement on assurances against the threat of nuclear weapons and on mutual respect for their systems and sovereignty. Hardly concrete progress, but there was enough for Pyongyang to trumpet to its people as proof of the triumph of the leadership's diplomacy.

In the meantime, the United Nations Security Council had passed a resolution criticising North Korea over the nuclear issue. Pyongyang dismissed it as unfair. But Security Council resolutions should not be treated so lightly, and the nuclear brinkmanship left a nasty taste in the mouth. North Korea could delude its population with claims of diplomatic victory, but the truth was that the country was now regarded with greater suspicion around the world than at any time before.

If only I hadn't gone to the Koryo Hotel that night, I could have left the country with more dignity. If only I hadn't had that final, late beer, I might have been spared the abrupt departure. If only a taxi had been waiting at the door, the last few months of my stay would have been less miserable. But at least amid the sense of lost dignity, of exclusion and of misery, and even as I admitted I had been stupid, I could cling to the knowledge that I was innocent.

Song Il was shocked when I'd opened my door that morning and he'd seen my face, bloody and bruised. He wanted to know what had happened. I was surprised he hadn't already heard, and for a moment I thought I might not be in such serious trouble, after all.

There had been a fight, I told him. I'd been waiting for a taxi and had got involved in a scuffle with a man who'd said some insulting things about me because I was a foreigner. Probably he'd thought I wouldn't understand. He'd seemed quite drunk. I confessed it had been foolish to lose my temper, but he'd started it and we'd only pushed each other around a bit. My injuries had been caused by all the other Koreans who'd appeared out of nowhere. They'd stopped me leaving; someone had come to ask questions.

Song Il went away. He returned at lunch time with Director Li. I'd been drunk, the security staff at the Koryo had told them. I'd hit the man and hurt him quite badly. No, I hadn't been drunk, I insisted. That's what they'd tried to make me say the previous night, in the interrogation in the hotel foyer, with all those people watching. A man I took to be a senior security officer had asked me over and over again if I knew what I'd done. He'd been on my left. Sitting on his far side had been a particularly nasty young hothead who'd suggested that torture was the best way of getting a foreigner to admit to his criminal actions.

Song Il and Director Li told me the man was quite badly hurt; he was in hospital. I couldn't have injured him that badly, I insisted. I'd been the victim, the one with the damaged face. I hadn't hurt anyone. At one point during the interrogation I'd got up and tried to leave. I'd got as far as the exit, but allowed myself to be pulled back. If I hadn't, someone who had seized my collar would have had his arm badly hurt in the revolving door.

The police wanted to interview me, Song Il and Director Li told me when they came later that day. The man's condition was worsening. My memories of the evening seemed hazy, they said. It would be better if I admitted I'd been drunk when the police asked. The girl in the billiard bar had told them I'd had several cans of beer. But now, I said, I remembered more about the scuffle with the man I was supposed to have hurt. I'd pushed him up against the wall, but I'd put my hand behind his head to protect him. I couldn't understand how I might have harmed him.

By the afternoon they were advising me as friends that it would be much better to tell the police I'd been drunk. I asked when they were coming? Soon, perhaps even that evening. The charge could be very serious, in view of the victim's injuries. But if I said I'd been drunk it wouldn't be so bad. I agreed. Do whatever you think is best, I told them.

They were soon back. The police would not be coming to see me. But the man was still in a serious condition. It would help my cause if I was to make some gesture, perhaps send medicines, to help him. Yes, they would take the money and buy what was necessary.

Two days later the patient was out of danger. Song Il and Director Li told me I could now forget the whole incident. I couldn't, of course; for a time I worried that I'd really harmed the man, but eventually I convinced myself that I hadn't.

For once I felt grateful for the lies and deceit that were such a part of everyday life in North Korea. I'd learned the hard way not to believe or trust anyone, and now I could argue quite reasonably, to myself at least, that there was no particular reason why the Koreans should have been telling the truth in this any more than they had at any other time. My own recollections contradicted what they told me, anyway. It was a convenient way of easing my conscience, I knew. But I saw no reason to dismiss it.

In the meantime I'd had a lot of visitors. My foreign friends had rallied round. I hadn't felt like going out and was pleased to see the sympathetic faces. Marek had dropped by to see how I was and an unusually subdued Kris had said it was a terrible thing to have happened. Madame Beatrice was away on vacation, for which I was grateful; she was the one foreigner who would have taken the Koreans' side.

But despite the concern of my friends, there was no-one I could tell what the worst of it had been: the silent, blank-faced crowd that had gathered to watch the humiliating interrogation; these were waitresses and cleaners, doormen and managers, people I'd talked to and joked with, shared cigarettes with and for whose children I'd bought chocolates. They'd watched in silence. Not one of them had shown any sorrow, any sympathy.

None of the Koreans I worked with ever mentioned the incident, leaving me guessing who had heard and who hadn't. For a while I comforted myself with the thought that perhaps those who knew had chosen or been told to keep it to themselves. Forlornly I also hoped that, if it had become public knowledge, the version being told might cast me in a more favourable light than that of the drunken foreigner lashing out at an innocent man.

Such illusions were to be shattered a couple of weeks later in the Rakwon Department Store. 'You bastard!' cried a young English-speaking Korean I knew from the hotel circuit. Normally quietly spoken and polite, he was shouting in Korean for all the shop to hear, 'Do you know what this bastard did? He should be in prison.'

I walked away. All I could think of to say, over my shoulder, was, 'Did you see it? You don't know what you're talking about.'

I had little interest in the events that unfolded over the following weeks and I never set foot inside the Koryo Hotel again.

There had been a parade and a mass game to mark Victory Day, the 40th anniversary of the end of the Korean War, in the last week of July. In September there was the 45th anniversary of the founding of the Republic, with the usual parade, the customary mass game and the inevitable evening dance in Kim Il Sung Square. Also in September my parents came out to visit me, as guests of the publishing house.

The original plan had been to invite them in recognition of my fifth year, but by the time all the organisation and logistics had been taken care of, it had become the publishing house's way of thanking me for my six and a half years of service.

We visited Kaesong and Panmunjom, where a remarkably relaxed officer told us that the last time so many British people had been there at one time had, to his knowledge, been during the War. We went to the Myohyang Mountains, where we stayed at the guest house I so loved. In Pyongyang we had official visits to the monuments, the museums and the revolutionary paraphernalia scattered across the city: Mangyongdae, the Juche Tower, the Grand People's Study House, the May Day Stadium.

One Sunday afternoon we went on a grand tour of Pyongyang on foot. Having first taken the underground to Moran Hill we walked down to the Arch of Triumph and from there to the pillar with Chollima on top; we climbed the steps up to the great statue of Kim Il Sung on Mansu Hill and then headed towards Kim Il Sung Square. But rather than walk across the square itself, we went through the passageway beneath the steps I'd stood on so many times at the great state occasions and round the far side of the Grand People's Study House, stopping for a while at the nearby fountain park. From there we walked to the People's Palace of Culture and the Potong Gate and on to the Changgwangsan Hotel Coffee Shop.

The visit helped ease my sense of shame and regret over getting involved in the seedy affair at the Koryo. My colleagues and my friends in the hotels and restaurants had all been as natural and friendly as ever. I thought I should thank the publishing house for inviting my parents and so, after they had left, I invited Director Li and Song Il to the expensive Japanese restaurant at the Ansan Club. It was quite like old times, laughing and joking. For the first time in many weeks I started to feel optimistic about the future.

Kim Jong Il had, several months earlier, been named Chairman of the National Defence Commission. There was strong speculation that by year's end he would be named to a leading post in either the State or the Party. For what it was worth, my bet was on him replacing his father as General Secretary of the Workers' Party of Korea, although a popular view among my foreign friends was that he might become President of the Republic. But somehow I couldn't see his father giving up the role of elder statesman of world politics.

Throughout the summer and autumn, a series of rallies were being held at which different sections of society declared their loyalty to Kim Jong Il. The armed forces were among the first to turn out to declare themselves, but there were also rallies by the League of Socialist Working Youth, the Democratic Women's Union and the Union of Agricultural Working People. I asked Director Li and Song Il if there were any plans for a rally by foreign language advisers.

I became a Saturday night regular at the Changgwangsan Disco. As a location I'd always found it rather uninspiring; just a long room with a bar at one end, semi-circular sofas and tables down both sides and a small dance floor at the far end from the bar. An incongruous bright red rose glowed on the wall behind the dance floor.

I had few memorable evenings there; generally I found myself drinking too much beer, while trying to salvage some sort of conversation from men who either moaned about the lack of excitement or who made impossible claims about the wild times they were having while all around them was misery. But I do remember one evening when the atmosphere was a little more animated than usual.

Kris, of course, was at the centre of things. There were a couple of the Czech officers from the Neutral Nations Supervisory Commission, who spent their weekdays inside the demilitarised zone monitoring observance of the Armistice. There was a good turnout by the African students; even the guys from Hamhung had been able to make it, as had most of the young Cubans, who were in Pyongyang because their parents were working at the embassy. There were some Syrian students, too, whom I knew only vaguely but who were nonetheless quite friendly. There were more embassy people, from Eastern Europe and North Africa. And then there was a crowd of engineers, German and French, from the Koryo. And Marek was there, too, a little tipsy and clearly enjoying himself, and he laughed at the story of the near-altercation I'd had at the Ryanggang Hotel, where an elderly lady was so shocked to see a waitress stepping out of a lift with me that she upbraided the poor girl for her immoral behaviour.

For some reason, that night at the Changgwangsan Disco everyone seemed to be drinking *pem sul*.[2] One of the African students invited me to a glass. It was a celebration, he said. No, really, I insisted. I didn't want snake liquor. I'd been drinking beer already and my stomach was turning as I watched him open the tap on the rubber tube coming from the base of the demijohn that stood on the bar and contained, I saw with revulsion, a great snake.

---

[2] Snake liquor.

But that was the whole point of the celebration, he told me as I reluctantly accepted the glass he handed me. It was a new snake.

In November elections were held to People's Assemblies across the country. I happened to be down in the courtyard in the morning of polling day and I ran into Song Il and two of our waitresses heading off to cast their ballots. They were dressed in their Sunday best. Song Il asked if I would like to come along.

The girls giggled and asked if I was going to vote. I said yes, I would, but I hadn't decided which Party to vote for. They looked confused but Song Il, who was rather more worldly-wise, suggested I might choose the Workers' Party of Korea, since there weren't any others.

What happened in elections in the Democratic People's Republic of Korea was that the Workers' Party put forward all the candidates and the people trundled out and voted for them. In theory there was the option of voting to reject the candidate, but since the Workers' Party had been very careful in choosing just the right man or woman for the job, this was not really the thing to do. In previous years the turnout across the country had been 100% and the votes in favour of the proposed candidates had likewise been 100%. However, in the elections of 1989 the Workers' Party had suffered something of a setback, when a mere 99.87% of the population had bothered to vote, although 100% of them had voted for the candidates imposed on them.

While I had no reason to doubt that 100% of the people did vote in favour of the candidates – to do anything else would have been futile, if not dangerous – I had always wondered, until the setback of 1989, about the turnout. What about those too ill to leave their homes and vote? There were, I was told, mobile polling stations that would visit such people. All right, then, I said, what about those who died, in between the electoral lists being published and the election itself? Well, there would be so few of them that the figure would still round up to 100%.

Mind you, I could understand why the turnout was so high when I saw how much fun an election North Korean-style really was. At the polling station – for the Ansan Guest House it was a nearby secondary school – there were crowds gathered and music was being played. The people were organised into large circles, dancing.

Taking the lead were, as usual on such jolly occasions, the old women, and they were pirouetting madly yet gracefully, coloured scarves held aloft, to the sound of some pretty uninspiring music being scratched out by a gramophone. I knew what was going to happen and so I tried as best I could to fade into the background. But it is hard for the proverbial sore thumb to become invisible, and it was with a shout of glee that one old lady spotted the foreigner in their midst. 'Have you come to vote?' she cried, to laughter from those around her. 'Vote for the glorious Workers' Party!' shouted another.

Fortunately Song Il and the girls emerged from the polling station and so I was able to bow and wave my way off before the inevitable request came for the foreigner to dance.

Later in November I was at the publishing house and had just finished a discussion of some texts when Yong Nam, who had joined the foreign affairs office after Ho Gwang had left to go into business, came to me in the lounge and said, 'Director Li wants to know when you intend to leave our country.'

I shrugged. It wasn't unexpected, but it was none the less unpleasant and brutal. After nearly seven years, there wasn't a nice way of being told you were no longer wanted.

'Your contract expires at the end of December,' Yong Nam said.

'But that's only a month away,' I protested. It was interesting, this mention of a contract. I'd found it strange the previous year when Song Il had turned up in my flat one day and produced a contract for me to sign. A mere formality, he'd insisted. So I'd signed, even though I'd been puzzled as to why after so many years without a contract – the only one I'd been given previously had been for an initial six months – I was now having to sign one.

It seemed that plans had been afoot to get rid of me a year before. I guessed I'd simply overstayed my welcome; perhaps I'd forged for myself too much independence, become too well known for the publishing house's comfort. By establishing myself in a wider circle, I was threatening the ultimate power they held over me, that of making me leave the country. The more my influence grew, it occurred to me, the greater the obligation would be on them to justify not renewing my contract.

It was a power they would have lost also, I reasoned, had I ever settled down and married. As I reflected on the greatest of the unanswered questions raised during my stay in North Korea I couldn't help thinking that, even as I'd been contemplating the possibility of making a lifelong commitment in North Korea, my employer must have been horrified by the prospect of losing the power to get rid of me. The irony was that had I ever married, I and the publishing house would have shared the same goal: of finding a way for me to leave the country.

I never found out what had really happened. As time passed, however, I became convinced that there had been an elaborate plan to bring us together, but something had gone wrong;

someone had not wanted it to happen. And I remembered how one of the girls in the Koryo had told me that the publishing house was bad, and it seemed significant that even as I'd been wandering from hotel to hotel in a vain attempt to bring some conclusion to the affair, the general director had been returned to his former position and the vice-director who had wanted to be my father and did nothing to help had been removed. But still there were no conclusive answers.

One of the clauses in my contract stipulated a three-month period of notice. I told Yong Nam, I would appreciate being allowed to stay until February so that I could sort out my affairs. There would be no problem with that, the message came back from Director Li. And presumably so that I could in return show my own goodwill, he asked if I might be able to recommend someone to replace me. It was a request that showed astonishing insensitivity, I thought. That aside, given how badly I felt I'd been treated of late, I couldn't see how they could possibly expect me to contact a friend back home and tell him or her what a wonderful experience was to be had in North Korea.

So I prepared to leave. In December Kim Jong Il wasn't named to any new senior posts of Party or State. Instead there was a surprise. His uncle, Kim Il Sung's younger brother Yong Ju, who had in the years before Kim Jong Il's emergence as his father's successor been widely regarded as the most likely man to take over, was named vice-president, marking a political comeback after almost two decades of obscurity.

Not that there was any hint that the dear leader's succession was in jeopardy; it was more a matter, it seemed, of keeping one's troubles in the family, because the Workers' Party of Korea had another surprise up its sleeve at the beginning of December. For the first time ever, it admitted that the targets of a national economic plan had not been met. The fault lay with the collapse of socialism and the loss of the markets of its former allies in Eastern Europe, as Korea Today explained:

> The disappearance of the world socialist market radically altered our country's external economic relations. This had a great influence on our revolution and construction and created great obstacles and difficulties in the way of economic construction in our country.
>
> At the same time the enemies' desperate war moves and offensive against our Republic aggravated the situation on the Korean peninsula to the extreme. Therefore, we had to direct great economic strength to increasing the nation's defence capability.[3]

There was more talk of remedying the situation by stepping up foreign trade. To this end new legislation had already been adopted – the Law on Foreigners' Investment, the Law on the Free Economic and Trade Zone and the Foreign Investment Banking Law[4] – although there was still no mention of how the country planned to resolve the great contradiction between promoting economic opening and maintaining ideological purity.

Hopes were being pinned on the Rajin–Sonbong Free Economic and Trade Zone, which covered an area of north-east Korea, north-east China and the extreme east of Russia. The plan was to offer tax breaks and other incentives to attract foreign investment and develop industry in a region with excellent port

[3] See *Korea Today*, 1994, 2.

[4] See *Democratic People's Republic of KOREA*, 1994, 4.

facilities. Six countries were involved: North and South Korea, Mongolia, China, Russia and Japan. Progress in what was an exciting undertaking was, however, constantly being held up by Pyongyang's persistent dissembling and failure even to turn up at some meetings, to the inevitable frustration of its partners – this despite some very strong statements from Pyongyang expressing its full commitment to the project.

But overshadowing all North Korea's external dealings was still the nuclear issue. Pyongyang's withdrawal from the Nuclear Non-proliferation Treaty had heralded a seven-month interruption in official contacts with Seoul. When talks had restarted in October 1993, such was the mutual mistrust that had once again built up that nothing came of them.

While North Korea stubbornly continued to reject inspections of its nuclear facilities, there could be no hope of improved relations with Japan or the United States or, indeed, the many Western European countries that had no objection to recognising both North and South Korea.

In January 1994 that most unlikely of envoys to North Korea, US evangelist Billy Graham, came and went again. According to reports, he brought with him out of North Korea a message from Kim Il Sung, addressed to US president Bill Clinton. The great leader was apparently keen to find a solution to the nuclear issue.

A month later and after nearly seven years, I would fly out of Pyongyang.

In the meantime I toured the city's hotel bars and restaurants, saying goodbye at the many places where, over the years, I'd become a regular customer. It occurred to me that, despite the massive efforts directed at transforming Pyongyang during the previous seven years, there had been little real change. There were a few more hotels and more hotel bars, but this just meant there were more empty rooms and tables for the staff to preside over. There were the new facilities, the stadiums and the sports halls. But they, like the hotels, went largely unused. There were trams on the streets and traffic lights, but the public transport was still overcrowded and the traffic police still stood at junctions directing a trickle of cars. The airport had been expanded, but still the arrival of two international flights meant a busy day.

But one change Pyongyang underwent in the time I was there cannot be so easily dismissed. The city's skyline is now dominated by possibly the world's greatest folly, a massive, towering symbol of the futility of the country's dreams of world prominence.

Work began on the 105-storey Ryugyong Hotel towards the end of 1987. Its opening was planned by the time of the 13th World Festival of Youth and Students in July 1989. But it wasn't finished. The shell was completed and it stands like a massive, useless hulk, a crane permanently at its summit over 300 metres above the ground. It was supposed to be covered in glass, but that never happened. From a distance the hotel dwarfs all the other buildings in Pyongyang, a city that impressed me with its greenness and thoughtful planning when I first saw a panorama of it from the top of the Juche Tower. Now it is different. From wherever Pyongyang is viewed, the eye is inexorably drawn to the towering, domineering pyramid. Up close, the vast foundation needed to support this monolith reinforces the impression of the enormity of the folly.

The story goes that in 1948 Kim Jong Il was standing on a hill with his mother, Kim Jong Suk, gazing down on Pyongyang. His mother told the little boy of how wonderful it was that a city of tall buildings was taking shape, where Koreans had previously been used only to living in single-storey shacks. 'You must build tall buildings for the people, of 30 or even 40 storeys,' the mother told her son. 'Mother,' he replied, 'I will build for the people housing 100 storeys high.' Hence the 105-storey hotel.

When the construction began, optimism was high. There was the chance that the 1988 Olympics might be shared with South Korea. Even if that didn't happen, it would still be among the most impressive of the facilities built specially for the 13th World Festival of Youth and Students, which promised the country an opportunity to raise its international profile. After that, who could tell what other major international sporting events might come along?

Underlying this optimism there seemed to be a genuine commitment to opening up, both economically and politically. The infrastructure was being prepared – road construction in Pyongyang and between major cities, the airport expansion, the international telecommunications centre, hotel building – for an influx of foreigners; legislation was being put in place to encourage foreign investment; and there was just a hint that the restrictions on foreigners, those purveyors of pagan ideology, might be eased.

But it all went wrong. The signs were there before Pyongyang's moment in the international spotlight in July 1989. The socialist brethren were already breaking ranks by allying themselves with the enemy in South Korea. Within six months of Pyongyang hosting its great gathering of socialist youth, communism was dead in Eastern Europe, and being buried.

And so the 105-storey hotel, as it is commonly known, stands as a symbol of dreams unfulfilled. Reflecting the fate of the deserted construction site, North Korea was left abandoned.

South Korea, by contrast, was flourishing by 1987. The economy had taken off and was outstripping that of the North, and the last of the military dictators was about to hand over power to those who, superficially at least, were democratic. And in 1988 the world gave its stamp of approval. While North Korea looked on in sulking isolation, the whole world descended on Seoul for a celebration of the greatest global sporting event.

North Korea, though, still insisted that it was the leading light in the international community, that its president was held in high regard by millions around the world as the elder statesman of world politics, as the champion of freedom, democracy and independence who had twice defeated and continued to stand up to the powers of world domination and imperialism. So Kim Il Sung was seen greeting like-minded world leaders. In the late 1980s and early 1990s Pyongyang hosted a series of meetings of the Non-Aligned Movement, in which North Korean officials tried unsuccessfully to present him as the organisation's leader.

As the last decade of the century arrived, a nuclear shadow stretched over the Korean peninsula. Ironically, for years Pyongyang had been condemning the United States and calling on it to remove its nuclear weapons from the Korean peninsula. But now the boot was on the other foot and North Korea found itself the object of international condemnation for its own nuclear pretensions.

While the drama on the international scene unfolded, life for North Koreans became harder and harder. So they tightened their belts. They were used to hardship; their forefathers had endured much worse during the liberation struggle against the Japanese and the war against the Americans. Poverty and isolation were the price they had paid before for defending their rights. They should be prepared to make sacrifices again, the people were told, until the day came when, with the triumph of the cause of socialism, they would all be enjoying the prosperity the great leader had promised them; the day when, fulfilling the dream of Koreans down through the ages, they would eat meat soup and rice every day, dress in silk clothing and live in a tile-roofed house.

But still they had another cause to fight for – reunification, when all the people of Korea would live together in happiness and prosperity. In the first half of 1994 they were given reason to hope that this particular promised land might be reached before long. The first ever meeting was planned between the leaders of North and South Korea.

Chapter 11

*T*he fable of the Frog in the Well is, I believe, well known across the Far East, and I suppose there is a slightly different version depending on whether it is told in China, Japan or the Koreas, either North or South. The basic idea is the same, though: that of a frog living in a well for whom the only world he knows is the circle of blue sky above his head.

The story I was told by a North Korean which, for all I know, could have been a personal interpretation, is this:

> The frog is teased by the birds that fly overhead every day, who make fun of him because he thinks that all there is to see in the world is his little patch of sky. The thought starts to grow in the frog's head that perhaps his world is a bit limited and it would be interesting to go and see where the birds are flying to all the time. So when one of them offers to carry him on his back to see, the frog agrees, and off they go. They fly and they fly and the bird points out to the frog all the wonders of Nature: the mountains and the forests, the seas and the rivers. The frog looks down and what he sees frightens him; he sees big, dangerous cities and filthy smoke, fighting and natural disasters, disease and poverty, and he implores the bird to take him back to his well. Only there, beneath the little patch of blue sky that he knows so well, does he feel secure.

The message of this North Korean version of the tale is clear. Don't believe what you hear of the outside world. You really are much better off where you are.

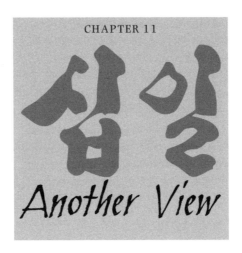

CHAPTER 11

십일

Another View

It was as if the great leader wasn't dead. In Pyongyang in the spring of 1995 his image was still all around me: on the chests of his people, in every room, and on the street corners. At the opera the audience still applauded as, at the end of the performance, his image appeared on stage against a magnificent setting sun.

It was less than a year since his funeral had been beamed across the globe and the world had witnessed the keening, breast-beating, uncontrollable anguish of his people. The historic summit with the South had not taken place, because the great leader was dead.

I'd left Pyongyang little more than four months before and was working in Beijing when the birds had wept and the double rainbow had risen over Mount Paekdu to mark the great leader's passing. The thing to do, I'd reflected, would be to go along to the North Korean embassy to sign the book of condolences. But I didn't. To my still bitter way of thinking, the great leader, who had gloried in things going right, should be held to account for the misfortunes of those who fell under his influence.

Even so, when the chance had come I had returned to his country. In April 1995 Pyongyang hosted an international festival of culture and I went and I saw that the great leader's death had changed nothing. It really was as if, as the magazine headlines put it: 'The great leader Comrade Kim Il Sung is with us forever'.[1]

I'd been mildly surprised, having left under such a cloud, to be allowed back into North Korea again. But they were letting anyone in this time, even Americans, for what I came to think of as the grandest and most bizarre public relations exercise ever undertaken anywhere in the world. The festival of culture was an excuse for throwing the country open; what many among the thousands of people who accepted the invitation anticipated was some demonstration of a North Korea willing to change under its new leader. What they got was a pro-wrestling tournament featuring, among a strange cast of characters, a fluorescent green-haired, well-muscled Japanese girl flinging herself headlong on top of her prone opponent. Presiding over the proceedings was not the dear leader but Muhammad Ali.

Such frivolity, it occurred to me, was out of keeping with a period of mourning. The planning must have been too far advanced at the time of the great leader's death, for the event to be cancelled.

It would be two more years before Kim Jong Il would return to public life. In the meantime, his country suffered a series of natural calamities that devastated the harvest, beginning with the flooding of the summers of 1995 and 1996.

Then in the autumn of 1997, Kim Jong Il, who had ruled the country for three years from behind the scenes in the capacity of

---

[1] For example, *Democratic People's Republic of KOREA*, 1994, 9.

Chairman of the National Defence Commission and Supreme Commander of the Korean People's Army, emerged from the traditional three-year mourning period for his father. He was named General Secretary of the Workers' Party of Korea, and it appeared as though it was business as usual.

Construction began of 10,000 new homes in Pyongyang, a throwback to the last years of Kim Il Sung's life, when Kwangbok Street and then Tongil Street had been built to provide new housing for tens of thousands of families. Nature, though, failed to play her part and the 1997 harvest was devastated by drought.

'It must be bad,' my friend told me. 'Even the cadres are thin.'

From time to time in Beijing, I would be visited by acquaintances and former colleagues from North Korea who were either there on business or passing through. They seemed more at ease than I'd known them in their own country, and more relaxed about talking to me. Even so, they still didn't reveal much.

I pointed out to my friend that he sounded somewhat detached, considering he and his family were in the thick of a famine. He wanted to know what the rest of the world was saying about the situation. That there was starvation, I said, that children were suffering. He thought for a moment and told me that things had always been pretty bad. But now his children were having to take food to school for their teacher. That's when he'd thought about the cadres.

I put an idea to him: 'Under Kim Il Sung, even when times were at their hardest, there wouldn't have been such an appeal to the outside world for help, such an admission that the system had failed the people.'

My friend considered the idea. He supposed I might be right.

So much for my theories, I thought. I'd been convinced that cracks were appearing in the Party's monolithic leadership. The acknowledgement, when the floods had come, that all was not well with their much vaunted agriculture, and that they needed help, must have been a bitter pill for the proud North Koreans to take. To allow the images of desperate mothers and pitifully thin babies to appear on the world's television screens must have been even harder to swallow.

But even as the people suffered, North Korea didn't let up on the glorification of its dead leader. In the autumn of 1997, his birthday, April 15th – the greatest national holiday – was designated the Day of the Sun and a new calendar was introduced that started with the year of his birth, 1912, henceforth to be known as Juche One. The year when the calendar was introduced would, therefore, be Juche 86.

And in Juche 86 North Korea announced that it had launched a satellite, which had the rest of the world protesting at the advancement of its missile technology. North Korea was surprised at the concern. The satellite was perfectly innocent; it was only up there to play the *Song of General Kim Il Sung*. The following year the mystery of why Kim Jong Il had not been named President of the Democratic People's Republic of Korea was solved when his father, whose embalmed body was by this time lying in state, was named President for Eternity.

It was all a reminder of the quaintness of the country I'd lived in. But now as an outsider – a stranger – I saw things as the rest of the world did and I questioned the principles and the ideology that produced such bizarre offshoots. The obsession with the great leader that had once seemed harmless, even beneficial as a unifying factor, now looked like the self-serving manipulation of an entire society's thinking aimed at preserving, through the exaltation of its figurehead, a political system lacking a sound moral basis. As for the claim that the purity of the ideology needed protection from pernicious outside influences, which had once made sense even though, as a pernicious outside influence myself, I, and hence my acquaintances, had been subjected to restrictions that in other societies would have been condemned as violations of our fundamental rights, it now looked like a desperate argument designed to delude an entire population into seeing the rest of the world as a sinister place best kept at arm's length, and to hide the unacceptable excesses of a regime from scrutiny by a world in which it had no place.

In this they had largely succeeded, as my own experience demonstrated. For seven years I was shielded from the North Korean reality. I learnt the language up to a point and I had friends, but still I barely scratched the surface of what North Korea was all about, what the people there really thought. The explanation of how this could be achieved was simple enough. On the one hand, restrictions and surveillance were imposed, preventing me from meeting ordinary North Koreans. On the other hand, it was a privilege, one they were anxious not to jeopardise, for North Koreans to be in a position that brought them into contact with foreigners. So senior government and Party officials would exercise their influence to have their children working as interpreters for foreign delegations; a university professor would be delighted if his daughter could find work as a waitress in one of the international hotels; for our elderly cook, his job was reward for the years he had spent fighting the Japanese. In a country where even living in the capital city was a privilege, everyone was careful about what they did and said, particularly around foreigners. The result was a population obsessed with casting themselves and their country in a faultless light. It was as if the propaganda became a part of their everyday life.

But that wasn't to say they didn't have much to be proud of. It was easy to forget, among the splendour and cleanliness of Pyongyang, that North Korea was a Third World country. So the boasts about feeding, clothing and sheltering the people, providing free education and health care – whatever the shortcomings – should not be dismissed lightly.

Seven years, though, is not enough to understand a country, and on reflection there is no reason why I should have come away with any greater knowledge of the society, the people and the politics than I did. In a sense, it's all laid out on a plate, or in books – the president's *Works* spring to mind – anyway. Never can a population have been given such clear and precise guidelines about how they should lead every aspect of their lives.

As for the grey areas, however – the things that aren't mentioned in the books – I have no better idea than any other outsider about the big issues that concern the world – the nuclear weapons programme, the arms sales, the camps for political prisoners and so on – other than to say that, while personally feeling horror about what might have been happening, I recognise that North Korea can offer justification, however dubious, for its actions. Without the powerful diplomatic bargaining chip of a nuclear programme, it would have no voice in the international community; however great the suspicion with which its exports and its partners are viewed in certain quarters, without its trade the economy would be in even worse shape; without ideological purity it would not be able to build a communist society.

But there was no justification for millions of children being left to face starvation. There had to be a point where ideology and national pride should be put to one side in the interests of saving an entire generation. To be fair, North Korea appeared to agree, when the floods hit and it launched its appeal for international aid.

With time my mood towards North Korea – it seems strange to lay the blame on an entire country, but in North Korea's case its monolithic system makes it quite plausible – healed, a process that accelerated after the middle of 1996, when I received the first of a series of faxes from Pyongyang, inviting me to return to my former job. Madame Beatrice, when she visited Beijing, told me the publishing house had been very pleased with the interview I'd given soon after my departure. A friend of a friend had been working for a major international news agency and I'd agreed to have a chat. I'd deliberately been positive in my views; after all, for the best part of seven years I'd struggled to form a fair and objective opinion of North Korea and I thought I'd be letting myself down by being bitter and overly critical, just because personal events had taken an unfortunate turn in the last few months of my stay. Now the invitation to go back, the knowledge that I wasn't *persona non grata*, made me feel comfortable that it had been the right thing to do.

I told Madame Beatrice that I wouldn't be going back. I didn't want to discuss the lingering anger and shame, so I said it was because of the food situation. But she had anticipated that and had spoken to the cook on my behalf. Even though the guest house's rations had been cut, the cook – an old friend – had promised to organise things so that I would eat well enough.

But that wasn't the point, I thought. The fact was, the rest of the population was going hungry; North Koreans were fleeing their country in search of food across the border in China, where they had to hide in fear of their lives. In the sure knowledge that such suffering existed, how could I accept any amount of food, however small?

There was also the ideological consideration. I'd never been a particularly strong supporter of North Korean-style communism; at best I'd admired the commitment to providing for all the people. I'd never really understood the philosophy the people were supposed to believe in, but I'd respected them for their belief. So I was disappointed that, in the deteriorating situation and as the need grew to ensure security, the army was said to be gaining in influence; even ideology could be jettisoned to ensure the regime's survival, it seemed.

But that wasn't the view from inside. Madame Beatrice insisted that life in Pyongyang went on as normal. And it occurred to me that I was beginning to see North Korea as the rest of the world did, to accept as truth sketchy and ill-founded reports for no better reason than they contradicted the official line and hinted at a darker side to the regime. But by doing so I was discounting my own experiences. While there, I had learned to appreciate a unique country, its strange politics and, above all, its people and their warmth and good humour. This was something I should never forget.

'Is there any news about Hwang?' the North Korean asked. He was referring to Hwang Jang Yop, a very senior Workers' Party of Korea official who had, until recently, been holed up in the South Korean embassy in Beijing. It was early in 1997 and Hwang was attempting to defect, a fact that North Korea had finally admitted when it labelled him a 'renegade of socialism' and allowed him, under pressure from the Chinese authorities, to leave the South Korean embassy safely.

The news was, I told my friend in the garden outside my apartment at Beijing's Friendship Hotel, that Hwang had left Beijing but was still not in Seoul, which was where he was presumed to be heading.[2]

---

[2] Hwang Jang Yop eventually arrived in Seoul on April 20th 1997.

Although the defection of such a senior official and close confidant of the leadership cast a shadow at the beginning of a year that was supposed to be an auspicious one for North Korea, when the period of mourning for Kim Il Sung would end, 1997 was marked by a number of successes in the international arena. Work began on the construction of two light-water reactors promised in the Nuclear Framework Accord signed at the end of 1994, under which an international consortium with the United States as a prominent member would finance the reactors and supply North Korea with large quantities of fuel oil until the construction was completed; in return, North Korea would freeze its nuclear weapons programme. By the end of 1997 there were signs of an improved relationship with Japan, when a number of Japanese women who had come to North Korea with their Korean husbands years before were allowed to return for their first visit home. Finally, four-way talks were held in Beijing, with the United States, China and South Korea, aimed at achieving a permanent peace on the Korean peninsula.

But the rest of the world was still uneasy. Only a year before, in 1996, North Korea had earned another ticking-off from the United Nations Security Council, after one of its spy submarines had run aground on the South Korean coast. The Security Council expressed 'serious concern' over the incident, in which more than 20 North Korean commandos spent several days on the run in South Korea, killing a dozen of their pursuers before either being themselves killed or captured. Finally, in December, Pyongyang expressed its regret, which was taken by the rest of the world as an apology for its actions.

By the late summer of 1998, North Korea was up to its old tricks again when another spy submarine was caught in South Korean waters. Of even more concern to the world at large was the test firing of a missile that flew over Japan and landed in the sea on the far side. Japan and the United States expressed outrage; later, Washington agreed to talks with Pyongyang in Berlin after the North Koreans had promised to halt such test firing.

At the end of 1999 the United States cast its shadow yet again. Earlier in the year President Clinton's special envoy William Perry, after a visit to Pyongyang, had urged a 'comprehensive and integrated' approach to North Korea's nuclear and missile programmes.[3] But by the year's end, such was the renewed mistrust between the two countries, fuelled by Washington's concern that North Korea was not keeping its side of the bargain under the 1994 Nuclear Framework Accord to freeze its nuclear weapons development programme, that Pyongyang was accusing Washington of making new preparations for an invasion of North Korea.

I couldn't help thinking that its enemies really left Pyongyang with no choice other than to resort to bloodthirsty rhetoric, hints at nuclear weapons programmes and provocative missile tests. There seemed to be an attitude, particularly in Washington, that North Korea was being unreasonable by not doing as it was told and abandoning its nuclear programme altogether and halting its sales of missiles and weapons to foreign regimes the US wasn't very keen on. For years the United States had imposed sanctions on North Korea, banning virtually all direct trade and investment, transport and financial settlements; whatever the justification for the policy, it seemed unreasonably harsh to try and extend it beyond bilateral limits by interfering in North Korea's trade with other countries.

North Korea saw itself as the victim of bullying, and its nuclear programme was the only diplomatic card it had to play. It had brought the United States to the negotiating table in 1994 and the

[3] See *Vantage Point*, December, 1999.

reward had been the nuclear framework agreement. As for the weapons sales, in a good year they were believed to account for as much as a third of North Korea's meagre foreign trade earnings. The country could quite reasonably expect an equally lucrative source of funds to be provided before it abandoned them.

North Korea was quite clear what it wanted from the United States: a peace treaty to replace the Armistice that had ended the Korean War; an end to the economic sanctions; and diplomatic recognition. On the face of it – and as far as any North Korean was concerned – there was nothing unreasonable in these demands. The United States, however, saw matters differently. North Korea should once and for all lay to rest suspicions about its nuclear programme, the Americans insisted, stop its arms sales to dangerous regimes around the world, renounce its support for terrorists, and tone down its anti-US rhetoric. Once all these conditions were met, there could be talk of peace treaties and diplomatic recognition. In view of Pyongyang's failure to acquiesce, they consistently rejected the demands of what they saw as a rogue, a pariah, state.

The United States has probably never realised the strength of feeling against it in North Korea. It is seen as responsible for the division of Korea, for the deaths of millions of Koreans during the war, and for preventing the reunification of the peninsula. Even though North Korea was, before Kim Il Sung's death, actively seeking diplomatic relations with the United States, it does not mean that the hatred of the ordinary North Korean for the Americans has been diminished. Anti-Americanism is such a strong unifying factor within society – on a par with the desire for reunification and the political ideology – that it is not in the leadership's interests to stop stoking it. One of the great ironies of the North Korean situation is that the United States has, by time after time setting itself up in North Korean eyes as the evil empire and the enemy of reunification – for example, by continuing to keep its troops stationed in South Korea, by holding Team Spirit, by imposing economic sanctions against Pyongyang, by bullying the country over the nuclear issue – effectively been lending support to a regime it would like nothing more than to see collapse.

I came to believe that North Korea's bloodthirsty rhetoric and sabre-rattling was a product of its frustration at not being taken seriously by the world at large, a world that it sees as hypocritical. Take, for example, the nuclear issue and the talk of war preparations. For years the United States – the enemy – had nuclear weapons stationed in South Korea; Pyongyang complained and no-one took a blind bit of notice. But with just a hint that the North might be thinking of acquiring nuclear weapons, the same enemy was demanding unrestricted access to see what was going on. North Korea cannot be trusted, the Americans argued. But North Korea, which does not see itself as a rogue state, pointed out that it had an obligation to defend its people, and it had never discarded the right to develop nuclear weapons to defend itself from the one country in the world that had used them.

Pyongyang's most consistent complaint against Washington is that, by stationing troops in South Korea, it is preventing the reunification of the Korean peninsula. The Americans would, no doubt, agree, pointing out that an invasion from the North is only too likely, were it not for the military deterrent in the South. Frankly, I don't know if North Korea would attack were the US army to withdraw. I doubt it would risk provoking unanimous international condemnation, unless the regime's fall was imminent and war seemed the only way for it to survive. The best way to stop that happening would be to help North Korea out of the corner it has been backed into, by extending diplomatic recognition, giving it the peace treaty it wants and allowing it free access to US and other world markets.

Perhaps that should have been done in the wake of the collapse of communism elsewhere. In the early 1990s, Tokyo and Seoul were clearly making overtures to Pyongyang, but not so Washington, which held back, demanding concessions before it would offer anything. Rather than recognise that in its greater isolation North Korea represented less of a threat, the United States chose to see the situation otherwise and pursued policies that appeared designed to push the Pyongyang regime towards the same fate that had overtaken its allies in Eastern Europe.

However it is looked at, the dire economic situation in North Korea can to some extent be blamed on the outside world. Even though the country's economic woes can largely be put down to the pursuit of self-reliance, a policy that is, because of its inherent inefficiencies, fatally flawed, the logic behind it is that of a country that sees itself under threat, from the imperialist superpower occupying the South and the militarist power to the East – Japan – that was a recent occupier and is now rearming. The threat is exaggerated in the interests of keeping the people in line, but the power in the South in particular has done little to dispel the fears.

If ever there was a view in those capitals that are antagonistic to Pyongyang that economic hardship might lead to the overthrow of the regime, it must surely long ago have been rejected. The North Korean people have proved time and again that they can withstand hardship. Those in Washington and other Western capitals whose concerns about the plight of the North Korean people are genuine, rather than a stick with which to beat a regime they dislike, must surely realise it is time to set aside ideological differences for the sake of humanitarian concerns.

Visitors to North Korea have two new mausoleums at which to pay their respects and which I have never seen. One is the

Kumsusan Palace, where the embalmed body of Kim Il Sung was laid in state in July 1995, a year after his death. The other is the tomb of Tangun, the legendary founder of the Korean nation.

I was in Pyongyang when the media and academic circles got very excited when a grave was discovered containing the remains of Tangun and his wife. The bones were shown to be 5011 years old.

I must confess it had all seemed rather unlikely to me. Firstly, Tangun's father had, according to the legend, descended from heaven to the Taebaek Mountains and had married a bear. The mountains, North Korea said, were the Myohyang Mountains and the bear reference should not be taken literally; Tangun's mother had been a member of a tribe called the bears. That it was Tangun in the grave they had no doubt, because the location and the age of the bones tallied perfectly with historical record. Thus admonished, I didn't like to ask how they'd managed to date the bones so accurately or how they knew he'd been married to the female bones lying alongside him.

The North Koreans were sure enough of themselves to build for their legendary ancestor a huge, domed white marble tomb reached by a magnificent, long white marble staircase,[4] the point being, I suppose, to give legitimacy to Pyongyang's claim to be the ancestral home of the Korean nation. It is also highly symbolic that not far away from the grave of the founder of the Korean nation and the source of the country's proud 5000-year history is the final resting place of that legendary figure of the modern era, Kim Il Sung.

In the same year – Juche 87, or 1998 – that Kim Il Sung's immortality was affirmed when he was named Eternal President

[4] The Mausoleum of Tangun was officially opened in October 1994.

of the Democratic People's Republic of Korea, South Korea elected a new mortal president, Kim Dae Jung, and he announced a 'Sunshine Policy' aimed at improving relations on the peninsula. There were soon signs of positive developments, when South Korean tourists were allowed to visit the Kumgang Mountains, the most beautiful mountains in the world, on the northern side of the demilitarised zone.

This new spirit of cooperation was in sharp contrast with the relationship four years earlier when, at the moment of the nation's greatest sorrow, the South Korean authorities had committed an act of betrayal that left the North uncomprehending in its fury. Seoul had refused to express condolences over the death of the greatest of Koreans.

But by the beginning of 1999 relations had improved sufficiently for Pyongyang to float the idea of high-level inter-Korean talks. Rather like the proposal made by Kim Il Sung over a decade earlier, though, there were a number of difficulties preventing the South Korean government from agreeing, not least of which was the invitation to the South Korean president to attend in his capacity as the leader of his party. Other preconditions included the old chestnuts of the cancellation of joint military exercises with the US and the abolition of the National Security Law.

Kim Il Sung's proposal for such high-level talks in 1988 came at a time when North Korea was faced with growing economic difficulties. Clearly back then he saw cooperation – if not reunification – with the South as the way forward, economically at least. Bring together the vast arable lands, the business acumen and the advanced technology of the South, the reasoning probably went, with the rich mineral resources and the hard-working labour force of the North, and it was a safe bet that sooner or later a pretty powerful economy would emerge.

But any optimism that might have existed in South Korea in 1988 about the potential economic benefits of reunification would soon be shattered by the German experience and the devastating effect the East's economy had on that of the capitalist West of the country.

Economic considerations aside, reunification became the great hope and belief for the people of North Korea. It would be the coming of a kingdom where all their wrongs would be put to right; not only would they prosper, but also the millions who belonged to separated families would be able to live together after long-lost brothers and sisters, parents and children, had found one another again. They would all enjoy true freedom; the Americans would have gone and without the great enemy occupying the territory the need for constant vigilance, for treating every stranger as a spy, would be lifted.

'What did the world's media say about the summit?' the Korean asked. It was the summer of Juche 89 – 2000 by the calendar I was used to – and the president of South Korea had just visited Pyongyang.

'People were impressed,' I told him. Each time they met me in Beijing, the Koreans I knew had come seeking the answers to questions: first about the famine, then about the defector, and now about the historic summit. But it wasn't so much information they were after, I thought, as it had been in the past when communism was falling in Eastern Europe and when China had opened diplomatic relations with South Korea and their own media hadn't told them. Now they seemed better informed. It was confirmation they were seeking.

I could have mentioned the successes that had been reported; the five-point joint declaration calling for concerted efforts towards reconciliation, cooperation and eventual reunification on the Korean peninsula; the emphasis on economic cooperation that promised massive South Korean investment in the North; the agreement to allow 100 elderly Koreans from each side to visit long-lost family members on the other.

But he already knew about that. So I told him that the dear leader had amazed the world by his confident and relaxed appearance on their television screens. How he had surprised everyone with his courtesy in meeting his guest at the airport, with his self-deprecating humour,[5] and with his impromptu walkabout among his adoring people.[6] It was reminiscent of his father, I said.

There were two significant and immediate results of the summit that highlighted for me the difficulty I still had in resolving the contradictions in my attitude towards North Korea. Firstly, within a month, the two Koreas agreed to reconnect a severed railway across the 38th Parallel.

So, the stranger said, South Korea has been browbeaten into offering the hand of friendship, left with little alternative other than to promote the steady development of economic cooperation as a way of easing the North's desperate economic plight. Otherwise it might be faced with having to deal suddenly and devastatingly, when reunification finally came, with an overwhelming economic mess that would rapidly undermine its own years of success and prosperity.

[5] Kim Jong Il was reported as remarking on his wife's absence from the banquet by saying that they should be counted among Korea's divided families.

[6] *En route* from the airport into central Pyongyang, the car carrying Kim Jong Il stopped and he got out and greeted the crowds lining the street.

The North Korean frogs, it seemed to me, were being given the hope of leaving their well, if only as far as a patch of sky that was not too unfamiliar.

Then, two months after the summit, the reunions were held in Pyongyang and Seoul of families, 100 members from each side, separated since the Korean War. It was gut-wrenching, tear-jerking stuff to see on the television those elderly people, faces etched with such a mixture of joy and sorrow as no outsider could comprehend, touching and holding and gazing into one another's eyes; mothers with daughters, fathers with sons, brothers with sisters, family they had not seen, had not heard from, for more than half a century, never knowing if they were waiting in vain.

And the friend – the comrade – inside me said: if ever there was a time for the outside world to hold up its hands and say there was a depth of suffering it did not understand here, that we all should come together, setting aside our ideological differences, to end this tragedy, then this was it.

It was a naïve thought, reminiscent of the much younger man who had set out on his life's adventure back in the spring of 1987 – or Juche 76 as it is now known – believing that international problems could best be resolved by ordinary people over a pint or two of beer. But it was a relief to know that, even after the years of emotional and moral battering that had turned excitement to cynicism, celebrity to doubtful expertise, and believer to friend and then outcast, I hadn't really changed. Maybe it was hidden a little deeper inside me, but the naïveté was still there.

Afterword

*I*n the ten years that have passed, almost to the day, since I left North Korea after a stay lasting seven years all but a month, I have lost contact with the various people who made my time there so colourful and educational. I know something of what has happened to some of the foreign characters included in these pages. Of those I have called Madame Beatrice, Philippe and Whitney, Kris, Miles and Marek, I can say of them all that none remains in North Korea.

I left Beijing in the winter of 2000, ending a period in which I could keep in touch with Korean former colleagues, either in person when they visited or indirectly via messages carried by these visitors. As is the nature of North Korean society, most of my former colleagues remain in the posts they occupied when I worked with them, although a few, thanks to their foreign language skills and, I presume, good contacts, have been able to make the coveted move into business.

Since 2000 much has happened on the Korean peninsula and little has changed. North Korea is little more than an onlooker to globalisation and keeps to the fringes of the world wide web. The World Cup was held in South Korea, but unlike when the Olympics were held in Seoul, North Koreans were not only kept informed, but even allowed to watch. And now that several Western countries, among them my own, have opened embassies in Pyongyang, I can be confident that no-one will ever experience North Korea as I once did.

As I write these words, North Korea is again the focus of international condemnation for its nuclear weapons programme. It is my fervent hope that some solution may finally be found to this issue that will allow the international community soon to extend the hand of friendship to North Korea and her warm, generous and long-suffering people.

Warsaw, Poland
February 2004

Bibliography

Korea Today, a monthly magazine published by the Foreign Languages Publishing House (Foreign Languages Press Group) in various languages, offers an interesting insight into how North Korea sees itself, South Korea and the rest of the world.

Democratic People's Republic of KOREA, a monthly pictorial magazine published by the Foreign Languages Publishing House (Foreign Languages Press Group) in various languages, is a lavish illustrated record of events on the Korean peninsula.

The Pyongyang Times, published every week by the Foreign Languages Publishing House (Foreign Languages Press Group) in English, French and Spanish, offers what passes for North Korea's idea of news.

Vantage Point, a monthly publication of the Yonhap News Agency in Seoul, provides a highly informative and fairly objective insight into developments in North Korea.

Andrew Holloway's *A Year in Pyongyang*, published on the website of Aidan Foster-Carter (www.aidanfc.net), provided some very useful reminders of the idiosyncrasies of life in North Korea at the end of the 1980s.

Index

The Last Empress
The She-Dragon of China
Keith Laidler

The unforgettable story of a woman whose lust for power ultimately destroyed her Destiny.

In 1856 Emperor Hsien Feng turned over an ornately carved jade name-plaque next to his bedchamber, an action with which he brought a much-desired new concubine to his bed and unwittingly sealed the fate of the Manchu dynasty. A centuries-old prophecy had foretold that Manchu rule in China would be brought to ruin by a woman from the Yeho-Nala tribe; in the darkness of the bed-chamber those words became reality. The Emperor was entranced with the young woman he had chosen, and from that time her power over him was ensured. Her name was Yehonala.

Forced to enter the Forbidden City at the age of sixteen Yehonala lost her family, her betrothed and the life she had sought. She was entering a world of opulence, scholarship, intrigue and power struggles; a world that had remained for centuries untouched by the outside world or the passing of time, ruled by etiquette and tradition but with danger in every word or gesture. The beautiful young girl proved herself equal to all the court. She rose to be one of the greatest female autocrats in history, the most powerful person in China, maintaining her power with a mixture of seduction, intrigue, manipulation and even murder.

'Laidler's Book is Meticulously researched and covers a fascinating period in Chinese History ...'
The Times

'A Riveting Story and Laidler tells it well ...'
Sunday Telegraph

'Engaging'
TLS

0470848812
£7.99

The Last Samurai
The life and Battles of Saigo Takamori
Mark Ravina

Provides a thrilling glimpse into Japanese feudal society and the customs, traditions and fighting spirit of the Samarai.

The dramatic arc of Saigo Takamori's life, from his humble origins as a lowly samurai, to national leadership, to his death as a rebel leader, has captivated generations of Japanese readers and now Americans as well – his life is the inspiration for a major Hollywood film, *The Last Samurai*, starring Tom Cruise and Ken Watanabe. In this vibrant new biography, Mark Ravina, professor of history and Director of East Asian Studies at Emory University, explores the facts behind Hollywood storytelling and Japanese legends, and explains the passion and poignancy of Saigo's life. Known both for his scholarly research and his appearances on The History Channel, Ravina recreates the world in which Saigo lived and died, the last days of the samurai.

The Last Samurai traces Saigo's life from his early days as a tax clerk in far southwestern Japan, through his rise to national prominence as a fierce imperial loyalist.

In **THE LAST SAMURAI**, Saigo is as compelling a character as Robert E. Lee was to Americans – a great and noble warrior who followed the dictates of honor and loyalty, even though it meant civil war in a country to which he'd devoted his life. Saigo's life is a fascinating look into Japanese feudal society and a history of a country as it struggled between its long traditions and the dictates of a modern future.

0471089702
£16.50

The Red Empires
A Tale of Love Divided
Patrick Lescot

The True Story of Li Lisan, first Chairman of the Chinese Communist Party, his Russian wife and their fight against two totalitarian regimes

As a youth in the 1920s, Li Lisan fled rural China for the seductive charms of Paris, where he met his aristocratic Russian wife Lisa. Here he joined the Communist Party and returned to China to become the first Chairman of the Chinese Communist Party and a key member of the Russian and Chinese revolutions. He rivalled Mao Zedong for this position and was to later suffer terribly at his hands.

The Red Empires moves between Paris, Russia and China, giving a highly evocative account of the cultural revolution as Russia and China moved apart in the 1960s.

0470090294
£16.99

Fleeting Rome
Carlo Levi

A nostalgic tour of Rome, its people and it's dreams, during the Dolce Vita era, through the eyes of one of the masters of twentieth century literature

Only a renaissance man could have described this glorious city in its heyday. And only Carlo Levi, writer, painter, politician and one of the last century's most celebrated talents, could depict Rome at the height of its optimism and vitality after World War II. In Fleeting Rome, the era of post war 'La Dolce Vita' is brought magnificently to life in the daily bustle of Rome's street traders, housewives and students at work and play, the colourful festivities of Ferragosto and San Giovanni, the little theatre of Pulcinella al Pincio; all vibrant sights and sounds of this ancient, yet vital city.

0470871830
£14.99

Adventure Capitalist
The Ultimate Roadtrip

The best-selling author of *Investment Biker* takes a fascinating journey through the world's economic situation in a convertible yellow Mercedes. This is the motivating story of entrepreneur Jim Rogers, dubbed 'the Indiana Jones of finance' by Time magazine, who made his fortune playing the stock market and then embarked on his lifelong dream adventure.

047086320X
£14.99